The Performing School

Education is increasingly preoccupied with performance: pupil performance, teacher performance and the performance of the school. This
specially commissioned collection of perspectives offers an analysis of the
new organisation of the teaching profession as it is reconstructed around
the notion of performance and the implications of a performance culture.
The Performing School examines the roots, directions and implications of
the new structure by drawing together insights from policy, research and
practice at this time of rapid change and debate. This unique volume
addresses three interconnected issues of modernisation and education:

*   What is the background to and significance of performance manage-
    ment in modernising schools and teachers at the present time?
*   What are the likely future effects of a performance culture on teaching,
    learning and schooling?
*   What will it take to ensure that performance management improves
    pedagogy and professionality beyond the narrow confines of performa-
    tivity, managerialism and market reform in education?

The Performing School will inform practice and debate amongst policy
makers in central government, professional associations and among
teachers, headteachers, governors, inspectors and researchers.

Denis Gleeson and **Chris Husbands** are both Professors of Education in
the Institute of Education at the University of Warwick.

D1113882

The Performing School

Managing teaching and learning
in a performance culture

**Denis Gleeson and
Chris Husbands**

London and New York

First published 2001 by RoutledgeFalmer
11 New Fetter Lane, London EC4P 4EE

Simultaneously published in the USA and Canada
by RoutledgeFalmer
29 West 35th Street, New York, NY 10001

RoutledgeFalmer is an imprint of the Taylor & Francis Group

© 2001 Denis Gleeson and Chris Husbands

Typeset in Galliard by BC Typesetting, Bristol
Printed and bound in Great Britain by
TJ International Ltd, Padstow, Cornwall

All rights reserved. No part of this book may be reprinted or
reproduced or utilised in any form or by any electronic, mechanical,
or other means, now known or hereafter invented, including
photocopying and recording, or in any information storage or
retrieval system, without permission in writing from the publishers.

British Library Cataloguing in Publication Data
A catalogue record for this book is available from the British Library

Library of Congress Cataloging in Publication Data
The performing school: managing, teaching, and learning in a performance
culture/edited by Denis Gleeson and Chris Husbands.
    p. cm.
    Includes bibliographical references and index.
    1. Educational accountability–Great Britain. 2. School management
and organization–Great Britain. I. Gleeson, Denis. II. Husbands,
Christopher T.

LB2900.5.P47 2001
379.1'58'0941–dc21   00-067377

ISBN 0–415–24779–9 (hbk)
ISBN 0–415–24780–2 (pbk)

Contents

List of figures and tables

List of contributors

Richard Arrowsmith is currently Headteacher of the Grove School, Market Drayton (Shropshire), having previously been a head for eight years in Nottinghamshire. He has recently chaired an education-business partnership (EBP) and directed a learning town project. In addition to his particular interests in promoting Lifelong Learning and Languages Development in School, he is also an active Fellow of the Royal Society of Arts (FRSA).

Stephen Ball is the Karl Mannheim Professor of Sociology of Education at the Institute of Education, London. He was previously Professor of Sociology of Education, and Director of the Centre for Public Policy Research, King's College, London. He is an Academician of the Academy of Social Sciences and Editor of the *Journal of Education Policy*. He is author of several books on education policy, including *Education Reform* (1994), *Markets, Choice and Equity* (1995, with Sharon Gewirtz and Richard Bowe) and *Choice, Pathways and Transitions Post-16* (2000, with Meg Maguire and Sheila Macrae). He is also editor of the four-volume *Sociology of Education: Major Themes*. His work has focused in particular on education markets and the theorisation of policy.

John Elliott is Professor of Education within the Centre for Applied Research in Education, which he directed from 1996–1999. He is well-known internationally for his role in developing the theory and practice of action research in the contexts of curriculum and teacher development, and has directed a number of funded collaborative classroom research projects with teachers and schools. These include the Ford Teaching Project (1972–1974) and, more recently, the TTA-funded Norwich Area Schools Consortium (NASC) on the 'Curriculum and pedagogical dimensions of student disaffection' (1997–2001).

Linda Evans is Senior Lecturer in Education at the University of Warwick's Institute of Education and Co-director of the Institute's Teacher Development Research and Dissemination Unit. Before becoming an academic she was a primary school teacher for fifteen years, working in socially disadvantaged areas in the north of England. She has researched and published widely in the fields of initial teacher education, teaching and learning in higher education and, in particular, teacher professionality and morale, job satisfaction and motivation. Her books include: *Teacher Morale, Job Satisfaction and Motivation* (1998) and *Managing to Motivate: a guide for school leaders* (1999).

David Gentle is Principal of Cockshut Hill Technology College, an 11–18 comprehensive school in East Birmingham. He was previously Head-teacher at Hodge Hill School, Birmingham and is reading for a doctorate at the University of Warwick.

Denis Gleeson is Professor of Education in the Institute of Education, University of Warwick. Previously he was Professor and Head of Department of Education at Keele University. His main areas of research interest are in the sociology of education with reference to ages 14–19 and post-compulsory education, policy and practice. He has directed major research projects in the area of further education and training and has published widely in the field, including the *Paradox of Training* (1989) and *Knowledge and Nationhood* (1996). Currently he is Co-director of a project known as 'Transforming Learning Cultures in Further Education', which is part of the ESRC's (Economic and Social Research Council's) Teaching and Learning Research Programme.

Helen Gunter is Senior Lecturer within the School of Education at the University of Birmingham. She has research interest in leadership and management in educational settings. Helen has published articles and books on theory and research including: *Rethinking Education: the consequences of Jurassic Management* (1997) and forthcoming in 2001 is *Leaders and Leadership in Education*.

Chris Husbands is Professor of Education at the University of Warwick, having taught at comprehensive schools in London, Norwich and Hertfordshire. He previously co-edited *Consorting and Collaborating in the Education Marketplace* (1996).

Pat Mahony and Ian Hextall are Professors of Education at the University of Surrey, Roehampton. Pat has published extensively in the areas of social justice and teacher education. Ian Hextall is Senior Lecturer in Education, at the University of Surrey, Roehampton and his publications have focused on the sociology of education and the politics of policy. Over the past five years Pat and Ian have undertaken two ESRC-funded projects on the restructuring of teaching. Their recent book is entitled *Reconstructing Teaching: standards, performance and accountability* (RoutledgeFalmer).

Martin Merson teaches at the University of Warwick and the Open University. His research interests and publications are in the area of the relationship between education and the changing nature of employment. He has previously taught in schools in England and Sweden.

Pat Sikes is a Lecturer in the Department of Educational Studies at Sheffield University. She is particularly interested in using biographical and narrative approaches to explore aspects of teachers' lives and careers. Her publications include: *Learning From Lives: Understanding Life History 20 Methods* (with Goodson, 2001, Open University Press); *Parents Who Teach: Stories From Home and From School* (1997, Cassell); *Teacher Careers: Crises and Continuities* (with L. Measor and P. Woods, 1985, Falmer).

John Smyth is Foundation Professor of Teacher Education at the Flinders University of South Australia, and Associate Dean (Research). He is Director of the Flinders Institute for the Study of Teaching. He has held a Senior Fulbright Research Award and the Palmer O. Johnson Award for the most outstanding piece of published research by the American Educational Research Association. His published work includes: *Remaking Teaching: Ideology, Policy and Practice* (with Shacklock, 1998); *Schooling for a Fair Go* (with Hattam and Lawson, 1998); *Teachers' Work in a Globalising Economy* (with Dow, Hattam, Shacklock and Reid, 2001); *A Critical Politics of Teacher Work: an Australian Perspective*.

Meryl Thompson is Policy Officer for the Association of Teachers and Lecturers (ATL) and has written extensively on teacher development and policy.

Geoff Whitty became Director of the Institute of Education, University of London in September 2000, having been the Karl Mannheim Professor of Sociology of Education at the Institute since 1992. His main areas of research and scholarship are the sociology of education, education policy and teacher education. He has directed major research projects on the impact of national education policies in England and undertaken comparative studies of education reform in other countries. His most recent books include: *Devolution and Choice in Education: The School, the State and the Market* (co-authored, 1998, Open University Press) and *Teacher Education in Transition: Re-forming Professionalism?* (2000, Open University Press).

List of abbreviations

Abbreviation	Meaning*
AARE	Australian Association for Research in Education
ASTs	Advanced Skills Teachers
ATL	Association of Teachers and Lecturers
BERA	British Education Research Association
CEA	Cambridge Education Associates
CfBT	Centre for British Teachers
DES	Department of Education and Science (from 1992)
DfEE	Department of Education and Employment (from 1994)
DTI	Department of Trade and Industry
ERA	Education Reform Act 1988
GCSE	General Certificate of Secondary Education
GEST	Grants for Education Support and Training
GTC	General Teaching Council (2000)
HEI	Higher Education Institution
HRM	Human Resources Management
ICT	Information and Communications Technology
ILEA	Inner London Education Authority
INSET	Inservice Education and Training
IPM	Institute of Personnel Management
LEA	Local Education Authority
LPSH	Leadership Programme for Serving Headteachers
MOTE	Modes of Teacher Education
NAHT	National Association of Headteachers
NASUWT	National Association of Schoolmasters and Union of Women Teachers
NLNS	National Literacy and Numeracy Strategies
NOF	New Opportunities Fund
NPQH	National Professional Qualification for Headteachers
NUT	National Union of Teachers

OfSTED	Office for Standards in Education
PAT	Professional Association of Teachers
PGCE	Postgraduate Certificate in Education
PI	Performance Indicator
PSHE	Personal, Social and Health Education
QCA	Qualifications and Curriculum Authority
QTS	Qualified Teacher Status
RAE	Research Assessment Exercise
SATs	Standardised Assessment Tasks
SCITT	School Centred Initial Teacher Training
SENCO	Special Needs Coordinator
SEU	Standards and Effectiveness Unit
SHA	Secondary Heads Association
SMART	Specific, Measurable, Attainable, Realistic and Timeframed
STRB	School Teachers Pay Review Body
TES	*Times Educational Supplement*
THES	*Times Higher Educational Supplement*
TIMSS	Third International Mathematics and Science Survey
TSO	The Stationery Office (was HMSO pre-1996)
TTA	Teacher Training Agency
TVEI	Technical and Vocational Education Initiative

* Please note that versions in full may appear upper or lower case in text according to usage

Introduction

The performing school: managing teaching and learning in a performance culture

Denis Gleeson and Chris Husbands

The stakes are high. Throughout the world governments are attempting to reform their education systems in the face of national and global change. In many advanced industrial societies, where both economic and natural resources are in decline, investing in human capital now constitutes a central platform of economic and education reform (Coleman, 1988). As governments increasingly articulate the rhetoric of a 'knowledge economy', traditional cultures and organisational structures for teaching are found to be wanting. The drive to improve indicators of educational performance, and to ensure that teachers are equipped and able to operate in rapidly changing professional environments, is leading to attempts to reorganise, reskill and reculture teaching. In some reform programmes the focus is on new forms of professional qualification, in others it is on flexibility and marketisation. A common thread in many, especially western, reforms is the increasing focus on the performance of schools, on the capacity of headteachers to measure that performance and on holding teachers more directly accountable for it through both rewards and sanctions. The idea of market performance and finance-driven education reform is not entirely new and, in the UK, has its origins in the 1988 Education Reform Act (ERA) and subsequent initiatives linking inspection, target-setting, league tables and performance management (Bridges and McLaughlin, 1994; Bridges and Husbands, 1996).

This book examines the Labour government's ambitions and extensive plans for the reform of the UK teaching profession set out in the Green Paper entitled 'Teachers: Meeting the Challenge of Change' (DfEE, 1998). New Labour won the 1997 election, famously, on a declaration that its three main priorities were 'education, education, education'. In the preface to the Green Paper, Tony Blair declared that 'the teaching profession is critical to our mission. First rate teachers and headteachers are indispensable to giving our children the best possible start in life'. The Green Paper developed the government's perception of what it called 'the imperative of modernisation'. In place of what it described as a profession dogged by low pay, poor status, unsystematic professional development, poor leadership and inadequate support, the Green Paper outlined a wide-ranging agenda for change. The agenda envisaged new staffing structures with rewards and incentives for high performance, systematic professional development, increased use of information and communications technology and a new culture of ambition and performance. The methods by which this agenda might be realised included the introduction of a performance threshold, progression beyond which introduces performance-related pay for experienced staff, new models of professional development, a 'fast track' route for able new entrants to the profession, and the development of a National College for School Leadership. The proposals were described by the Prime Minister as the most thoroughgoing reform of the teaching profession since the introduction of compulsory schooling in 1870. According to teacher and head-teacher associations, the reforms are the most dramatic since payment by results was abolished a century ago. A key policy question in the UK is how to deliver such reform with a diverse teacher workforce, many of whom feel demoralised and who are widely seen as 'underpaid and under siege' (Marsden, 2000).

The questions posed by performance management and the new wave of education reform demand detailed examination. In response this collection examines the implications for policy and practice of the government's modernisation of the teaching profession. *The Performing School* reflects the preoccupation of the reform agenda with the linked concepts of 'performance' and 'performativity'. It examines the relationships between pupil performance, teacher performance and the performance of the school, as well as the wider question of the relationship between educational and national economic performance. The book critically addresses theories of management, teaching and learning and the likely short and long run implications of performance management for the way schools, and those who support and work in them, operate. We talk about 'the performing school' because of the increased emphasis in policy and practice on those elements of a school's work which can be subjected to management and measurement, and the profound consequences of this emphasis for the 'performance' of a school's 'performers': its pupils, staff and leaders. We use this metaphor of performance to structure the book, considering the meanings and impacts of the performing school for school leaders ('liontamers' and 'jugglers'), teachers ('high-wire artists' and 'acrobats') and as a policy initiative (with the concepts of 'ringmasters' and 'big tops'). Our contributors explore the new relationships being constructed and the wider implications for society of this performance culture. The book is not simply concerned with analysing performance management, but also with the values and measures attached to educational performance, and its impact on the culture of schooling and professional relationships in the delivery of high-quality teaching and learning.

Although the book is clearly derived from policy developments in England, the changes it addresses have a wider significance. The New Zealand government has, for example, recently published its proposals for the introduction of performance-linked pay; several American states have revised their current performance management arrangements; and, in Australia, there is a White Paper on teacher reform in Victoria. Thus, whilst being firmly grounded in current English education developments, *The Performing School* explores work on school effectiveness, school improvement and critical policy analysis applicable across a range of cultural contexts. The immediate focus of this book is, therefore, on how different aspects of performance management, appraisal, inspection targets, standards and development-planning, impact on the construction of what Smyth and Shacklock (1998) call the 'preferred teacher', and the consequences of this construction for pedagogy, practice and professionality. Our contributors do not necessarily agree in their analysis, but they share a common interest in seeking to describe and understand the shifting nature of schooling and the reshaping of the teaching profession. This collection, based on their original research and professional experience, seeks to establish coherence in three ways:

- a focus on a common issue – the notion of performance management and the implications of an emerging performance 'culture' in secondary education;
- an internal structure identifying principal themes: teaching, learning and policy and management; and
- an analysis which considers the world of education beyond the narrow confines of performance, managerialism and market reform.

This book is bounded by a real and seismic shift in education policy and the way schools are run. Throughout the world, governments have largely abandoned the belief that effective education systems are characterised by legislative *laissez-faire* and professional autonomy. Bill Clinton's belief that 'what we earn will depend on what we learn, and how well we can apply what we learn to the workplaces of America' (quoted in Halsey *et al.*, 1997 p.8) is mirrored by New Labour's conviction that 'in the twenty first century knowledge and skills will be the key to success' (DfEE, 1997). Both legitimate sharply interventionist education policies in which accountability, system development and outcomes are subjected to management both at what can be described as macro-educational and micro-educational levels. At macro-educational levels, state direction prescribes the operating environments for schools with increasing precision, structured forms, curriculum, assessment regimes, all of which are increasingly managed. At micro-educational level, governments exhibit increasing interest – through a concern with 'effectiveness' and 'improvement' – in direct interventions in pedagogy, professional development and institutional management. Performance management is a policy device, which binds together micro- and macro-educational intervention. Over the next few years, pupils, parents, teachers, managers, researchers and policy-makers at all levels of the education service will be involved, in some way, with the concepts of performance management and measurement.

References

Bridges, D. and Husbands, C. (eds), (1996), *Consorting and Collaborating in the Education Marketplace*, Lewes: Falmer Press.

Bridges, D. and McLaughlin, T. H. (eds), (1994), *Education and the Marketplace*, Lewes: Falmer Press.

Coleman, J. S. (1988), 'Social capital in the creation of human capital', in *American Journal of Sociology*, 94, Supplement, pp.S95–S120.

DfEE (Department for Education and Employment), (1997), *Excellence in Schools*, London: DfEE.

DfEE (1998), *Teachers: Meeting the Challenge of Change*, Cmd. 4164, London: DfEE.

Halsey, A. H., Lauder, H., Brown, P. and Wells, A. S. (eds), (1997), *Education: Culture, Economy and Society*, Oxford: Oxford University Press.

Marsden, D. (2000), 'Preparing to Perform', in Centre Piece, Vol. 5, Issue 2, Centre for Economic Performance, LSE, London.

Smyth, J. and Shacklock, G. (1998), *Remaking Teaching: Ideology, Policy and Practice*, London: Routledge.

Part I
Liontamers and jugglers?
Challenges and opportunities
in managing the performing school

The first section of the book explores performance management from the perspective of school leaders, who will need to mediate the dynamics of performance management policy in the context of their own schools. Chris Husbands' opening contribution explores the relationships between the complexity of schools as institutions with multiple goals and competing agendas, and the sharp focus of performance management. He argues that whilst performance management offers school leaders and policy makers a policy technique which closes the circle between macro- and micro-level interventions in schooling, the extent to which it prioritises the short-term and immediate – the 'clear, concise and measurable' phenomena beloved of performance management policy – raises issues about whether it will deliver the inclusive, successful education system on which the modernisation project depends.

This ambivalence about performance management underpins the remaining contributions in this first section. Chapters 2 and 3 explore performance management from headteachers' perspectives. David Gentle and Richard Arrowsmith ask penetrating questions about whether performance management arrangements – hastily assembled and introduced with apparently scant regard for the realities of school management and delivery – can contribute positively to school improvement and effectiveness. Both headteachers highlight complexities and contradictions in the concept and approach. For Gentle, these complexities turn on the extent to which headteachers can transform their current internal management arrangements into leadership, line management and team coherence arrangements on which successful implementation of performance management depends. For Arrowsmith, the complexities relate both to teachers and to pupils, and the extent to which the rational planning assumptions which operate performance management literature speaks to a culture of schooling which depends on the capacity of teachers to inspire, enthuse and motivate young learners. The final contribution in this section, by Meryl Thompson, draws together these policy issues at the level of the school. Thompson is cautious about the ability of large-scale reform programmes – such as performance management – to transform teacher and school practice. However, she goes beyond such reservations to highlight the transformative potential of performance management if, or when, the opportunities are seized to take the twin preoccupations with pupil performance and staff development as the basis for a new model schooling, in which school leaders are able genuinely to pursue their own improvement agendas.

1 Managing 'performance' in the performing school:

The impacts of performance management on schools under regulation

Chris Husbands

Schools, of course, are complex institutions. School management involves making a constant and unending set of judgements between competing priorities, based on principles which are difficult to reconcile. The rights of individuals must be balanced against the needs of groups; the need to prepare learners for examinations must be balanced against the requirement to equip them for the unpredictable demands of adult life; the pressure to provide knowledge must be balanced against the need to equip learners with personal and study skills. In a finite amount of time, a decision must be made about the best way to use time and to allocate it between competing curricular and pastoral demands each of which has individual merit. In a changing context, schools must consider how most effectively to mediate the demands of different interest groups for new curricular, pedagogic, assessment and managerial approaches: too much change, and the established routines on which all institutions depend are at risk; too little, and the most successful of schools atrophies.

The relationships between attainment and motivation, between curriculum and assessment, between the proper concerns for pastoral care and for pupils' academic achievement, between individual needs and general provision, between the demands for time, resources and development of different curriculum priorities are complex. In key areas, school leaders make often intuitive judgements, between the short-term and the long-term, between the pastoral and the academic, between what is desirable and what is possible, between what appears urgent and what may be most important, between the demands, aspirations and expectations of pupils, parents, staff, governors, local authorities and government.

Over the past two decades, the imperatives on schools to respond rapidly to imposed change from central government have markedly increased. The introduction of performance management from 2000 represents the culmination of increased policy, public and research interest in the quality, effectiveness and measured improvement of schools over some three decades. What is at issue, therefore, is the nature of the school response; put crudely, what will performance management do to the cultures of school management and to the ways in which school managers mediate the pressures on them and their staff and pupils?

New Labour and the closing of the management circle: the operation of national performance and school policies

New Labour's aspirations for the education system are ambitious: 'our vision is of nothing less than a new and stronger fabric for our society. We want all our young people to emerge from school with a sound basic education, committed to continuous learning and equipped with the personal skills they need to succeed as individuals and citizens. We want people of all ages engaged with learning. We want opportunity for all. We want a nation equipped for the challenges and opportunities of the new millennium' (Blunkett, 1999). The diagnosis is that 'for most of the last 150 years, mass education has been of at best fitful concern to English political leaders, left and right. In consequence, central government has taken scant interest in standards too often dismissing as a matter of local concern what was in truth a chronic failure of national leadership and responsibility' (Blair, 1999). In place of this neglect, Labour in opposition promised 'rigorous assessment of pupil and school performance, and action based upon it to raise the standards of the worst schools to that of the average and the standard of the average to that of the best' (Blair, 1996).

After the 1997 election, the new Labour government, whilst making important changes in school governance, largely accepted the frameworks of curriculum, assessment and accountability which had been introduced through the 1980s and 1990s (Halpin and Whitty, 1997; Gray and Wilcox, 1996). Onto a structure of largely autonomous schools operating in a marketised environment (Bridges and McLaughlin, 1994; Husbands, 1996), Labour grafted the activist role for the Department for Education and Employment (DfEE) which Michael Barber, himself installed as head of the new Standards and Effectiveness Unit (SEU), had presaged in advising 'politicians with a passion for education', 'how to do the impossible' (Barber, 1996). The SEU, the Standards Task Force, the DfEE standards web-site and the Qualifications and Curriculum Authority (QCA) took lead roles in identifying and disseminating perceived 'good practice'. National targets were set for pupil attainment in literacy and numeracy at age eleven, with nationally defined pedagogic strategies to support the achievement of the targets within five years. Circular 11/98 required that secondary schools set and circulate to parents targets for the number of pupils attaining given levels in national curriculum and GCSE assessments (DfEE, 1998). LEAs (local education authorities) were required to develop education development plans for approval by the DfEE that mediated the relationship between national and school-level targets. Through national strategies, approved schemes of work, and school-level targets, the DfEE defined, in greater detail and more extensively than ever before, the expected outcomes for specified facets of schooling, and established mechanisms for close monitoring of progress towards these outcomes.

In government, Labour progressively marshalled the entire education system around this reform agenda. The Secretary of State was not immune from the drive for reform: his task now was 'not to tinker in Whitehall', but to lead a newly activist and interventionist Department 'to promote successful change in every classroom in the country' (Barber, 1996). Civil servants were urged by the then Permanent Secretary at the DfEE to acknowledge histories of the failure of 'educational and social reform at the implementation stage', and to recognise the need to 'become more focus[ed] on the issues of the day' (Bichard, 1998). School leadership was to be overhauled, with prime ministerial recognition for leading headteachers and a national college for school leadership. Whilst the Prime Minister described teachers as often 'excellent . . . and dedicated' (Blair, 1999), the Green Paper has observed that the culture of the profession had too often been defensive and reluctant to change (DfEE, 1998). Where previous reform efforts had been abandoned 'by governments without the courage or the strategic sense to see them through to impact on pupil performance', the task of root and branch reform and restructuring would this time be seen through (Barber, 2000 p.23).

The Green Paper on the reform of the teaching profession, which emerged after eighteen months of the new government (DfEE, 1998), provided a clearer framework for the management of national, local and school targets through the restructuring and reculturing of the teaching profession. The introduction of programmes for performance management, linking teacher performance to promotion above a national threshold, with further financial rewards for high performing schools – which was trailed in the 1998 Green Paper on the teaching profession, but which has not appeared in pre-election statements and policy papers (Labour Party, 1997) – provided the final, connecting link in the chain. The mechanisms through which performance management would reshape schools and school management were outlined in a series of technical and procedural papers for headteachers, teachers and governors published through 2000. They suggest both a clinically straightforward series of assumptions about the ways in which performance might be managed, and a wide ranging sense of its potential impact on the whole culture and practice of school management. Performance management is intended to focus headteacher and governor attention on 'what, with encouragement, support and high expectations . . . pupils can achieve', based on 'the integration of performance management with the overall approach to managing the school' (DfEE, 2000a p.1). Thus, performance management redirected the focus of school management around a deceptively simple proposition: 'where schools and individual teachers are clear about what they expect pupils to achieve, standards rise' (DfEE, 2000b p.3). Targets are to be set annually in the performance management cycle for both headteachers and teachers who have successfully passed a performance threshold. Under the DfEE's performance management regulations, governors are required to set at least two 'clear, concise and measurable objectives' for headteachers each year, one of which must relate to pupil progress and one to leadership and management (DfEE, 2000c). In order to pass successfully through salary thresholds, teachers must adduce a range of evidence about their professional competence, including evidence that their pupils 'achieve well in relation to their prior attainment making progress as good or better than similar pupils nationally' (DfEE, 2000b).

English schools, and particularly English secondary schools, have always been concerned – rightly – with pupil achievement in external examinations. What is new here is not the emphasis on pupils' cognitive outcomes, but the sharpness of the focus on performance management, the range and depth of statistical and comparative data on which analyses might be based and, as an over-arching issue, the centralisation of the management of school, teacher and pupil achievement. What is imposed is simultaneously limited and expansive. It is limited in the extent to which performance management focuses school leadership onto the core tasks of enhancing pupil progress against measurable criteria; but expansive in the extent to which the language and assumptions of performance management describe a cultural refocusing of schooling. The DfEE's guidance on performance management polices, and its training materials for external advisers, insist – though the language can in the year 2000 only be aspirational – that 'performance management works best when it is an integral part of a school's culture . . . based on a shared commitment to continuous improvement' (DfEE, 2000a p.4).

English schools, as a result, stand at a critical policy and developmental cusp. Charged with spearheading the government drive for improvement in pupils' life chances as a key element in the strategy to combat social exclusion, they must sharply focus their efforts as never before on the management of teacher performance in order to improve measured pupil performance There are three direct connections: first, teachers' central focus is pupils' (test and examination) performance. Second, headteachers must focus on the management, deployment and development of teacher performance in order to enhance pupil performance. And third, governors must set targets for pupils' performance based on prior attainment data and national attainment targets. School targets can be derived from national targets; and teacher and pupil targets from school targets. In the short term, it is almost certain that the sharper focus and defined targets brought by performance management systems will deliver higher levels of attainment in external tests and examinations, of which there are now a plethora: one study by the Professional Association of Teachers (PAT) suggests that the typical English pupil now takes some seventy-five tests between entry to school and the age of eighteen (PAT, 2000). In these tests and examinations, the marshalling of institutional effort, the focus on defined short-term targets and the management of time, resources and curriculum around maximising short-term performance will, in the majority of schools, demonstrate the 'success' of performance management. It is less clear that the structures of performance management will in the medium term produce a 'nation equipped for the challenges and opportunities of the new millennium'. In the third section of this chapter I want to explore some of the ways in which performance management, as a policy translation of Labour's aspirations, is likely to impact on what we know about the behaviours of institutions, and especially schools, under regulation.

Managing performance under regulation

The regulatory framework within which schools operate tightened in the late 1980s through the introduction of the national curriculum, tightened again in the 1990s through the publication of examination results; and with the introduction of regular OfSTED (Office for Standards in Education) inspections has been more sharply tightened than ever. One way to interrogate the impact of performance management is to consider the ways in which institutions respond to regulatory frameworks. Any assessment or evaluation framework impacts on the behaviours it is intended to measure. For policy-makers, therefore, the key task is to design assessment and evaluation tools which impact virtuously on behaviour and which do not have negative unintended consequences. There is little doubt that much of the DfEE guidance quoted already assumes that performance management can only impact virtuously on schools' behaviour:

teachers will 'have a proper opportunity for professional discussion with their team leader . . . best practice is characterised by a commitment to attainment and welfare of pupils . . . an appreciation of the crucial role that teachers can play [and] an atmosphere of trust between teacher and team leader which allows them to evaluate strengths and identify areas for development (DfEE, 2000a p.3). It is in fact difficult to find any evidence of the direct virtuous impact of centrally planned change (Fullan, 1991, 1994; Finnan and Levin, 2000; Elliott, 1998).

There are a number of reasons for this. Of course, pupil outcomes are of enormous individual significance and schools have a social and perhaps moral obligation to maximise individual student attainments, raise aspirations and enhance employment and educational opportunities. However, translated from measures of individual attainment to institutional indices of success on which careers and institutional fates depend, pupil outcome measures begin to serve quite different purposes. Performance management is 'high stakes' policy-making for schools: on it depends not only institutional reputation and reward, but also teacher career development, and headteacher and teacher remuneration. Campbell's Law suggests that 'the more any quantitative social indicator is used for social decision-making, the more subject it will be to corruption pressures and the more apt it will be to distort and corrupt the social processes it is intended to monitor' (Campbell, 1977).

Throughout the 1990s, external performance measures of pupil attainment at school level have become increasingly public. Headline indicators have emerged: the average A-level points score at age eighteen, the percentage of pupils scoring five or more GCSE grades at A*–C as the key indicator at age sixteen, the percentage of pupils scoring level 4 or above at age eleven, and so on. Such indicators increasingly shape the allocation of resources and time in schools. In primary schools, attention during year six can most productively be focused on techniques which will support level 3 pupils in securing a level 4; in secondary schools the application of mentoring and revision techniques particularly to pupils predicted to score a grade D. For those pupils in receipt of additional attention and support, such techniques are almost certainly helpful and beneficial, but the point is that in these cases school effort is shaped by pressure of the social indicator, and, in many cases, attention is directed away from other pupils: those already likely to secure a level 4, who might with additional extended support realise further potential; those who have no realistic chance of securing a grade C however much support they receive. Less laudably, anecdotal evidence suggests that in some competitive settings, expectations of outcomes may influence admission decisions at primary, secondary, and particularly sixth-form level; or that in some settings the focus on testing itself – as opposed to the study and personal skills which equip learners to manage their learning – may narrow the curriculum. Different measurement techniques – alternative ways of calculating GCSE scores – or different measures, for example holding schools to account for the proportion of their pupils who begin and persevere with a musical instrument, would produce different measures and dictate different management actions. The more an indicator is used for social decision-making, the more subject it will be to corruption pressures.

In managing performance against any external targets, managers can only focus on those margins of organisational performance which are likely to engender enhanced institutional performance. A multinational company cannot reduce its overall environmental impact other than through a careful process of audit and the setting of short-term, measurable targets which will contribute to enhanced overall organisational performance. Schools must respond in individual ways, and successful management strategies involve the sequencing of marginal management strategies which enhance overall institutional success against medium-term targets. This approach to school improvement is now entrenched in statutory targets and buttressed by non-statutory guidance: targets for school improvement should be SMART (i.e. specific, measurable, attainable, realistic and time-framed); they should be focused on institutional priorities and should not be located in the 'historic' (past performance) or 'comfort' zones (DfEE, 1999). As an individual school improvement strategy, in the short term, management by marginal targets can bring about important successes (Gray *et al.*, 1999). However, Gray's study suggests, based on a sample of twelve improving schools, that improvement strategies organised around examination results, whilst useful for those pupils whose success was enhanced, tended to focus management activity on *tactical improvements*, entering some pupils for additional examinations, providing support for borderline candidates, reviewing syllabuses and homework policies – what one head called 'the improvement game'. Rarer, though more systemically effective, were strategic improvements which reviewed approaches which might help to raise achievement levels across the institution, whilst rarer still were 're-engineering' approaches which considered fundamental issues of teaching and learning. The relevance of Gray *et al.*'s research here is that the logic of performance management is most likely to encourage a search for tactical improvements which bring about short-term improvements. Gray and his collaborators question the long-term potential of tactical improvement to bring about systemic structural improvement: 'modest amounts of external pressure had undoubtedly helped to make the case for improvement. In this of all areas, however, it was difficult to mandate or impose the conditions of change' (Gray *et al.*, 1999 pp.145, 151). Whilst SMART targets provide short-term managerial routes to improvement, and thus may be important staging posts in school development, longer-term and systemic changes may demand more profound rethinking of structures and processes.

There is, in the long term, a potential tension between the rhetoric of New Labour's aspirations for an inclusive education system, which generates the capacity for lifelong learning, and the short-term consequences of target-focused, results-based schooling. The former encourages a focus on the long-term, structural constraints which impede achievement and success; the latter encourages a focus on the next set of results, the next cohort's attainments. Effective schooling is, of course, partially measured by examination and test results, and critics of assessment and review arrangements who forget this underplay the importance of credentials to pupils' life chances in a competitive labour market. However, not all the outcomes of schooling are short-term and not all are quantitative. Pupils learn many things in schools where it is difficult to quantify or measure the outcomes: they become involved in community activities, they learn musical instruments and play in school orchestras; they participate in school plays and school sports teams; they engage in community programmes and voluntary activity. They learn mathematics, science, art, and they also develop individual sensibilities and understandings of themselves and others. The 1988 Education Reform Act (ERA) captured something of this in its emphasis on the role of the school curriculum in promoting spiritual, moral, social and cultural development. Mary Warnock commented that 'of all the attributes that I would like to see in my [own] children or in my pupils, the attribute of hope would come high, even top of my list' (Warnock, 1986 p.182). Richard Pring has written persuasively about the contribution of education and schooling to what he calls 'the community of educated people' (Pring, 1996). Carol Taylor Fitzgibbon, whilst allowing that the pre-eminent outcome indicator in education is generally student achievement, nonetheless goes on to outline a series of process indicators, including the breadth and intrinsic value of education experiences, and longer-term outcome indicators of education including long-run retained knowledge and understanding and adult-reported quality of life as valid components in a measurement system. She concludes that 'one of the aims of indicator systems is to attach value to that which is measured' (Fitzgibbon, 2000 pp.260, 261). These tensions surface periodically in performance management policy guidance: 'best practice is characterised by a commitment to the attainment *and welfare* of pupils [emphasis added]' (DfEE, 2000b), but schools are encouraged to focus on 'clear concise and measurable' goals which, by definition, address issues of attainment rather than welfare. There is little specific guidance on how, in a performance management culture, concern for children's welfare, or their cultural, aesthetic and social education, might be manifested.

Here, as elsewhere, schools will have to make choices about the allocation of staffing, resources and institutional effort between competing, and in many cases equally pressing and valid, demands on their efforts and energies. As a result, tensions are inevitable between the culture of focus on comparative pupil performance – what DfEE guidance characterises as attainment reaching a standard 'as good as comparable pupils nationally' – and between other cultural traditions in English schooling, however much the latter might in the long-term contribute to pupil achievement. The now well-established literature on management economics explores the response of organisations to multi-objective regulatory frameworks. Selznick (1957) found that in settings where organisations were asked to meet multiple and competing objectives, few were structurally capable of meeting more than four or five complex targets simultaneously. In settings where there were perceived conflicts between the competing demands of different objectives, priority was given to the short-term, most pressing and most easily measurable target.

It may well be, as Gray's team suggests, that, historically, schools in difficulty gave insufficient attention to the analysis of data or the attainment of high pupil outcomes; but it is by no means clear that improved educational experiences and improved outcomes will derive from performance-based targets (Gray *et al.*, p.145). Indeed, the improvement literature is largely unanimous in seeing sustained improvement as a cultural rather than technical pursuit (Hargreaves, 1995; Fullan, 1995; Brighouse and Woods, 1998; James, 1999; and for case studies, Barker, 1999; Duffy, 1999). It is difficult to see how these tensions can be resolved for schools, but they are likely to result in the refocusing of school management on the attainment of narrow and partial, albeit important, short-term outcome measures.

Government policy towards the teaching profession has been influenced by Michael Fullan's maxim about the significance of both pressure and support (Barber, 2000), what some observers have termed 'carrot and semtex'. Performance management, in both general terms and detail, draws on the two. For successful schools, able year on year to meet and exceed pupil performance targets, the rewards in both status and remuneration promise to be considerable. For the successful school and the successful teacher, higher status, higher pay, and focused professional development are traded against greater accountability. There is, as Linda Evans indicates in Chapter 7 of this volume, a set of assumptions about the direct malleability of teacher motivation underpinning the trade-off.

This assumption about motivation is, I think, also to be found in the assumptions about school culture which underpin the DfEE's model of performance management. It is, of course, clear that professional dialogue as a structured component of school management and planning – about teacher objectives and professional development needs, about the relationship between individual teacher development and institutional development – is to be preferred over an absence of such dialogue. The DfEE's guidance on performance management does, indeed, refer to the provision of 'appropriate and effective personal training and development to ensure job satisfaction, a high level of expertise and progression of staff in their chosen profession' (DfEE, 2000c). But it stands in contrast to the force of other elements of performance management. What is at issue is the extent to which the dialogue, on which developing professional cultures depend, can be legislated through the structures of performance management. In some cases, the ecology[1] of schooling will be supportive. In others, the dynamics of change, the responsiveness to pupil needs will no more be developed through performance management than they have been through any other systemic attempt to impose policy-driven change on schools. School development, teacher development and teacher effectiveness depends on the exercise of imagination, on rigorous self-evaluation and on the involvement of the whole school community in change processes (Hopkins, Joyce and Calhoun, 2000).

This chapter began by exploring the differences between the complexity of day-to-day school management and the clarity of the government's ambitious aspirations for an education system which has at its core the concern for all individuals to fulfil their personal and educational potential. Performance management has been constructed as a largely technical tool, which relates government policy aspirations for short-term measurable improvements in outcome indicators, to mechanisms for the delivery of policy at school level. In the hands of gifted headteachers and team leaders, working in school cultures where improvement and development are well established, performance management policies will probably consolidate already successful practice. In schools where insufficient attention is still given to strategies for improvement and development, performance management may contribute to short-term performance gains, following from the Hawthorn effect. The real policy difficulties for schools, and, later, for the government, largely derive from the fact that we now have exceptionally detailed and sophisticated measures for tracking the performance of the school system in relation to examination and test results, but poor or undeveloped measures for tracking the attainment of the other desirable and important outcomes of schooling. Schools are complex, multi-objective institutions with a commitment to enhancing the quality of pupil learning experiences and their long-term life chances as well as their examination attainment. Where school reputations, teacher career development and remuneration are related only to measured attainment against well-developed indicators in one area of their wider purposes, the likelihood is that performance management will focus largely, if not exclusively, on achievement against that measure. In the short term, marginal strategies can contribute to school improvement. In the medium term, they may prevent more fundamental and long-term approaches to restructuring schooling and reshaping learning. In the long run it is far from clear that target-based performance management strategies can sustain the sort of dynamic, inclusive and successful education system on which the achievement of New Labour's aspirations depends.

Note

1 I am grateful to Vicki Pite for the term, the concept, and much helpful discussion about performance management and school cultures.

References

Barber, M. (1996), 'How to do the impossible: a guide for politicians with a passion for education', University of London, Institute of Education, Inaugural Lecture.

Barber, M. (2000), 'High expectations and standards for all – no matter what', *Times Educational Supplement*, 7 July 2000.

Barker, B. (1999), 'Double vision: forty years on', in H. Tomlinson, H. Gunter and P. Smith (eds), *Living Headship: voices, values and vision*, London: Paul Chapman, pp.73–85.

Bichard, M. 'Modernising the policy process', Lunchtime seminar, DfEE, 25 January 1999, and at *http://ntweb1/Gen_Brf_&_Speeches/Speeches/Michael%20Bichard/pmpa.htm*.

Blair, T. (1996), 'Twenty Years On', The Ruskin Lecture, Ruskin College.

Blair, T. (1999), 'The Romanes Lecture', University of Oxford, 2 December 1999.

Blunkett, D. (1999), 'Tackling Social Exclusion: Empowering People and Communities for a Better Future', London, DfEE, and at *http://www.dfee.gov.uk/socialexcl*.

Bridges, D. and McLaughlin, T. (eds), (1994), *Schools in the Marketplace*, Lewes: Falmer Press.

Brighouse, T. and Woods, D. (1998), *How to Improve Your School*, London: Routledge.

Campbell, D. T. (1977), 'Keeping the data honest in the experimenting society', in H. W. Melton and D. J. H. Weston (eds), *Interdisciplinary dimensions of accounting for social goals and social organisations*, Columbus Ohio: Grid Inc.

DfEE (1998), *Target Setting in Schools* (Circular 11/98), London: TSO, and at http://www.dfee.gov.uk/circulars/11_98.

DfEE (1998a), *Teachers Meeting the Challenge of Change*, London: DfEE.

DfEE (2000a), *Performance Management in Schools: Performance management framework*, London: DfEE.

DfEE (2000b), *Threshold Standards*, London: DfEE.

DfEE (2000c), *Education: Schoolteacher appraisal (England) Regulations 2000*, London: DfEE.

Duffy, E. (1999), 'Leading the creative school', in H. Tomlinson, H. Gunter and P. Smith (eds), *Living Headship: voices, values and vision*, London: Paul Chapman, pp.105–13.

Elliott, J. (1998), *The Curriculum Experiment*, Milton Keynes: Open University Press.

Finnan, C. and Levin, H. (2000), 'Changing school cultures', in J. Elliott and H. Altrichter (eds), *Images of Educational Change*, Buckingham: Open University Press, pp.87–98.

Fitzgibbon, C. T. (2000), 'School Effectiveness and Education Indicators', in D. Reynolds and C. Teddle (eds), *International Handbook of School Effectiveness Research*, London: Falmer Press, pp.260–1.

Fullan, M. (1994), *Change Forces: Probing the Depths of Educational Reform*, Lewes: Falmer Press.

Fullan, M. (1995), 'The school as a learning organisation: distant dreams', in *Theory into Practice*, Vol. 34 (4), pp.230–45.

Fullan, M. and Stiegelbauer, S. (1991), *The New Meaning of Educational Change*, London: Cassell.

Gray, J. and Wilcox, B. (1996), *'Good school, bad school': evaluating performance and encouraging improvement*, Buckingham: Open University Press.

Gray, J., Hopkins, D., Reynolds, D., Wilcox, B., Farrell, S. and Jesson, D. (1999), *Improving Schools: performance and potential*, Buckingham: Open University Press.

Halpin, D. and Whitty, G. (1998), *Devolution and choice in education: the school, the state and the market*, Buckingham: Open University Press.

Hargreaves, D. (1995), 'School effectiveness, school change and school improvement: the relevance of the concept of culture', in *School Effectiveness and School Improvement*, Vol. 6 (1), pp.23–46.

Hopkins, D., Joyce, B. and Calhoun, E. D. (2000), *The new structure of school improvement*, Buckingham: Open University Press.

Husbands, C. (1996), 'Schools, markets and collaboration: towards new models for educational polity?' in C. Husbands and D. Bridges (eds), *Consorting and collaborating in the educational market place: developing new relationships in schools and higher education*, Lewes: Falmer Press.

James, C. (1999), 'Institutional transformation and education management', in L. Bush, R. Bell, R. Bolam, R. Glatter and P. Ribbins (eds), *Educational management: redefining theory, policy and practice*, London: Paul Chapman, pp.129–41.

Labour Party (1997), 'Labour's education summit', 27 April 1997.

PAT (Professional Association of Teachers), (2000), *Tested to Destruction?: a survey of examination stress in teenagers*, Derby: PAT.

Pring, R. (1996), 'Values and education policy', in J. M. Halstead and M. Taylor (eds), *Values in education and education in values*, London: Falmer, pp.104–17.

Selznick, P. (1957), *Leadership in administration*, Evanston, Illinois: Row, Peterson.

Warnock, M. (1986), 'The education of the emotions', in D. Cooper, (ed.), *Education, Values and the Mind*, London: Routledge, p.182.

2 Managing performance management in the performing school

David Gentle

As of September 2000, new arrangements for performance management, backed up by the obligatory compelling legislation (DfEE, 2000a p.1), came into force to supersede terminally ailing appraisal systems. The purpose of this chapter is to raise several practical issues that may well have an impact on the immediate and middle-term management of schools as leaders strive to implement the requirements of performance management legislation within the context of current improvement strategies. As with much legislated change, it is highly likely that within a short period of time the issues raised here may either have been resolved by practitioners or have been rendered superfluous by further change.

Much of the official DfEE documentation on performance management has the now familiar style of extolling its virtues in terms of enhanced teacher development, job satisfaction, staff progression and raising standards through meeting the needs of children (DfEE, 2000b p.1). School leaders will have the responsibility of ensuring that these expectations are met more effectively than, for instance, those associated with appraisal. In view of the fact that the DfEE documentation tends to describe, rather than define, performance management and that the principles of performance management are adopted from consultants with limited experience of schools, an appropriate starting point might be a definition from outside the world of education.

'Performance management is a strategic and integrated approach to delivering sustained success to organisations by improving the performance of the people who work in them and by developing the capabilities of teams and individual contributors' (Armstrong and Baron, 1998 p.7). Taking an overview of the literature, there are four main characteristics of performance management arising from the definitions (Hartle, 1995 p.12). First, it is a process rather than an event. Performance management must permeate the school culture on a day-to-day basis and must not be considered simply as an annual form-filling exercise to gain instant reward.

Second, the process must be used to generate an increased understanding of what the organisation is trying to achieve and how this can be accomplished. Staff must have a shared picture of what success looks like and what they are aiming to achieve. Third, it is a way of managing people to ensure that aims are met through appropriate lines of accountability. Fourth, it is about people sharing in the success of the organisation to which they have contributed.

Historically, the performance culture has arisen through an emphasis on decentralised managerial and financial control within a climate of increased concern for accountability and value for money (OECD, 1993 p.13 and Tomlinson, 1992 p.1). What has slowed down the process has been the lack of a judgemental framework (Murlis, 1992 p.55), rather than any ideological reticence about performance management. This has been particularly the case within the education system where the imposed parameters have determined that there has been a transition from professionalism to managerialism (Flynn, 1990 p.56).

The DfEE also emphasises that performance management works best when it is an integral part of the school culture and that the consequences are raised standards, continuous professional development, involvement of all staff in planning, improved management and equity through openness and fairness (DfEE, 2000b p.4). It convincingly promotes the benefits for teachers (workforce) and pupils (customers). There is, however, an argument that establishing performance management systems within schools will give a reason, if one is needed, to deflect blame for under-performance from the political to the professional arena. Clearly, it is intended that performance management processes should have links with pay (DfEE, 2000a p.4) through the use of the review statements in decision-making with regard to promotion and progression. Sir Keith Joseph's abandoned ideas of performance-related pay in the early 1980s (Heywood, 1992 p.131) have now been revived in a different form by a Labour government.

Two pieces of advice may be appropriate for the unsuspecting school leader who believes that performance-related pay will automatically lead to increased staff morale. First, the joy of the majority of staff who go through the threshold or otherwise gain salary increases will be as nothing compared to the misery of those who do not. Second, a reference to Maslow's hierarchy of needs will confirm that, although satisfactory pay is required to fulfil basic need, there are four higher levels involving self-fulfilment, esteem, companionship and safety (Trethowan, 1987 p.49). Performance-related pay can be a motivating factor, will reward high achievers, can encourage a transparent system, reinforces high levels of expectation and can be used to facilitate change. However, finance does not guarantee sustained motivation. Measuring performance, particularly qualitative, can be difficult. It can focus on the individual rather than teams, it can lead to a narrow range of targets and can be short term.

Within the documentation it is somewhat confusing that the term 'appraisal' is stated as synonymous with 'performance management' (DfEE, 2000a p.3). Again, it may be best to look for an explanation beyond the world of education, where there are broadly two schools of thought. The first is that performance management is closely linked to the growth of accountability (Bell, 1988 p.2). This is taking the old commercial model of, for example, commission based on sales – whereby teachers are rewarded according to mainly quantitative output. The second, and more appropriate, is that performance management helps employees to understand what they need to do to perform more effectively (Hartle, 1995 p.52). The key areas are continuous improvement and employee development through consistent and transparent processes.

Most teachers will no doubt feel able to accept the general principles of performance management and will look forward to realisation of the clear benefits. However, as with much innovation within education, the devil will be in the detail. I want therefore to pose a series of questions that might be asked by school managers in relation to the practical aspects of performance management.

Who is my team leader?

The team leader is responsible for carrying out the annual review of the teacher (DfEE, 2000a p.4) and is clearly a key person (DfEE, 2000b p.5) with regard to collating and presenting evidence of the teacher's achievements and consequent objectives. It is therefore important, particularly as teachers may have no say in the matter, that the team leader structure is appropriate. In most schools this may well be very similar to that which operated for appraisal (Trethowan, 1991 p.45). Thus, in a large secondary school, heads of department, assisted by their deputies and other postholders, will be team leaders for members of their department. Similarly, the head will be the team leader for all members of the leadership team and they, in turn, will be team leaders for heads of department.

Although this may well be the most expedient model, it does present a number of challenges. Most heads will be comfortable with the benefits of having a clear structure within which they can mould the leadership team. Management, leadership and developmental objectives will flow naturally from such a relationship. However, the head is unlikely to be an expert in relation to the variety of subjects taught by members of the team, or indeed in any subject, perhaps. Similarly, it is unlikely that members of the leadership team will have, between them, expertise in all subjects of the curriculum. The head of modern languages may end up being assessed by a team leader whose knowledge of French is as a consequence of a weekend trip to Paris. Conversely, the head of year seven who teaches mathematics will find themselves being assessed by the head of department who may have little knowledge of the management objectives related to being a head of year.

All of this demonstrates a simple principle. That is, teachers very often have more than one line manager. For example, a head of year is line managed by the head of department within which they teach and also, usually, by an appropriate deputy head. This is not considered to be a major problem outside education where individuals are often members of several teams. Within schools, there must be a system whereby subsidiary team leaders input relevant objectives to the review process for each teacher. Such a process will involve the teachers themselves in collating objectives and will also necessitate discussion between team leaders. It will be necessary to include in the school policy an agreement about the proportion of management and teaching objectives. Thus, if there were to be four objectives altogether, for a classroom teacher these might all be teaching-related; for a middle manager there could be two teaching and two management; and for a deputy head there might be three management and one teaching.

Within the above structure, there is still scope for the deployment of local knowledge in determining the team leader system. Although compliance with a logical, transparent structure is essential, there are areas for compromise, particularly within the department. This might well be the case, for instance, with the highly experienced head of year where care must be taken in matching this person with an appropriate subject postholder. If all else fails, then the head of department will need to be the team leader. Schools where heads of year are remunerated at a higher level than heads of department may find that this challenge verges on being a problem. However, in general terms, there are advantages for developing the system outlined in that it will increase communication between middle managers and give all staff a broader understanding of whole-school issues.

How will performance management affect morale?

It is clearly intended that information from review statements may inform decisions about promotion and pay (DfEE, 2000a p.4). It is also clear that teachers who are unsuccessful in achieving promotion or pay advancement, particularly if the issue is common knowledge with other staff, are unlikely to be happy. This situation would be exacerbated if school planners, or even parents, made decisions about which group those teachers perceived as weaker should be given to teach. Would it be acceptable, for instance, for the most able mathematics set to be taught by a teacher who had failed to cross the threshold? On social justice grounds, would it be acceptable for pupils in lower sets to be taught by such teachers? Given that the consequences of review could be unpalatable for staff, it is even more important that the process is continuous, systematic and fair. Teachers must be clearly directed towards personal professional development that will address any perceived weaknesses. In this way, if pay progression is refused on the basis of evidence from the review process, then the teacher will see that they have failed to take the steps that were clearly signalled to them for improvement. Even for successful teachers, life is now made difficult through the introduction of a multiplicity of career routes. Should they go for management or advanced skills, fifth management allowance or assistant head? Career progression becomes more risky than buying shares.

The cycle of plan, monitor, and review must be followed meticulously with consistency across the organisation, with preparation time for both the reviewer and the teacher whose work is the subject of review, a clear focus for review and predetermined time schedules. Monitoring must be a continuous process with ongoing review of progress, an aspect that is not adequately emphasised within the guidance and which might be difficult to implement given constraints in schools. The minimum requirement of at least one lesson observation per year is unlikely to prove satisfactory for effective monitoring.

All current professional guidance documents, quite rightly, emphasise that as soon as serious deficiencies are identified in a teacher's performance, then separate capability procedures will be triggered (NASUWT/SHA, 2000 p.4). This enables a wider range of evidence to be considered (Trethowan, 1991 p.69) and also removes a substantial area of negativity from the performance management process.

What about collegiality?

There is evidence to suggest that collegiate approaches towards school improvement are far more effective than the efforts of those working in isolation. Having made this generalisation, it should be pointed out that not everyone agrees. Some research has shown, for example, that working in teams brings about a phenomenon called social loafing whereby people working in team settings exert less effort than they would do individually (Armstrong and Baron, 1998 p.257). Whichever view is taken, any process that potentially raises the contribution of the individual is to be welcomed. There is a clear argument that performance management can be used to communicate school vision, culture and aims thus reducing the possibility of value conflict within teams. The strategy mentioned in a previous section, of middle managers collating objectives for individuals, will also serve to develop collegiality beyond conventional teams.

The proposed structure of team leader performance management will serve to strengthen the lines of communication and management within department teams in particular; but will also depend for its success on the abilities of team leaders to develop their own performance management skills. There is no reason to assume that the only way teams can operate effectively is under a flat management system and every reason to expect that clarity of roles and responsibilities will enhance team performance. Difficulties will arise in a few circumstances. For example, if a team leader is judged as not meeting the standards for threshold assessment this may give rise to a lack of confidence on the part of team members. In this case, it might be questioned as to how a team leader could have been allowed to be in such a position and why appropriate action had not been taken earlier.

What is a good lesson?

For the majority of teachers, performance in lessons will be the main factor for discussion at the review. It is therefore critically important that school leaders have a consistent concept as to what constitutes a good lesson, that this is communicated to all staff and that the methods of data collection reflect the school's priorities. Hitherto, many schools would have been using an *ad hoc*, if any, method of lesson observation within their whole school self-evaluation policy. In this respect, help is at hand since the associations (the National Association of Schoolmasters and Union of Women Teachers; the Secondary Heads Association; the National Union of Teachers) (NASUWT/SHA, 2000 p.7 and NUT, 2000 p.12) and the DfEE (DfEE, 2000c p.20) have produced useful guidelines and associated standard forms. This is not the case for the existing OfSTED pro-forma that, in character, is likely to prove vague, subjective and provocative. The lesson observation time/events log suggested by the DfEE is a more helpful starting point, being based on recognised qualitative research techniques and aspiring to be objective. In cases of disagreement between the team leader and teacher, the time/events log could be a relatively neutral document for reference. All three suggested classroom observation checklists are very similar but schools will need to adapt the wording to suit their particular ethos. Some of the wording in the DfEE model is either inconsistent or susceptible to multiple interpretations. For example the terms 'discipline' and 'class management' are used interchangeably and without definition. Clearly there is a need for INSET (Inservice Education and Training) to ensure that all team leaders are adopting a consistent approach to classroom observation. Following a lesson observation there must be feedback within a few days otherwise the time spent will have been wasted. A proven starting point for this meeting is to agree the facts on the time/events log and for the team leader to ask the teacher for their opinion as to how the lesson went. From this point, the team leader will lead a two-way discussion to identify strengths, areas for development and teacher comment to record on the classroom observation feedback record. This, in turn, will inform the annual review statement.

Although in most cases such review statements will be uncomplicated and agreed, there is nonetheless considerable potential for professional disagreement about issues of lesson quality. Such disagreement has traditionally been seen as legitimate, and in some cases as productive. But if review statements are to form the basis for decisions about promotion and pay, then disagreement assumes a different dimension.

Which groups have I got next year?

One of the great benefits of the threshold assessment process has been to focus teachers' attention on the use of information about prior attainment in setting expectations for pupils and subsequent analysis to show that progress has been made (DfEE, 2000d p.4). Disappointingly, the lesson observation guidance (DfEE, 2000c p.20), because it refers to a single lesson, cannot convey such a clear line regarding demonstration of progress. For many teachers, progression is conveyed over sequences of lessons. Thus, most schools will wish to make pupil progress over a period of time a significant factor in relation to evidence presented at the annual review. Managers must demand that progress of a class with a particular teacher over a period of time is shown to be at or beyond that which is expected in relation to prior attainment and national norms. As a consequence, it may increasingly be the case that teachers will realise that it is to their advantage to be assigned teaching groups where they have a reasonable chance of demonstrating satisfactory measurable progress. It is certainly the case that schools in difficulties or those in challenging settings will find recruitment and retention increasingly difficult unless additional policy models on teacher pay and recruitment are implemented. Schools must have systems of collating predictive data based on several assessments and distributing this to all the staff. Everyone within the establishment must have a clear idea of the potential of each individual student in each subject area. Given this, teachers are even more likely to be selective about the groups that they would wish to take. It might be argued, for example, that progress is easier to demonstrate at key stage four than at key stage three due to increased separation of subjects. It is also the case that progress will appear to be more rapid when prior attainment results are lower than expected. Consequently teachers may wish to take over a group previously taught by a weak colleague. It must be considered that progress is generally not uniform across the whole ability range and consequently teachers will be looking to take classes at a level where progress has historically been good. Staff will be unwilling to take groups where attendance is poor, since it is somewhat difficult to demonstrate satisfactory progress with a class of persistent truants. Tensions may also arise due to the fact that progress is easier to measure in the core subjects.

Colleagues compiling the school timetable may find that teachers are no longer willing to teach outside their main specialist area, since they may well be unable to show good subject knowledge and understanding. Nor will they be willing to share classes with a less competent colleague. A further challenge is presented by the use of cover staff. Many secondary schools employ full-time cover teachers on their permanent staff. Although from the school's point of view, this is generally more effective than daily-rate cover, the teacher concerned will have more difficulty in demonstrating several aspects within the lesson observation guidance. Incidentally, this raises issues about staff employed by cover agencies and those on teachers' conditions of service employed by the local education authority at the centre. Overall, teachers are likely to be less obliging in terms of the classes that they are willing to teach.

What are my objectives?

Objectives are an important tool for the school manager in shifting staff towards actions that are in accord with the school improvement plan. They can be used to encourage compliance with the school culture, bring about higher student achievement or indicate ways of improving unsatisfactory teacher performance. Objectives will be about pupil progress, associated professional development and, in relevant cases, management or leadership (DfEE, 2000 p.14). Much has been written about the nature of objectives in as much as they should be clear, concise, challenging yet realistic, appropriate, measurable and time-related. It might also be suggested that they should be flexible in order to respond to change over time. Views vary as to how many objectives there should be. Associations recommend three on the grounds that more would be confusing and time-consuming (NUT, 2000 p.8), whereas the DfEE suggests between three and six. In view of the fact that objectives should be specific, rather than generic, it is likely that managers would prefer six since it could be argued that twice as much can be achieved. Irrespective of the number of objectives, concerns remain. First, a finite number of objectives may lead to teachers confining their activities to their pursuit at the expense of everything else. This is similar to the boundary tactics employed by schools to attain a higher percentage of five A*–C grades and prior to the realisation by the DfEE that this could be countered by frequent changes to regulatory procedures. Second, there may be an assumption that if a teacher meets his or her objectives then salary progression is automatic. The contradiction arises in linking these two concepts together whereby a teacher who meets pupil progress objectives but fails in other aspects of their work cannot reasonably expect progression.

Further difficulties may arise from the requirement for objectives to be measurable. Education and other public services have already suffered from the consequences of attaching importance only to that which is easily measurable (Flynn, 1990 p.113). Many schools will need to develop strategies, such as questionnaires, interviews and surveys, for assessing qualitative issues in order to retain a balance in accord with all of the school aims. There is the opportunity to set objectives in relation to team performance (Trethowan, 1991 p.41; Armstrong and Baron, 1998 p.287) thus, to some extent, rebuilding aspects of collegiality that may have been lost through other aspects of performance management. A further area that is not clear is the status of objectives when the two parties cannot agree. Despite the fact that this is raised in the guidance (DfEE, 2000a p.5), there remains the critical issue of what happens when a disputed objective is not achieved.

What is the future for professional development?

As with appraisal, one of the biggest carrots offered to teachers from performance management is the issue of their own professional development (DfEE, 2000b p.3). It is hopefully not intentional that the DfEE describes the importance of team leader discussions about professional development, omitting any mention of implementation. It is clear that the credibility of performance management depends largely on the capability of the school to deliver appropriate professional development identified within review statements. There must be a system for collating professional development needs and incorporating delivery through a well-planned, financially viable development planning cycle. This might prove difficult given that the professional development coordinator is not permitted to know the identity of staff having a particular need. Coordinators will play a key role in ensuring the effective delivery of identified needs and in collating feedback from participants, assuming issues of confidentiality have been resolved. Since professional development is linked to objectives, which are in turn about student and school improvement, there might be a more restricted package of opportunities available for staff. This is particularly so in relation to professional development for career advancement and pursuit of higher qualifications, where it is not always possible to establish a link with the school improvement plan. A somewhat unexpected bonus has been the degree of professional development achieved through hours of thought when completing the threshold assessment application form. Many members of staff have considerably advanced their thinking, particularly about varied teaching strategies, using information about prior attainment, measuring students' progress, wider professional characteristics and, perhaps above all, taking responsibility for their own professional development. From the perspective of the school manager, the clear link between student achievement, the school improvement plan, objectives and subsequent professional development, will be generally welcomed. It gives the opportunity to promote whole-school priorities, for example with regard to literacy, numeracy and ICT (Information and Communications Technology), and also to develop a climate in accord with the school vision statement.

Who pays?

There are at least four major areas associated with performance management that have clear resource implications (OECD, 1993 p.75). First, there are start up training costs for heads, governors and whole staff training days. Second, there are continuing operational costs. Staff associations require that schools should provide additional staff time for team leaders to meet staff and conduct classroom observations during the teaching day. The total time budget must be within the 1,265 hours of teacher-directed time and include all aspects of performance management such as the recording of objectives. Activities will need to be planned in such a way as to use cover teachers for whole days and not parts. Difficulties have already arisen with the threshold process. Although it could be argued that a member of staff should consider it reasonable to spend four hours or so completing the application form for the probability of gaining £2,000, heads are not so enthusiastic about spending endless weekends assessing them for no additional reward.

Third, performance management, as with appraisal systems, raises staff expectations about effective delivery of identified professional development needs. Given that professional development coordinators will need to be more systematic about planning delivery, there is an imperative that adequate funds for training are delegated to schools and not earmarked for government-determined priorities. From a teacher's point of view, performance management may stand or fall on this basis. Fourth, is the issue of the ongoing salary bill. Some promises have been made about funding threshold payments and costs associated with the new leadership scale for a few years. However, these payments, together with double increments, fast-tracking, incentives for shortage subjects, retention allowances, leadership scales, advanced skills teachers, and any other future whim, have considerable implications for longer-term budget profiling. Perhaps the master plan is that schools are compelled to make expensive 'weak' teachers redundant in order to meet financial targets.

What about school self-evaluation?

It has already been emphasised that performance management must be built in, not built on, to existing systems. Previous sections have referred to building in performance management in relation to the whole-school leadership dimensions of communicating vision and mission, planning the budget profile, target-setting, implementing improvement plans and coordinating staff development. What has not been mentioned is the interrelationship of performance management and whole-school self-evaluation processes. This can be a complex issue, complicated by the apparent similarity of aspects of each dimension, particularly classroom observation. In a large secondary school at departmental level the connection is relatively straightforward since the team leader network for performance management is virtually concurrent with the departmental line management system. It is therefore possible to use evidence from departmental self-evaluation to inform the continuous process of performance management and, similarly, to use classroom observation within performance management as one element of self-evaluation.

Unfortunately, beyond the departmental level this relative simplicity is not present, since members of the leadership team will not generally be managing the performance of the same people that they line manage. As with many challenges within education, the more thought the issue is given, the worse it appears. The solution, then, is to keep it simple. The leadership team can be regarded as a central clearing-house for information. Evidence for consideration within the self-evaluation cycle will come to the leadership team from at least two directions. First, will be the evidence from leadership team members in relation to the area of responsibility that they have. The member with responsibility for curriculum would, as a natural part of their duties, contribute evidence in relation to the quality of teaching and learning. In doing so they would no doubt use other members of the leadership team to observe lessons. This person would also report on the effectiveness and outcomes of departmental self-review. Second, members of the leadership team would input supplementary evidence derived from their performance management of middle managers. One of the benefits of the system is that school leaders engage in exchanges through collating and analysing evidence, thus leading to collegiate professional development and giving rise to strategies for school improvement.

Conclusions

There are, no doubt, many more practical issues that will arise through the implementation of performance management. This might be particularly so in aspects that have not been mentioned such as managing poor performance, managing leadership teams and the plight of the head teacher, for which there is likely to be limited sympathy. Overall, a fully integrated performance-management system can integrate the major functions of the school. An effective performance-management system will involve all staff in analysis of input, process and output data leading to planning for continuous development and improvement. All members of the school will gain from a fair, objective and transparent system that promotes shared expectations, attitudes and behaviour leading to strategies for improvement.

References

Armstrong, M. and Baron, A. (1998), *Performance Management*, London: Institute of Personnel and Development.

Bell, L. (1988), *Appraising Teachers in Schools*, London: Routledge.

DfEE (2000a), *Performance Management in Schools: Guidance Notes*, Sudbury: DfEE.

DfEE (2000b), *Performance Management in Schools: Performance Management Framework*, Sudbury: DfEE.

DfEE (2000c), *Performance Management in Schools: Model Performance Management Policy*, Sudbury: DfEE.

DfEE (2000d), *Threshold Assessment: Application Pack*, Sudbury: DfEE.

Flynn, N. (1990), *Public Sector Management*, Hemel Hempstead: Harvester Wheatsheaf.

Hartle, F. (1995), *Transforming the Performance Management Process*, London: Kogan Page Limited.

Heywood, J. (1992), 'School Teacher Appraisal: For Monetary Reward, or Professional Development or Both?' in H. Tomlinson (ed.), *Performance Related Pay in Education*, London: Routledge.

Murlis, H. (1992), 'Performance-related Pay in the Context of Performance Management' in H. Tomlinson (ed.), *Performance Related Pay in Education*, London: Routledge.

NASUWT/SHA (2000), *Model Performance Management Policy*, Rednal: NASUWT/SHA.

NUT (2000), *Managing Performance Management*, London: NUT.

OECD (Organisation for Economic Cooperation and Development), (1993), *Private Pay for Public Work*, Paris: OECD.

Risher, H. and Fay, C. (eds), (1995), *The Performance Imperative*, San Francisco: Jossey-Bass Publishers.

Tomlinson, H. (ed.), (1992), *Performance-related Pay in Education*, London: Routledge.

Trethowan, D. (1987), *Appraisal and Target Setting*, London: Harper and Row Limited.

Trethowan, D. (1991), *Managing with Appraisal*, London: Paul Chapman Publishing Ltd.

3   A right performance

Richard Arrowsmith

I came to my performance management training in the last four weeks of a year in which we had: had an OfSTED inspection; introduced asset management; planned for the new sixth-form curriculum; debated whether and then how to implement the new key skills qualification; gone through the threshold process and received 52 applications; run the longest Dialogue 2000 project in the country; begun preparing the specialist college bid; prepared for the revised national curriculum; sketched in the issues for citizenship; run our first summer literacy school and follow-up programme; and coped with a very high level of staff absence and illness in an extremely difficult budget year. Already on the horizon for next year are the coming of 'connexions', and the new code of practice for special needs.

I begin writing with this list, not as a prelude to a whinge, but because it describes a true context for this latest significant change. In other schools, there would have been different items on an equally overcrowded list, but few teachers would have been sitting idly by waiting for a nice new initiative to implement. Major planning issues now come along on average at the rate of one per month for teachers; each with an emphasis on the processes of planning, implementation, monitoring, review and evaluation. They all go into the melting pot and we teachers do our best.

But how can this be the way any government seriously intends to build a new service? We cannot believe, with all its data and information systems, that the government does not know the weight of the demands made on schools and the serious danger of having an 'implementation culture' for schemes which never become embedded because there is not enough time to embed them. I do believe that heads and their management teams have become very adept in absorbing, conceptualising, consulting and implementing new initiatives. These are things that many schools do well because of the calibre of the senior management in schools. However, there is a cost to this both personally and professionally. For every new job taken on, something somewhere goes less well in their professional or personal lives.

As an illuminating aside, we received two invitations to the training event: one invited us to arrive from 8.45 for a 9.30 a.m. start. The other contained a programme clearly showing that the event started at 10.00. The regional organisers, facing busy heads who had arrived too early, distanced themselves from this irritating niggle, saying that the DfEE had set the times and sent both letters. Surely someone was not sitting in the DfEE setting the times of training events up and down the country? I assumed not until, sitting through Anthea Millett's recorded message ("I expect most of you will know me . . ."), I had the uncomfortable feeling of being one of several thousand headteachers who would all be receiving the same message between 10.10 and 10.20 a.m. in far-flung venues and then trooping off to discussion groups to follow a programme which was being carefully scripted by the DfEE. Unfortunately the Orwellian sense of all this was rather undermined by the knowledge that the script was changing daily as DfEE civil servants attempted to adapt their script and the processes it described, in the light of conference questions from the previous few days. From the assembled ranks came deep rumblings of discontent: Headteachers Behaving Badly.

Does no-one see the dangers of this mania for control? Teachers are required to be performance technicians, and heads to become systems managers. Why do we keep hearing about the need for heads to be creative, imaginative leaders with flair and vision when there is so little scope to demonstrate those skills, and when it is always someone else who has all the visions? Is the real purpose of performance management to keep the engines of some vast national machine purring quietly and in perfect tune, and to make minor adjustments with appropriately sharp tools when necessary?

The question arose during the training day as to whether heads were cynics, idealists or frustrated romantics. This was because the nature and tone of the training put us in an odd position. One is made to feel strangely unpatriotic by questioning the motives or procedures of major initiatives. The government clearly wishes to improve educational performance even if it does not yet have a broader educational vision, and it is quite challenging for a head of eleven years' experience to know why it does not feel better to be in such an improved and beneficial climate. It may be that this government shares with its predecessor the view that the only way to improve schools is the way it has decided and although no-one can doubt the extent of the consultation process on this issue, it has not been about 'whether', it has been about 'how'. It is no secret how badly some regional meetings went. Did the government ever seriously consider dropping the initiative as a result? Was a significant alternative ever considered which might have achieved the same or even better outcomes? What was the real agenda? Listening to the earnestness of ministers like David Blunkett and Estelle Morris, it seems such a pity that many heads still feel that they are in opposition and have to develop those skills which enable them to 'render unto Caesar that which is Caesar's and render unto God that which is God's' (as Professor Tomlinson memorably described it when he spoke at the Shropshire heads' conference in 1998). We are by no means all on the same side yet.

An overview of the proposals

Of all the skills headteachers have developed or possess intuitively since this bizarre world of education was invaded by politicians half a generation ago, two must rank as essential for survival: that of forming good judgements and that of making good decisions based on them which will stand up to close and unrelenting scrutiny hours, days and weeks later. Our basic instincts for headship may not have changed very much during this period. We still want our institutions to succeed and are proud of them: they are our life's work. I have yet to meet the colleague who champions mediocrity and low standards. We want our staff to enjoy a working atmosphere which challenges them professionally, but is sufficiently comfortable to make them want to keep coming back for more. We want our students to enjoy the opportunities which we know exist out there, and we want to provide a service which compensates for the crumbling at the edges of our society as the unrelenting pressures on work and marriage cause such damage. We know that learning pays.

Most people left that training day disgruntled (that is to say, remembering John Arlott, few were actually 'gruntled'). The most impatient left at midday. Then began that transitional period between being told what to think and thinking for oneself. Many of us, furious at the shambles of the threshold payment, were not won over to performance management. It is hard for heads to stand up in front of staff and propose something we do not fundamentally believe in: there have been too many such impositions in recent years.

In detail, the package for performance management is not wholly unattractive. Talking about your work and setting goals for yourself in a well-structured framework is a good form of professional development. Having to think hard about opportunities for training and having to relate inset to these goals is very sound for a profession which, perhaps because of tiny training budgets throughout this enormous period of change, has tended to muddle through on the job rather than take time out to observe, reflect and envisage how things might be. I am not quite sure how much tension there could be between a profession which became highly trained, articulate and inquisitive, and a government wishing to maintain rigid systems for the curriculum and (who knows from what the Prime Minister says from time to time?) for teaching methodology. Such a day seems a long way off at the moment however. But if performance management beds down successfully, it could well be in the field of staff development that we see the most beneficial outcome. The decision to increase the number of opportunities for staff to study school systems abroad may be the beginning of a remarkable expansion of expertise and understanding on the part of colleagues, many of whom in many schools are currently too tired, demoralised or confused to engage in serious professional debate or in development projects beyond those they have to undertake in their classrooms and departments.

A mechanism for increasing the scope and responsibility of subject leaders is much needed and many heads will use performance management as the lever to achieve something they have been wanting to achieve for some time. We have to move away from the old model of the head of department advocating departmental staff like a gatekeeper to rebuff management incursions. There are still pockets of such resistance in many schools. The subject leader needs to be the voice of the management within the department and this uncompromising line-management model will move us further along this road.

It is also challenging for individual teachers to have to embrace developments at department and school level and to consider realistically what part they can play in them. It will be beneficial to team-building processes for everyone to have a considered view on what their contribution is to the whole. Just as it is good and right to negotiate reports with children so that they cannot dismiss them by saying 'well, she doesn't like me anyway' or 'I'm no good at German', so it is good and right to engage all staff in school developments. It is too easy for hard-pressed teachers to view the school plan as something other people do while they themselves get on with things in their classroom. I have a feeling that this part of the process will not be too difficult to implement. Advice, ideas, untapped expertise and volunteers have always lurked beyond the traditional middle-management posts. Deeper-rooted monitoring processes will be beneficial too. Most schools have developed such systems to a degree in recent years and the chances are that great care has been taken to avoid the 'big-brother-is-watching-you' approach. Peer monitoring, more open departmental discussions, clearing agendas in order to focus on teaching and learning; all have been subtle, sensible, realistic and acceptable ways of opening classroom doors and minds which had been closed for a long time. It was for this reason that some schools, during the early days of the appraisal initiative, adopted very successful 'pool' models of appraisal; these may have been on the soft side, but they undoubtedly served to make appraisal acceptable to an untrusting profession. How will schools cope with a more managerial and top–down model when they have experienced something better? This was a real dilemma for a colleague at our training event, who was clearly already running an excellent monitoring system and was gloomy at the prospect of rigidity in the model she was being told to implement.

This issue – the managerialist underpinnings of the DfEE's performance management model – will hit many schools where the management team is working extremely well and in a spirit of friendship, mutual trust and interdependence. It will need yet another 'trick' for heads to bring a sense of purpose and worthwhile outcomes to planning, monitoring and review sessions with such close colleagues. The performance management approach perhaps works in some cultures outside teaching, but not in others. Performance management seems a risky strategy when you consider how much teachers rely on each other and support each other in management teams through the issues which arise both predictably and unexpectedly every day of the year. I feel sure that if studies of outstanding teams were made and lessons learned, this simplistic approach of performance management would not be recommended as a means of improving such teams still further. It seems odd that the Prime Minister should be criticising comprehensives for their one-fit-for-all approach (which has failed to bring about the transformation of the education system) while advocating a one-fit-for-all performance management system in order to bring about the transformation of the teaching profession. It is another of the ironies and contradictions which run through the management of education at national level.

The monitoring aspect of performance management feels rather thin. It is easy to see how the planning and review meetings could be very focused and could therefore achieve a lot; but the amount of time between them will create some difficulties. The expected three to four hours devoted to monitoring will be lost in the weeks and months set aside for the purpose and it will be difficult for both parties to keep the spirit of the planning meeting going. However, any attempt either to telescope the process overall, or alternatively to suggest that more monitoring should be carried out would precipitate a crisis in school planning.

On balance and with reservations, performance management adds up to a package which I would feel able to recommend to staff as an updated version of the appraisal system which failed to take root. It is a little harder to sell to staff than appraisal was: the language and tone of the little brown pamphlet sent to all teachers convey a different climate: 'your head teacher will decide which colleague has the best overview of your work' (DfEE, 2000) is not a comforting line for teachers with little confidence in their head of department, or indeed their head, or who work in a number of teams.

In the pack sent to headteachers, the phrase 'the head teacher must ensure that team leaders carry out their responsibilities' is not a comforting line for those many subject heads who are not going any further in the profession and who are ill at ease with the many new demands on them. The performance management model which has emerged has not made it any easier for heads who have been seeking ways of rethinking traditional structures in schools and finding room for more cross-curricular positions of responsibility to replace the traditional subject model. The current national curriculum surely cannot survive long into the twenty-first century and will logically be replaced by something more integrated, more competence-based and less subject orientated. As and when that happens, a government which is not currently looking beyond the standards agenda will have to rethink its performance management model and may regret the lost opportunity to make early inroads into school structures which desperately need a rethink. One cannot argue with the sentiment that there should be ways of rewarding high-quality classroom teachers through tough thresholds; but if the other side of the coin is to devalue imaginative management and planning through the reinforcement of traditional structures, then heads will have been dealt a poor set of cards in the long run. We should not overlook the fact that although we need excellent classroom teachers, we also need excellent managers, planners and leaders. I believe the absence of any incentive for this is a flaw which will lie dormant for a number of years only to hit us in the face in a few years time like the current recruitment crisis is hitting us now.

Opportunity or threat?

There will be serious grounds for criticism of performance management if it is implemented with an undercurrent of staff fear. I know there will be many schools where heads, staff and governors have worked successfully to create a good climate of genuinely high professional standards. In such schools, this measure will slip in – possibly with some resentment – but will not undermine that morale which comes from being on board a good ship. But these are the A and B grade schools. As we all know from our GCSE crusades, it is the C/D borderline schools that need the most attention: our challenge is to bring them up. Will fear of governors reading their reviews and blocking their promotion, fear of having a bad review, fear of having to work with a head of department in whom they do not have total confidence all come together and make this many times more difficult to work with than it need have been? This may be the consequence of the link with pay. While understanding the rationale and the rhetoric put forward by defenders of the idea, I think it really is a risk. Some cynics may take the view that OfSTED is based on and engenders a climate of fear; but few would deny that it has contributed to driving up standards in schools. It may be worth the risk, but what does it say about the sense of professionalism which this government talks so much about?

Is performance management a threat or an opportunity? It is a crucial question, but like all big questions there is no clear-cut answer. In theory, it is almost certainly an opportunity, but in the real world we inhabit, it contains several elements of threat. But headteachers are skilled at turning threats into opportunities: 'The trick is', we were told at our instruction day, 'to make staff see that performance management is an opportunity and an entitlement'. In its rhetoric, the DfEE appears to recognise this ability we have; yet if there is one comment I could make which points to a major failure of strategic planning, it is that they underestimated or ignored the vital importance of winning the hearts and minds of headteachers on this issue. We do not understand why it has to be this issue at this time. It has caused us a lot of problems, involved us in yet another hugely bureaucratic exercise – perhaps the largest ever – and has awakened the spirit of militancy which has been quiet for a while. It did not have to be like this, but somewhere in the slippage between two key phrases uttered on television by Mr Blair and Mr Blunkett: 'Let us never forget that it is the people who have put us into power'; and, within a year, 'Our flagship policies are not negotiable'; lies that elusive arrogance of power which has been written about elsewhere many times and which played its part in the court action taken by the NUT (National Union of Teachers) leading to the government's recent embarrassment.

Staff will perceive certain key differences of performance management from appraisal. I suspect the government has been mischievous in pretending that appraisal was more deeply rooted than it is in our schools. It knows the true picture but is impatient to move forward and does not want to fight old battles again. This model is more authoritarian and top–down. It is also intended to become more integrated into the school's routines in the respect that a process is in progress throughout the year and immediately repeats itself the next year. It was possible for some appraisals to be all over in a couple of weeks and not revisited for another two years. The intention this time is cultural change, not another task to be added to the many. It remains to be seen how feasible the annual cycle will be and

I am surprised how relatively little emphasis has been given to this area. It is certainly difficult to see when to begin the annual cycle so that each part happens at the optimum time. Clearly a good time for planning is the run up to the end of the financial year when development planning and inset budgeting are taking place. In another sense, though, it is a bad time since the start of a school year is also a good time with new classes, renewed aspirations and a fresh set of targets all coming into the picture. A good time to review is also the start of the school year when the main set of results is available, but this would have required us to have set the targets after Christmas, half-way through the school year! In any case, the summer term is the worst term for monitoring in secondary schools. The government's answer to this problem has been to pose us an impossible conundrum: to tell us that we have the freedom to decide when the cycle should begin, but to require all staff to have set targets by February – thus determining for us when the cycle should begin!

However, overshadowing all these possible administrative problems and staff reactions is the connection between performance management and pay. We have yet to hear the end of this. This is such a cultural change for education that I believe the government has made a tactical mistake in not stimulating greater debate and seeking to win over headteachers to its point of view. While it is accepted practice in some parts of industry, in others it has been tried and rejected. Tune into any governing-body meeting which is discussing this issue and you will find both viewpoints represented. It is dangerous ground and I am not sure the DfEE has conducted its own risk assessment!

We must not forget that we are not implementing this initiative at a moment of opportunity. The bizarre threshold caper has not bought peace. Staff are resentful of the hours they had to spend during their half-term working on difficult forms which were written for a future audience, and heads are furious about the position it has placed them in. Teachers think that if the intention was to kick-start performance management by virtually creating a point ten on the salary scale, politicians should have had the courage to do that and face out the flack. Many feel that they deserve the payment, and receipt of it will not change much, I am afraid. It may turn into a serious miscalculation in the face of overwhelming opposition.

In many schools, a sense of trust has grown up among the staff and an initiative like performance management can be implemented if it can be seen to be furthering teachers' professional development and contributing to a better education for the students. However, this trust does not yet extend beyond schools. While no-one doubts that this government has made considerably more money available to education, many teachers look on with cynicism at the growth of empires at the periphery of education. The ongoing costs associated with the national curriculum, QCA (Qualifications and Curriculum Authority), OfSTED, the national testing and data industry, the TTA (Teacher Training Agency) and others are colossal. How much have they really improved or influenced what goes on in classrooms? Has it really been the only way? Has it been the best value? Governments tend not to ask these questions of themselves, only of others.

Whether this will turn into a transformational change, or become yet another thing which we do not have the time to do properly, remains to be seen. The annual time-scale will almost certainly slip unless the flow of new initiatives slows down. I am not especially confident that it will not go the way of appraisal, but I do know that it probably depends on the ability of heads to present it as an opportunity and an entitlement, and to find ways of sustaining the momentum in years to come. I cannot yet see it sustaining itself by its own virtue and value because, at the moment, it does not appear to have enough of either. How true this is of so many things we have had to do in the past fifteen years to suit hostile or impatient politicians who confuse professionalism with accountability and meeting targets. It is difficult to see how professionalism can be re-defined through imposing new systems. Surely it needs to grow outwards from within.

I come back to the question, 'why this issue now?' when there are so many other priorities and urgent needs for money. The outcome of the introduction of the threshold will add £100,000 to the annual salary bill of the school where I work, money on an unthinkable scale after the years of cutbacks. Within two years, with such money, we could have transformed our school environments and made them ICT-rich. This would surely be a higher priority. I understand that the government is concerned at the low level of staff morale (though I cannot see why it should be such a surprise to them), but it is precisely because of the low motivation of students, especially boys, at the arid curriculum and the lack of exciting resources in schools that most staff feel so badly about their job, and why recruitment is so difficult. As so often, we have the sense that the DfEE is aiming at the wrong target and that strategic thinking at the highest level of planning is fundamentally misdirected.

In a world dominated by media slogans, the phrase 'out-of-touch' strikes an uncomfortable chord when we consider how well-meaning and idealistic politicians of integrity and calibre, in the hope of transforming the profession, have presented schools with an issue which is so difficult to manage and believe in. For teachers wanting to explore notions of professionalism which liberate them to show their ability and use their initiative, to inspire children, to earn respect from the immediate audience and within a wider society, this measure still has the feeling of submitting to a great plan. It has to be built around the school development plan, the department development plan and the school targets. The essential dilemma between control and letting go, which lies at the heart of the standards and wider educational debates, has been further highlighted by performance management; the government has made a predictable choice.

Will it work? One undoubted consequence will be that schools will add another bureaucratic procedure to the many already in place. Something will happen! Teachers do not believe they have the clout of hauliers and will take this on with a certain resignation. A process will emerge which, in OfSTED speak, is 'broadly in line with national averages'. But is this the stuff of transformation? Can heads pull off the trick of making this the change agent we have been waiting for? It would take an optimist to say yes.

It may be that somewhere the government has made it clear why it believes that performance management has come to the top of the priority list at this moment in time. All the attention stimulated by the debate has been on the 'how?' and not on the 'why?'. When we come to look back on this frustrating period, it may be that someone asks how schools went for so long without any measures specifically aimed at increasing the motivation of students. The focus on systems, standards, inputs and outputs, data and teacher accountability has been relentless during my eleven years as a head. I struggle to recall a piece of legislation which, when implemented, would have increased children's enjoyment of education and made them want to come to school a little bit more. This latest measure is, in my view, several years too soon. There is not yet enough for teachers to look forward to in their jobs for them to enter into the spirit of performance management in the right frame of mind. Should we not be pursuing more radical ideas to bring the excitement back into teaching? Why not rethink the timing of the school day? Why not blur the edges between what is compulsory and what is voluntary? Why not consider incentives for success? Why not examine whether the national curriculum entitlement and the notion of choice and diversity are for many children contradictory? Why keep sticking plasters over wounds with inconsequential gimmicks to stimulate recruitment when so many potential teachers are being put off by existing teachers?

Like all heads, I will continue to work my hardest to improve the quality of education in the community I serve. That, to me, means a lot more than just raising standards. This latest directive will go into the funnel of the 'implementation culture' referred to above and dedicated senior and middle managers will strive to make a success of it. If, in the end, it simply adds to the inevitable mediocrity which results from an endless stream of new initiatives, the kindest epitaph for performance management would be either that it was the right thing at the wrong time in the sense that the climate is not yet right for this to be a transformational innovation; or that it was the wrong thing at the right time in the sense that if the government's only priority is 'performance, performance, performance', a more teacher-friendly and less centralised system needed to have been entrusted to headteachers.

Reference

DfEE (2000), *Performance Management for Teachers: Consultation Document*, London: DfEE.

4 Towards professional learning communities?

Teacher development and teacher culture in performance management

Meryl Thompson

Introduction: performance management and predefined professional expectations

What are the implications for teacher culture and teacher development of the introduction in England of the statutory system of performance management? It is apparently designed to establish a performance culture working to measure teachers against predefined expectations of levels of performance. The expectations have, of course, not originated from within the teaching profession. They have been mandated by the 'new' Labour government, working more often with think-tanks, focus groups, management consultants, civil servants and privatised training agencies, than with educational practitioners and researchers into school and teacher effectiveness. This alone has implications for teacher culture, and for the sorts of relationship between policy-makers and practitioners which are envisaged. In this chapter, I explore the nature of these predefined expectations of teachers; the operation of these expectations at three levels in the performance management context. I also consider their implications for teacher culture and teacher development. The three levels of expectation are: first, the expectation that the new professionalism of the government's key Green Paper (DfEE, 1998) will 'modernise' the teaching profession, give it higher status and function to recruit, reward and retain high quality teachers; second, the expectation of new levels of professional skills defined by the performance threshold standards, which is seen as a key stage in a continuum of expected teacher development from novice to advanced skills teacher (DfEE, 2000a); and, finally, the expectation of continuous improvement inherent in objective-setting and review which is part of performance management (DfEE, 2000d).

Performance management has been introduced, replacing the largely defunct arrangements for appraisal of 1991, as an integral part of the implementation of the 1998 Green Paper. The School Teachers' Review Body (STRB), which advises the Secretary of State for Education on teachers' salaries, explains:

> the . . . new performance management arrangements involve annual review by teacher and manager of priorities and objectives in order to strengthen and support teachers' work, to plan professional development, and to inform pay assessment at relevant career stages. A sound system of performance management is fundamental to the successful operation of any arrangements under which improved performance is reflected in pay . . . In the longer term the successful development of performance management and the recognition of its value by teachers will be the foundation for the success of the new pay arrangements.
>
> (STRB, 2000 pp.16–17)

These are high stakes, even when limited to using monetary incentives to reward, recruit, retain and motivate. However, performance management is also linked to non-pay incentives, such as better training and development opportunities and good career prospects, which, in evidence to the STRB in 1999, the DfEE said are often just as important in recruitment and motivation. Performance management is at the very centre of the government's modernisation programme (Thompson, 2000 p.12).

'New professionalism' and the status of the teaching profession

In the Green Paper's ambitious vision of a 'new' professionalism, teachers must be prepared to meet pre-defined levels of performance, for the reform strategy will have failed if measured improvement is not the outcome. The characteristics the Green Paper says teachers must exhibit in a modern profession are to:

- have high expectations of themselves and of all pupils;
- accept accountability;
- take personal and collective responsibility for improving their skills and subject knowledge;
- seek to base decisions on evidence of what works in schools in this country and internationally;

- work in partnership with other staff in schools;
- welcome the contribution that parents, business and others outside a school can make to its success; and
- anticipate change and promote innovation.

These themes are, in general, carried through in both the existence of, and the detailed arrangements for, performance management and threshold assessment. They impose or presuppose an acceptance of account-ability, the responsibility for improvement and high personal expectations. Performance management, especially through the role of the team leader, represents collective responsibility. The threshold standards also look for pupil progress which demonstrates, 'care and attention to all pupils'; 'an up-to-date knowledge of good practice in teaching techniques'; 'an active contribution to the policies and aspirations of the school', and 'contributing constructively' to work teams. In addition, the vision appears to be carried through into the opportunities provided in new DfEE programmes for international professional development and best-practice research scholarships.

But for the external imposition, it would be difficult to argue that a closer definition of professionalism would not have positive implications for teacher culture. I have argued elsewhere that a statement of the teaching profession's norms, values and principles would facilitate greater consistency and shared understanding of professional values across the professional community. It would make professional socialisation more effective, would highlight the extent of the responsibilities of the teaching profession, and could help to raise morale, self-confidence, sense of purpose and commitment within the profession (Thompson, 1997 pp.25–9). There is also a convincing similarity with the three broad value areas derived by my earlier analysis of the characteristic activities and actions which underpin effective teaching practice: an *ethic of care*, which includes positive relationships with the child and relations with the home and community; an *ethic of competence*, which includes good learning relationships, knowledge of pedagogy, intellectual accountability, and professional development; and an *ethic of professional commitment*, including contributing to the profession's competence but also to debate on the profession's purposes, values norms and standards (Thompson, 1997 pp.30–1ff.).

At the moment, however, 'new' professionalism is projected largely as a predetermined expectation of government. Consequently, it may only have a limited impact on teacher culture, for no definition of professionalism is 'likely to be internalised in that profession's own consciousness of itself, unless it corresponds to the profession's own deepest intuitions of the service it has to offer and the values which are consonant with that service' (Rodger, 1995 p.84). Others question the extent to which an ethical perspective can 'infuse a profession like teaching when the profession is not in significant control of its ideals and practice' (Macmillan, 1993 p.189).

The issue of professional ownership will remain central to whether this performance culture reprofessionalises or deprofessionalises teachers, with consequent implications for teacher culture and teacher development. Not unless performance management leaves teachers with a sense of control of their values and practice, can it contribute positively to a renewed professionalism. Increasingly, the government has made explicit use of Michael Fullan's juxtaposition of the importance of pressure and support in successful change processes (Fullan, 1991; Barber, 2000). The Green Paper emphasises both: increased accountability, but improved professional development; increased focus on measured performance, but the potential of improved pay and conditions. At the very least, it can be argued, the government's emphasis in the Green Paper on professional development, and the recognition that it is an incentive perhaps as important in staff recruitment and motivation as pay, puts teacher development centre stage in the performance culture, and acknowledges an organisational role in establishing a motivational culture.

Both pressure and support are carried through into performance management. The DfEE's *Performance Management Framework* is not strong on clarifying the concept, but the closest it gets to a definition emphasises that performance management 'is a way of helping schools improve by supporting and improving teachers' work, both as individuals and as teams'. The DfEE's *'Model' Performance Management* policy puts into governors' mouths the statement that: '*We* want to improve school performance by developing the effectiveness of teachers, both as individuals and as teams' and has governing bodies, and thus headteachers, accepting the rationale that: 'Performance management means a *shared commitment* to high performance. It helps to focus attention on more effective teaching and monitoring to raise the quality of teaching and to benefit pupils, teachers and the schools. *It means providing appropriate and effective personal training and development to ensure job satisfaction, a high level of expertise and progression of staff in their chosen profession* [emphasis added].'

If this is so, then the implications are profound. The DfEE is trying to use the introduction of performance management to require schools to become 'learning organisations' by mandating the characteristics of a public commitment to the learning of every individual; creating a learning partnership with all stakeholders; centering management processes on the enhancement of human potential; and operating in a culture of continuous improvement, development and growth (West-Burnham and O'Sullivan, 1998 p.46). The extent to which this cultural transformation of schools is new can be evidenced from much current headteacher development work. Pat Collarbone's revision of the National Professional Qualification for Headship (NPQH) noted that 'overtly missing from the present NPQH conceptual model is the role of head teacher in developing organisational learning . . . Yet collegiality, teamwork and, indeed sustained development of the organisation, require organisational learning' (Collarbone, 2000 p.30). At the same time, the Leadership Programme for Serving Headteachers (LPSH) found that serving headteachers most common weaknesses were in holding people to account, and in developing potential in others. There are therefore reasonable expectations of support through performance management, for which many headteachers and perhaps the vast majority of governors are quite unprepared. Schools, at the moment, are more likely to show the slow and bureaucratic change characteristic of prescriptive organisations; or the rapid intuitive change of entrepreneurial organisations, which do not really have time to think; or the lack of capacity for continued change characteristic of unlearning organisations (West-Burnham and O'Sullivan, 1998 pp.31, 38–9).

The inertia of existing school management cultures will be hard to break. Roland Barth went right to the heart of teacher culture, and perhaps to an ambivalence towards the public sectors, when he wrote of teachers' professional development: 'In schools we spend a great deal of time placing oxygen masks on other people's faces while we ourselves are suffocating' (Barth, 1990). The widespread reluctance of the teaching profession, and their managers and employers, to focus on upskilling, continuing professional development, and investment in people, has, it could be argued, resulted in:

- the widespread and largely uncriticised, even by the accountability-conscious OfSTED, failure to implement the Education (School Teacher Appraisal) Regulations 1991, despite their emphasis on teacher development;
- the continuing tendency to begrudge teachers time away from schools and classes for professional development, resulting in prospective headteachers being required to spend weekends training for the NPQH and teachers training under the New Opportunities Fund (NOF) programme for ICT in 'twilight' time and by distance learning;
- the introduction of the National Literacy and Numeracy Strategies (NLNS), requiring radical changes in teaching skills and the use of new teaching methods (or why else were they needed?) by a cascade process using headteachers and coordinators, both frequently unskilled

and untried in relation to developing other adults, which, it was quickly realised, 'alone could not provide the resources or the in-depth learning needed to transform instructional capacity' (Earl *et al.*, 2000b p.6); and

- a general lack of acknowledgement that the skills of coaching and mentoring, observing and giving feedback, are critical to teacher development, resulting in hit-and-miss support for student teachers and newly-qualified teachers, notwithstanding the supposedly higher demands of the standards required for qualified teacher status (QTS) and the induction period.

Certainly if the expectations of new professionalism are to be fulfilled then all this will have to change. Appraisal failed, at least in part, because teachers simply did not see that it resulted in professional development opportunities. The funding made available to schools was too limited or diverted to other priorities. The new DfEE programmes of international opportunities and best practice research scholarships and the plans for professional bursaries offer innovative and exciting opportunities that were simply not there in 1991. Funding is necessary but not sufficient: valuing professional development requires a change of attitudes to put teachers first (Thompson, 1998 pp.208–9). It also requires a change of attitude in teachers, because while 'continuous learning and the improvement of our practice should be at the core of teacher professionalism in many instances this is not so' (Sachs, 1997 p.268). As Michael Fullan says, 'We are not a learning profession' (Fullan, 1993).

Predefined expectations: threshold standards

All this may change, however, with the introduction of one of the other predetermined levels of performance linked to performance management – the *Performance Threshold Standards.* Performance management is not linked to the threshold standards only because it is a way of managing the allocation of post-threshold performance-related pay. There is a clear indication in the DfEE's *Performance Management Framework* of a potentially more influential impact on teacher culture and development. It states: 'Over time performance reviews will form part of the evidence which teachers will be able to cite and heads consider in making their judgements', and 'Annual reviews will help teachers identify areas on which they need to focus to meet threshold standards'.

Some of the immediate attitudes of teachers to the threshold are not likely to be as relevant in the future. For example, a telephone survey of 504 teachers, commissioned by the Association of Teachers and Lecturers

(ATL), found that 80 per cent of those eligible to apply had applied for threshold assessment; but two-thirds had done so to increase their level of pay; 16 per cent because it was expected of them; and only 16 per cent to get recognition for the work they do (Opinion Research Corporation International, 2000 p.2). One in five thought that the headteacher did not have the core competences to assess their standard of teaching and only four out of ten respondents felt that the threshold standards accurately describe good teaching (Opinion Research Corporation International, 2000 p.5). Of those not applying, a third stated it was because the process was too time-consuming, and another third was composed of teachers near retirement or moving into the leadership group. It is, however, likely, that in the future virtually all teachers will apply, not least since it is intended that no teacher will be able to move into the leadership (i.e. management) group unless he or she has 'crossed the performance threshold'. Consequently it seems equally likely that teachers will be persuaded that one of the benefits of performance management is to establish evidence towards threshold standards, and that for this reason alone the threshold standards will have an all-pervasive effect on teacher culture and teacher development. The quality of these standards and the extent to which they represent a higher level of professional skills and characteristics, as well as teachers' trust and respect for the professional integrity of the standards and of the process of assessment, therefore, become key issues.

The DfEE has devised the threshold standards. They consist of five areas, which set out eight standards; successful applicants are expected to meet all eight standards. The areas are: knowledge and understanding; teaching and assessment (which includes three standards – planning to meet pupils' individual learning needs; using a range of appropriate strategies for teaching and classroom management; and using information about prior attainment to set well-grounded expectations for pupils and monitor progress to give clear and constructive feedback); pupil progress; wider professional effectiveness (including two standards – taking responsibility for their professional development and making an active contribution to the policies and aspirations of the school); and professional characteristics. These professional characteristics, although adapted and modified by the DfEE, were established by a research contract given to Hay McBer (Hay McBer, 2000) to identify the competencies associated with high levels of teacher effectiveness. They require teachers to demonstrate that they challenge and support all pupils to do their best through inspiring trust and confidence; building team commitment; engaging and motivating pupils; analytical thinking; and taking positive action to improve the quality of pupils' learning. The other standards are offered with no evidence-based rationale, either as to their content or their implicit weighting. Of these pupil progress has created the most immediate concern because of the shadow of payment by results. Its precise definition and the manner of its assessment were, therefore, of considerable significance. Pupil progress was originally termed 'pupil performance' but is defined now as a standard where: 'Teachers should show that as a result of their teaching their pupils achieve well in relation to their prior attainment, making progress as good or better than similar pupils nationally'. It was argued in justification that 'Pupil progress over school years is likely to reflect teachers' teaching much more than pupil background (which will already have had the most of its effects on pupils' levels of achievement when they start the year at the school)' (DfEE, 2000c).

Headteachers have been offered far more advice on how to make this assessment than in the other areas. They are asked to make a professional judgement as to whether the progress made by the teacher's pupils is at least within the range expected in the light of the local and national context of the school and in reaching that judgement, they must consider a variety of factors, including the representativeness of the evidence; the extent to which it demonstrates care and attention to all pupils; the consistency of value-added progress in relation to prior attainment; and whether the evidence suggests that pupils have made progress at least within the range that would be expected of similar pupils nationally (DfEE, 2000c). What implications for teacher culture has this emphasis on measuring pupil progress against published assessment? Perhaps too frequently, the implications of introducing performance management are confined too closely to the apparent dissonance between the professional values of teachers and the climate likely to be created by directly relating performance to differential levels of pay. In preliminary findings from a major ESRC (Economic and Social Research Council) research project, designed to map the implementation of the Green Paper, 56 per cent of respondents disagreed with the statement that: 'The principle that individual teachers' pay should take some account of pupil progress is a good one'; only 27 per cent agreed. In contrast, 79 per cent agreed that: 'The best way to reward good teaching is to raise existing salary levels for all teachers'; and only 12 per cent disagreed (Marsden, 2000 p.18). Responses such as these are sometimes taken as evidence that teachers consider they should be financially rewarded irrespective of their competence. But teachers are not necessarily rejecting the link between teaching and pupils' progress as a reasonable expectation; but rather, they are rejecting the link as fair evidence on which to base a fair reward. For when teachers are asked about teacher effectiveness, only 25 per cent cite the main factor among experienced teachers in their own school as 'different levels of teaching skills', compared to 32 per cent who cite differences in motivation and morale, 22 per cent the ability to motivate pupils, and 14 per cent that some teachers have a very difficult workload (Marsden, 2000 p.19).

Teachers, it seems, are sensitive about fairness as to context. What makes pupils 'similar'? What circumstances will and do affect teachers' work? What effects do behaviour, background and ability have? What is an 'expected range'? Threshold assessment of pupil progress will surely encourage a teacher culture increasingly sensitive to such issues. It will surely also increase teachers' critical awareness of a number of issues, including such questions as how 'value-added' impacts can be assessed if underpinning assessment data can be called into question and how to identify and value pupil progress in areas where there are no standardised tests, especially in the value-laden areas of artistic, moral, cultural, personal and social development.

There are implications for performance management too, since an annual objective for every teacher related to 'pupil progress' is a statutory requirement. But here there are critical differences. In its advice on evaluating progress in threshold assessment, the DfEE adds two further general points it says are worth noting:

- The exercise of professional judgement by the head teacher will necessarily have elements of subjectivity but should be closely informed by available evidence. The role of the assessor is designed to maximise objectivity and reliability.
- The purpose of the assessment of pupil progress is not to produce complicated hierarchical rankings of teachers. Indeed there are only two distinctions necessary on the basis of the data submitted – that it shows progress that is at least within the range that would be expected in the light of the local and national context of the school – or that it does not.

(DfEE, 2000c)

Yet in performance management there is no external assessor to maximise objectivity and reliability. The team leader's role at the review stage of the performance management cycle, before turning attention to the next set of objectives, is set out in the DfEE's *Model Performance Management* policy, and involves:

- reviewing, discussing and confirming the teacher's essential tasks, and objectives;
- recognising strengths and achievements and taking account of factors outside the teacher's control;
- identifying areas for development and how these will be met; and
- recognising individual professional development needs.

It is also explicitly required that the team leader should evaluate the teacher's 'overall performance', including an 'assessment of the extent to which objectives have been met and the teacher's contribution to the life of the school during the review period. It should take account of the stage the teacher is at in his or her career e.g. teacher with 2–3 years service, advanced skills teacher, senior manager' (DfEE, 2000c).

Furthermore, we must not forget the implications of using the other seven threshold standards in performance management. Teachers and team leaders build up evidence of, for example:

- thorough and up-to-date knowledge of their subject and the way they take account of wider curriculum developments, especially in ICT;
- consistent and effective planning to target individuals and groups effectively and to ensure good year-on-year progression;
- using strategies for teaching and classroom management which motivate different individuals;
- evaluating pupils' progress in relation to national, local and school targets and setting realistic but challenging targets for improvement;
- their wider professional effectiveness by the responsibility they take for their professional development and the active contribution they make to the policies of the school; as well as
- the professional characteristics of inspiring trust and confidence, building team commitment with colleagues and in the classroom, engaging and motivating pupils, analytical thinking and taking positive steps to improve the quality of pupils' learning.

Teachers will be working towards predetermined areas of expectation where differentiated performance criteria have simply not been defined. Team leaders may be working on little more than personal intuition and what experience they have been able to accumulate.

The implications for teacher culture and teacher development of complicated, hierarchical rankings made by headteachers or colleagues in their role as team leaders based upon unmoderated subjectivity are almost too serious to contemplate. It cannot create positive outcomes for either. Nor is it consistent with the principles of fairness and equity, which the *Model Performance Management Policy* (DfEE, 2000b) promise. It is likely to damage relationships between teachers and their team leaders. By predetermining a link between performance management and threshold standards, before these are understood widely across the profession, this is what the DfEE could achieve.

Team leaders, including headteachers acting as team leaders, will need substantially more training and experience to operate these standards diagnostically and developmentally, since they must be relative to the standards already expected in induction and those standards even better rewarded by the status and salary of advanced skills teachers. It is unclear how, for example, the induction standard 'sets clear targets for improvement of pupils' achievement, monitors pupils' progress towards these targets and uses appropriate teaching strategies' differs from the supposedly more challenging threshold standard to: 'consistently and effectively plan lessons and sequences of lessons to meet pupils' individual learning needs'. Similarly, progression is unclear from the induction standard for 'other professional requirements' which expects newly qualified teachers to take 'responsibility for their own professional development, setting objectives for improvements and taking action to keep up-to-date with research and developments in pedagogy and in the subject(s) they teach'; to the threshold standard for 'wider professional effectiveness' which expects teachers to take 'responsibility for their professional development and use the outcomes to improve their teaching and pupils' learning' or to the threshold standard for professional knowledge and understanding which requires an up-to-date knowledge of their teaching subject.

Expectations and improvement: target-setting and review

This brings us to the implications of the last predetermined level of expectations inherent in objective setting and review in performance management. The regulations make objectives related to developing and improving the schoolteacher's professional practice and pupil progress statutory requirements, and insist that professional accountability and professional development are at the heart of performance management. The annual cycle of performance management provides the basis for visible and acknowledged continuing improvement and lifelong learning. But it is only through the managerial responsibilities set out in the School Teachers' Pay and Conditions document that performance management can operate. These reside in the responsibilities teachers have to contribute to the professional development and, in particular, the appraisal of their colleagues.

The extent of the responsibilities of the team leader, formerly understood as the line manager or appraiser were grossly neglected in the DfEE's hastily-assembled performance management training directed solely at headteachers. Although in small primary schools the headteacher may be the team leader, for all other teachers the norm will be for the role of team leader to be delegated to the colleague 'who has the best overview of a teacher's work'; or to 'others who hold significant management posts within the team' (DfEE, 2000b p.3). Since the DfEE also recommends that each team leader should undertake the performance review of only between four and six colleagues, there are thousands of teachers who will be taking on these responsibilities with little awareness, notice or training. Very belatedly, the role of developing team leaders emerged as a responsibility for DfEE-accredited performance management consultants; but even this can only happen in those schools that recognise its importance, as schools decide what training to purchase. Even then the training programme for the consultants offered no additional training materials for them to use with team leaders and only the most cursory discussion of the extent of the responsibilities and the depth of their own developmental needs as consultants.

The team leader's role is key in achieving the expectations of the other two levels which could have the most profound positive influence on teacher culture and teacher development. We have considered the team leader's role in review and the need to understand the predetermined levels of expectation and how the standards should be measured for accountability purposes. It is now time to consider the breadth of the role more fully. At each stage of the performance management cycle, as set out in the DfEE's *Model Performance Management* policy, the supportive and developmental role of the team leader is explicit. At the planning stage, the team leader's role is to ensure that each teacher understands what his or her objectives involve, is in a position to achieve them, and understands when and how they will be reviewed. The team leader needs to focus these objectives on issues over which a teacher has direct influence, to see that they are clear, concise and measurable, and to ensure that the teacher's own individual objectives relate to the objectives in the school development plan and any departmental or team plans, as well as to professional needs. At the monitoring stage, there is an expectation of skilful observation and of full, constructive and timely feedback, offering the teacher an opportunity to discuss what went well, what might be done differently or better next time. Finally, the performance review is described as 'an opportunity for teacher and team leader to reflect on the teacher's performance in a structured way, to recognise achievements and to discuss areas for improvement and professional development' in order to raise performance and improve effectiveness.

The existence of the performance threshold and its standards, combined with the responsibilities and expectations of the team leader in performance management, surely imply that the role of the team leader will be to assist the teacher to develop towards the threshold standards. If so, then the implications are all-pervasive for teacher culture. 'Coaching has to become the most significant working relationship in the school'

(West-Burnham and O'Sullivan, 1998 p.62). But such a role cannot be fulfilled without high-quality personal and interpersonal skills and the development of mutual trust, confidence and respect which are central to the coaching relationship (West-Burnham and O'Sullivan, 1998 pp.52–3).

The extent of teachers' confidence in their team leaders' skills, therefore, becomes central to an assessment of the impact of performance management on teacher culture and development. In a survey of teachers following threshold assessment, one-third of the respondents did not agree that their team leader was good at coaching and developing them; and a fifth said that the team leader did not take a close interest in their professional development. Significantly, in my view, it also found that teachers who were confident of passing the threshold were twice as likely to regard their managers as good at coaching and developing them and more likely to trust their managers and feel that they took a close concern in their professional development (Opinion Research Corporation International, 2000 p.3).

Lack of trust and confidence may be an unavoidable feature of existing teaching cultures. Like its predecessor, appraisal, performance management is about power delegated to the team leader – 'the power of knowledge, access, secrecy, bias, prejudice and idiosyncratic ways of thinking' (Townsend, 1998 pp.53–4). In teaching there can be a detectable performance orientation pervading the content and practice of giving feedback. It is highly evaluative and sees the purpose of feedback as to judge the performance of others, which is also encouraged by the dominant discourse of 'performance'. Such judgementalism does not promote the optimum processes and levels of learning, rather it may damage learning relationships between teachers, by encouraging teachers' negative views of their abilities, helplessness and lack of persistence in the face of difficult tasks and thus lead to lower standards (Watkins and Whalley, 2001). If team leaders do not understand how to establish a learning orientation, nor understand teachers as learners, for example, and that very important things such as how teachers think, are not 'observable' – then the expectations of new predetermined levels of performance cannot be met.

Team leaders will also require an understanding of andragogy – the theory of learning as applied to adults – recognised now in the NPQH (National Professional Qualification for Headteachers) (Collarbone, 2000 p.30). For example, understanding that the psychological factors which influence adult learning are characterised by valuing the experience of learners; establishing collaborative learning relationships; and engaging in reflection on experiences (Tennant, quoted in West-Burnham and O'Sullivan, 1998 pp.49–50). Coaching requires the recognition that adults go through transitional phases and that these influence their perspectives on learning, and that adults learn for specific purposes and must be motivated to want to learn (Collarbone, 2000 p.30). Yet in the present context of performance management, one of the hardest roles for the team leader may be to motivate. Teachers' excessive workload is undeniably a key feature of their present culture and will influence their perceptions of the value of performance management. Marsden found that 88 per cent agreed with the statement: 'It is very hard for teachers like me to improve our performance because we already work as hard as we can', and only 6 per cent disagreed. He also found a general scepticism about the professed goal of raising pupil achievement and a strong suspicion that there is a hidden agenda of minimising the cost of uprating teachers' salaries and of getting more work out of them. Teachers' perception of the new system is that it is 'punishment-centred' (Marsden, 2000).

Notwithstanding the present context, there are also high expectations of teachers' self-motivation in performance management, as well as in new professionalism and the threshold standards. The DfEE's performance management material recognises the value of teachers who reflect, in advance of their performance reviews on the work of the year, on strengths and achievements and on areas for development. It is entirely consistent with the understanding that, when adults change, they most often change themselves, especially where change is sustainable. However, there is little appreciation that reflection and coaching are inextricably linked. The purpose of both is to facilitate the process of internalisation and so develop understanding and thereby the capacity to act autonomously. Arguably without coaching *and* reflection, learning will not take place. Reflection needs a stimulus, such as 'an appropriate questioning process; a means of comparing experience; the support of materials and strategies; and a coach to facilitate it' in order to produce a consolidated and internalised experience (West-Burnham and O'Sullivan, 1998 pp.73, 81).

In summary, therefore, many of the expectations of new professionalism and of professional growth towards new performance threshold standards depend on the role of the team leader during the process of performance management in encouraging and enabling teachers' continuous learning. The logical consequence, which would have positive benefits for teacher culture and teacher development, should be that training for team leaders in the interpersonal and professional skills of mentoring and coaching should be the highest priority in the implementation of performance management.

There is one further predetermined level of expectations, represented by the process of objective-setting in performance management, which is clearly regarded as critical throughout performance management, and the team leader has a key role to play. What 'performance' is to mean is defined precisely in the regulations, where it is stated quite categorically that the objectives *shall* include objectives relating to developing and improving the school teacher's professional practice and pupil progress, thus continuing the twofold approach to development and accountability, support and challenge. The *Model Performance Management Policy* states: 'Each teacher will discuss and agree objectives with their team leader'; and 'Objectives should be challenging but realistic and take account of the teacher's job description and their existing skills and knowledge base.' It also commits the school to the following principles, again to be secured by the team leader, namely that objectives:

● are written clearly and concisely and are measurable;
● focus on issues/matters over which a teacher has direct influence/ control and take into account fully the wider socio-economic, cultural and other external influences on pupils; and
● should relate to the objectives in the school development plan or team plans as well as to his or her own professional needs.

These are principles which have their origins in theories of goal-setting and its impact on motivation and performance achieved by directing attention and effort, providing a gauge by which to judge success and encouraging persistence. But the DfEE's model ignores the point that goals (objectives or targets) do not influence actions until teachers make them their own, and that goal-setting processes should therefore be highly participatory (Leithwood *et al.*, 1999 pp.8–10).

As the DfEE's international critical friends observe, initiatives aimed at fostering motivation by target-setting must not ignore the idea that 'motivation is influenced by more than external actions. Teachers' motivation is a function of their goals, their beliefs about their own capacities, and their beliefs about the extent to which they will be supported in their schools' (Earl *et al.*, 2000b p.5). If performance-based reforms are to be successful, the standards set for students need to be valued by teachers if they are to have an effect on their practices. But often they are not, and what teachers do value goes unrewarded. For example, setting the same standard for all students can send a message to teachers that individual differences are being ignored. Schools that want to influence how teaching and learning actually happen in classrooms, it is argued, may have to distinguish these 'vertical' standards from 'horizontal' standards. For example that all children should have the chance to be involved in meaningful problem-solving (Leithwood *et al.*, 1999 p.56). However, again it is left to team leaders to bridge what may be a serious mismatch between teachers' beliefs about standards and those pre-determined in performance management; and again these are complex demands on the team leader. How objective-setting is handled in schools and the extent to which, as organisations, they recognise the energising effect of such 'personal' goals, will have a key impact on teacher culture and development, and again on whether performance management deprofessionalises or reprofessionalises.

Also, both objective-setting and reviewing will require considerable skill in data analysis and evaluation, since the assumption is that performance data will drive change by contributing both rewards and sanctions. Even for the highly consistent NLNS (National Literacy and Numeracy Strategy), the evaluators found, for example, a wide variation in knowledge and expertise about interpretation and use of data and that it was not at all clear to what extent people in LEAs and schools have the skills necessary to interpret and use data for wise decision-making. The way data is used is 'often relatively unsophisticated' (Earl *et al.*, 2000a p.19). It is even doubtful whether we have good enough data if objective-setting is to promote professional growth. For as Carol Fitz-Gibbon says, for this we need 'good information. But years of work will be needed to get the information systems working at every level in such a way that they have maximum positive impact and avoid the negative impact which can arise from poorly conceived systems which threaten rather than inform, distract rather than energise, and demoralise rather than promote professionalism' (Fitz-Gibbon, 1996 p.4). Just to counteract this, and certainly to translate data into appropriate action, teachers, and team leaders in particular, need to become more skilled in interpreting performance data as part of the implementation strategy for performance management. So far this, too, has been neglected.

Performance management and professional cultures

Performance management is an example of an attempt at large-scale reform of the most complex kind. Not only is it a systemic, standards-based or performance-based large-scale reform, it is at the same time part of the essential additional effort and development needed for any large-scale reform to be sustained. For it amounts to an attempt to 'upgrade the system context' by revamping the policies, incentives, standards, compensation and overall requirements for the teaching profession, including administrative leadership to create a strong teaching profession and a corresponding infrastructure, without which no reform is possible (Leithwood *et al.*, 1999 p.4; Fullan, 1999 p.16). So to evaluate its likely consequences and effects it should be assessed against other large-scale reforms.

Analyses of large-scale reforms suggest that variations in their success can be explained by their influence on 'will' (motivation); 'capacity' (including beliefs in one's capacity); and 'situation' (the collective capacity of the organisation) (Leithwood *et al.*, 1999). The warning from the international evaluators of the NLNS applies with even greater force to the ambitions for performance management. 'It is not possible to *make* schools or LEAs operate effectively. They become effective through local capacity-building and the development of a strong teaching profession' (Fullan, quoted in Earl, 2000a p.12). But building the capacity of teachers in literacy and numeracy alone, they say, is likely to require professional development and supervision for many years to come. There is even some doubt as to whether the strategies are the source of the gains in outcomes. They conclude that, even in relation to these well-resourced and planned strategies, sustaining their implementation 'will require extensive capacity building in directions not yet anticipated, in addition to a continued commitment on the part of headteachers and teachers'. In considering the earlier failure of appraisal, West-Burnham and O'Sullivan identify the lack of resources, lack of confidence in the competence and capability of appraisers; the limited infrastructure available to support the meeting of appraisal targets; and the fact that many schools lacked a fully developed strategy for human resource management into which appraisal could be integrated (West-Burnham and O'Sullivan, 1998 p.92). The lack of these essential capacities still applies.

The implementation of performance management seriously lacks 'cross-over structures', agencies structured to mobilise commitment and capacity, 'will and skill', and are key to protecting and sustaining both because they build on dissemination and diffusion as they go (Fullan, 2000 p.17). The one-day training events for headteachers and the training for the DfEE-accredited performance management consultants, to be employed by the nine regional consortia, compare very poorly with the structure provided by the national directors and offices and the twelve regional directors, promoting training and interaction, for the NLNS, and its over 600 LEA coordinators. It is highly unlikely that the DfEE can generate the critical mass required for the implementation of performance management to be a success. Indeed, it may come to rue the decision to remove responsibilities for performance management from LEAs and to so downplay their role compared to that played at the implementation of appraisal. For what the introduction of performance management lacks is the input of professional development agencies and the strengthening of institutions responsible for training education personnel, which Michael Fullan argues are critical to support large-scale reform.

In this context, then, what is the likely impact of performance management on teacher culture and teacher development? Could it succeed? Paradoxically it could.

Nonetheless, performance management could still add capacity and strengthen the profession even within the predetermined expectations and despite the structural deficiencies in its implementation. Schools are now expected to be learning organisations, which create the conditions in which adults will commit themselves to continuous, collective, professional learning. Headteachers are now expected to be able to undertake the role of both assuring the professional skills of teachers against national standards for threshold assessment and giving developmental feedback. This is an entirely new responsibility, which is surely to become more exacting and exact over time and to feature more prominently in head-teacher training programmes. Each school has to become a professional learning academy. Headteachers, through the agency of performance management and the skills of team leaders, are now to assume leadership of school-based professional growth and development. As is argued for similar reforms in Australia, this can have a dramatic effect on teacher culture, with each headteacher having 'the opportunity to develop a unique learning community for their school; and consequently they are freer to delegate inside the schools in ways which encourage leadership and innovative practices from their experienced teachers' (Sachs, 1997 p.267). There is the opportunity for headteachers and senior managers 'to wrest learning back for the profession' and reinvent schools as truly learning organisations and reengineer their structures and processes for lifelong learning (West-Burnham and O'Sullivan, 1998 p. 31).

But to do so schools must be managed as organisations designed to strengthen teachers' capacities, since high motivation and low ability cannot change performance (Leithwood, 1999 p.7). We know a great deal about how teachers learn best. Teachers learn 'by studying, doing and reflecting, by collaborating with other teachers, by looking closely at students and their work; and by sharing what they see' (Darling-Hammond, 1997 p.319). The consistent emphasis is on schools which have community-like characteristics and take a collective responsibility for students' learning. The whole panoply of expectations incorporated into performance management can act as a catalyst, through a focus on student learning and its legitimation of teachers' professional discussion and collaboration. But it is the 'idea of belonging to a community' which then changes 'the way we think about teacher learning. Its importance lies in the fact that it changes the relationship of teachers to their peers, breaking the isolation that most teachers have found so devastating. In supportive communities, teachers reinforce each other in a climate that encourages observing students, sharing teaching strategies, trying out new ways of teaching, getting feedback, and redesigning curriculum and methods of instruction' (Lieberman and Miller, 2000 p.58). If the introduction of performance management fast-forwards schools towards becoming professional learning communities then it will have a positive impact on teacher culture and teacher development.

The paradox, too, is that in large-scale reform the importance of the place where reforms take place – the school and the classroom – has been consistently underestimated. But it is now recognised that reform is likely to be influenced positively by places where there are:

- expectations that teachers are responsible not only for the quality of instruction in their own classrooms but for department and school-wide decisions likely to influence their classroom practices as well;
- structures in the school that minimise teachers' isolation and foster dialogue and discussion;
- organisation of physical space to support such dialogue and discussion;
- norms and opportunities for teachers to learn from others not only inside their school but outside as well;
- systematic training in effective team or group problem-solving processes (Fullan, 2000 p.20).

All are features of strong professional learning communities, which, it is argued, advance reform because the more the school works collaboratively on improvements at the school level the more it engages critically with external standards and policy.

Furthermore, if schools now use the opportunities of performance management to practise the 'positive politics' of defining their own reform agenda, then performance management could act as an antidote to the deprofessionalising impact of reform constantly imposed from above, and escape from the mindset that teachers are just implementing someone else's agenda (Fullan, 2000 pp.19–20). Schools which use performance management to develop a strong sense of collaborative professionalism, which critically evaluate the significance and value of the threshold standards and all other standards, and which consider critically the role of the headteacher in organisational learning and the role of the team leader and take positive steps to enhance their capacities, could alter the course of the impact of performance management and take back professional ownership of these externally-determined expectations.

Performance management does reflect the 'new social realities of teaching', taking it from individualism to professional community, from teaching at the centre to learning at the centre, from 'technical work to enquiry', 'control to accountability', classroom concerns to whole school concerns, from a weak knowledge base to a stronger, broader one; and from 'managed work to leadership' for as teachers redefine and augment their roles they become leaders in curriculum, instruction and teaching (Lieberman and Miller, 2000 p.52). Yet, despite the fact that the introduction of performance management is so embedded in the government's new professionalism, it is not understood: it is doubtful whether teachers in England understand that the introduction of performance threshold and performance management is aimed at revitalising teacher professionalism and as such influences their occupational and professional identity. This may have implications for the existing teacher culture for 'new' professionalism, simply imposed could just become a different version of a 'common-sense' professionalism, which is developed passively and not self-consciously (Friedson, quoted in Sachs, 1997 p.267).

But new professionalism, like any other version of professionalism, needs the internalisation of values, the motivation from true professionalism, because the desire for continuous learning, the eagerness to innovate and to experiment in order to improve practice, in the last resort cannot be imposed or mandated. The government should understand that this too needs high support. Far more attention should be given to presenting the performance-related initiatives in a debate about teacher professionalism and involving teachers in that debate. Securing professional ownership should be seen as the key performance indicator of these reforms and not professional compliance, for as Michael Fullan says 'reform will never occur on a large scale until teachers and others get out of the mindset that they are always implementing someone else's reform agenda' (Fullan, 2000 p.9). The General Teaching Council (GTC) will need to assert its key role in advising on standards of teaching, standards of conduct for teachers, the role of the teaching profession and the training, career development and performance management of teachers. It will have to do so as it fulfils its statutory responsibilities to establish a code laying down standards of professional conduct and practice expected of teachers. To construct such a code it must analyse, reassess and, if necessary, re-state the values implicit in 'new' professionalism and put under early scrutiny Hay McBer's research into teacher effectiveness, which has become the basis of alleged 'professional characteristics'. It should also begin the debate about the appropriateness of private bodies such as the Centre for British Teachers and Cambridge Education Associates, in effect, being in control of the criteria for reaching the threshold standards through the management, on behalf of the DfEE, of the external assessment arrangements; that is, the moderation and the verification of those standards, which will have so much influence on teacher culture and teacher development.

The GTC should also be expected to comment on the appropriateness and accuracy of the performance threshold standards. As Leithwood *et al.* comment in relation to all performance-based reform: 'Standards for teachers should be based on an empirically valid theory of teacher performance. Enough research has been generated by now to form the basis for a set of teaching standards able to stand the test of both professional and academic scrutiny. The ability to stand up to such scrutiny will contribute to the development of a broad consensus among teachers about the importance of using such standards as a guide to their own practice' (Leithwood *et al.*, 1999 pp.56–7). For this reason the government should encourage, not curtail, such scrutiny. The academic educational community also has a proactive role to play as researchers knowledgeable about effective teaching and its characteristics. It should see teachers as its key audience and disseminate the research to empower teachers and bring them into the debate. Similarly, educational researchers into effective schools, into organisational management and motivation, and educational philosophers and moralists, all have a role in influencing the implications of performance management for teacher culture and teacher development.

But far more will need to be provided to give this 'high support' and capacity-building. As international observers have commented it is much cheaper to provide incentives for large-scale reform than it is to develop significant individual or organisational capacity. 'Several days a year in a professional development workshop simply will not translate into transformed instructional capacity' (Leithwood *et al.*, 1999 p.61). The same is true for the capacities needed by team leaders and the professional development needed to support the capacity of professional communities. If the intended relationship between new expectations of professional performance and performance management are to be taken seriously as a strategy for improvement, it will require a radically different approach by the DfEE to mould professional development and its quality. The capacities of teachers as learners must be developed by prioritising training in the skills and competences of teachers as mentors and coaches and by resourcing the time for professional collaboration. The capacities of teachers as researchers and as users of research must be strengthened by the continued involvement of higher education, through teachers' increased involvement in research opportunities. The DfEE's focus must be on effective and accessible means of disseminating everything that can contribute to enhancing teachers' capacities. Since the aim of performance management is improved teaching and learning, it must also be accompanied by investment in, and development of, high-quality teaching and training materials (Fullan, 2000 p.18). Above all, professional development must be redesigned to support the capacity of professional communities in networks, for this large-scale change cannot be achieved if teachers and headteachers identify with only their own schools and classrooms and not those of others.

The teaching profession faces a challenge if it is to secure control of its own future and the outcome will have an immeasurable impact on the quality of teacher culture and teacher development. 'Reclaiming teacher professionalism is an ongoing struggle. It requires energy, commitment and the ability to think strategically' (Sachs, 1997 p.273). To turn these predetermined expectations into a revitalised professionalism should be the strategy. Academic and policy-making communities have a significant part to play, but the teachers, team leaders and headteachers who use their energy and commitment to create stronger professional communities through performance management will have reclaimed professionalism through community, capacity, and collaboration.

References

Barber, M. (2000), 'High expectations and standards for all – no matter what', *Times Educational Supplement*, 7 July 2000.

Barth, R. (1990), *Improving Schools From Within*, San Francisco: Jossey Bass.

Collarbone, P. (2000), 'Aspirant Heads', in *Managing Schools Today*, June/July 2000 pp. 28–32.

Darling-Hammond, L. (1997), *The Right to Learn*, San Francisco: Jossey Bass.

DfEE (1998), *Teachers: meeting the challenge of change*, London: DfEE.

DfEE (2000a), *Threshold Standards*, London: DfEE.

DfEE (2000b), *Performance Management in Schools*, Ref DfEE 0051/2000, London: DfEE.

DfEE (2000c), *Threshold Standards: proposed handling of analysis of pupil progress*, DfEE, March 2000.

Earl, L. *et al.* (2000a), *Watching Learning; OISE/UT Evaluation of the implementation of the National Literacy and Numeracy Strategies; First Annual Report*, Ontario Institute for Studies in Education, University of Toronto, January 2000, London: DfEE.

Earl, L. *et al.* (2000b), *Watching Learning; OISE/UT Evaluation of the implementation of the National Literacy and Numeracy Strategies; Summary: First Annual Report*, Ontario Institute for Studies in Education, University of Toronto, January 2000, London: DfEE.

Fitz-Gibbon, C. T. (1996), *Monitoring Education Indicators, Quality and Effectiveness*, London: Cassell.

Fullan, M. (1993), *Change Forces: probing the depth of education reform*, London: Falmer Press.

Fullan, M. (1999), *The Return of Large-Scale Reform*, Ontario Institute for Studies in Education: University of Toronto.

Leithwood, K. *et al.* (1999), *Large-Scale Reform: What Works?* Ontario Institute for Studies in Education: University of Toronto.

Lieberman, A. and Miller, L. (2000), 'Teaching and Teacher Development: A New Synthesis for a New Century', in R. S. Brandt (ed.), *Education in a New Era*, Alexandria, Virginia: ASCD, pp.47–66.

Macmillan, C. J. B. (1993), 'Ethics and Teacher Professionalisation', in K. A. Strike and P. L. Ternasky (eds), *Ethics for Professionals in Education: Perspectives for Preparation and Practice'*, New York: Teachers' College Press.

Marsden, D. (2000), 'Preparing to perform', in *CentrePiece'*, Vol. 5, Issue 2, Summer 2000, pp.16–20.

Opinion Research Corporation International (2000), *Survey of Attitudes on Performance Threshold (Post-application period)*, London: ATL.

Rodger, A. R. (1995), 'Code of Professional Conduct for Teachers: An introduction', in *Scottish Educational Review*, Vol. 27, No. 1, May 1995, pp.78–86.

Sachs, J. (1997), 'Reclaiming the Agenda of Teacher Professionalism: an Australian experience', in *Journal of Education for Teaching*, Vol. 23, No. 3, pp.263–75.

School Teachers' Review Body (2000), 'Ninth Report, 2000', London: HMSO.

Thompson, M. (1997), *Professional Ethics and the Teacher: towards a General Teaching Council*, Stoke-on-Trent: Trentham.

Thompson, M. (1998), 'Turning Round the Titanic: Changing Attitudes to Professional Development for the Teaching Profession', Ch. 19 in C. Richards *et al.* (eds), *Primary Teacher Education: High Status? High Standards?* London: Falmer Press, pp.201–14.

Thompson, M. (2000), 'Performance Management: new wine in old bottles?', in *Professional Development Today*, Summer 2000, pp.9–19.

Townsend, F. (1998), 'Appraisal: As a Process of Betrayal', in *International Studies in Educational Administration*, Vol. 26, No. 1, 1998, pp.45–56.

Watkins, C. and Whalley, C. (2000), 'Extending Feedback Forward', in *Professional Development Today*, Autumn 2000.

West-Burnham, J. and O'Sullivan, F. (1998), *Leadership and Professional Development in Schools: How to Promote Techniques for Effective Professional Learning*, London: Financial Times Pitman Publishing.

Part II
Highwire artists and acrobats?
Professional cultures and school contexts

In the second section of *The Performing School*, our focus moves from leading and managing schools to the professional cultures which performance management may engender. The contributions pursue some common themes. Performance management is not simply a technique for more effective management of the teaching profession, although it is frequently presented as a relatively neutral best-practice approach to staff development, improved pupil performance and structured organisational development. It also depends on some assumptions about teacher culture, teacher morale and teacher development. These assumptions are identified and subject to scrutiny in this section.

Martin Merson opens the section, setting the Green Paper in a wider concept of staff management in fordist and post-fordist settings. Merson queries the intellectual frameworks of the Green Paper, seeing in them effectively the impulse to exercise fordist control over the teaching profession. In the long run, for Merson, the tensions between fordist management and non-fordist teaching cultures will prejudice the grander project of the modernisation of teaching. In this sense, modernisation is a contemporary myth.

For Pat Sikes, issues of teacher performance are also issues of teacher development and, beyond that, issues of the relationship between the values teachers hold and their own life histories. As Sikes demonstrates, teaching style, teaching approach and the values of the teacher are complex. She advocates teachers giving a clearer voice to articulating the relationships between their own values, their life experiences and their teaching. However, even here she detects ambiguities and perhaps possibilities in cultures of performance management, showing neatly how a church school's incorporation of performance management went beyond what Mahony and Hextall have characterised as 'performing and conforming', to become a celebration of the fundamental values which the school professed. Linda Evans asks parallel questions about teacher morale and motivation. For her, the motivational power of performance-related pay – the headline issue in performance management – is conservative. Drawing on both current research in staff development and her own empirical work, Evans gives at best a guarded and conditional answer to the motivational power of performance-related pay. There are motivational consequences, but, as Evans shows, these are as dependent on other elements in workplace and teacher culture as on purely financial grounds.

John Smyth's contribution concludes the section. Smyth draws on Australian experience in implementing fast-track promotion programmes and state-managed programmes of teacher development to raise questions about the cultural values and norms which underpin the concept of the 'preferred teacher'. For Smyth, something fundamental about schooling in an open and democratic society is at stake, and he argues for a teacher culture which can articulate alternative models of professionality and development if, in the long term, education is to serve the demands of a complex society.

5 Teachers and the myth of modernisation

Martin Merson

Introduction

This chapter seeks to analyse the proposals and assumptions in the 'Consultation Paper, Teachers meeting the challenge of change' (DfEE, 1998a). It is argued that although the paper is framed as being about modernising the teaching profession and raising standards of teaching and learning, it is really an attempt to address the problem of recruitment and retention in the teaching force. It is further argued that the paper is written with the economic and employment legacy of the New Right, it is also firmly based in the tradition of teacher criticism, developing such criticism to embrace the culture and structure of the teaching profession. It is suggested that the policies proposed in the Consultation Paper will amount to a further intensification and regulation of teachers' work and a narrowing of their professional skills.

Framing the problem

It is arguable that the most important policy problem that confronts the Consultation Paper (DfEE, 1998a) is that of improving the recruitment, retention and motivation of good teachers – for without good teachers, the pursuit of standards is compromised. There is not only a recruitment problem, as the recent flutter of financial incentives for graduates to train would suggest; but there is also a crisis in morale for serving teachers (House of Commons, 1997); there is also evidence that many teachers are planning to leave the profession. However, governments rarely present policy problems in a straightforward manner, rather they reformulate them to suit their particular ends. Lindblom (1968), writing about USA policy-making in the sixties, claims that there is often room for controversy over what the problem actually is, and that there is opportunity for the reinvention of problems to provide new policy goals. Hence the problem of teacher recruitment, retention and motivation is reconstructed in the Consultation Paper not as a problem of pay and conditions or the treatment of teachers over the last two decades of criticism but as the problem of a profession which is in need of 'modernisation'. The teaching profession is described in the paper as failing to keep up with the times, poorly led and with an outdated structure and culture.

This process of modernisation is presented as inevitable; there is no choice. This furnishes modernisation with the status of being beyond political debate. Prime Minister Blair, in his 1999 party address, stated 'You have no choice, this is inevitable. These forces of change driving the future don't stop at national boundaries. Don't respect tradition. They wait for no-one and no nation. They are universal'. Hence the agenda for modernising the teaching profession is presented as inevitable in the foreword to the Consultation Paper, 'the status quo is not an option'. The term 'modernise' itself does not invite debate or scrutiny, for to be against modernising implies a commitment to the past, a failure to adapt to the present and the future, and the trap of luddism.

The modernisation of the teaching profession is to be accomplished by ensuring that its culture, structure, rewards and conditions are congruent with other professions in a modern economy. According to the Consultation Paper, a modern profession will be productive in achieving high standards, it will be accountable and flexible in its response to changing demands from a modern society: it is intended that it will be attractive to able and ambitious graduates:

> We need to give them [teachers] better support, leadership and recognition . . . We need a modern professional structure capable of achieving our goals. But the status quo is not an option. After decades of drift, decisive action is required to raise teaching to the front rank of professions. Only by modernisation can we equip our nation for the new century.
> (Foreword to *Teachers meeting the challenge of change*, DfEE, 1998)

Such a reformulation of the problem gives apparent justification for the government to intervene in the professional arrangements surrounding the leadership, management and deployment of teachers. Such a reformulation will meet the need of the government to attempt to solve the recruitment and retention crisis through better pay for some, whilst at the same time implementing a series of mechanisms which will strengthen state-regulation of the teaching force. The paper proposes that teachers will be subject to annual appraisal, their work will be judged against a set of non-negotiated detailed prescriptive standards, there will be more flexibility in the pay rewards for individual teachers with less transparency, there will be a shift towards the negotiation of local pay deals and within schools there will be a considerable transfer of power to management.

There are some 400,000 teachers in service in England and Wales and the age distribution is such that the average is forty-one, with 61.8 per cent of the service aged forty or over. Nearly 20 per cent are aged fifty or more compared with only 17 per cent under thirty. This suggests that the recruitment crisis will be amplified as the tranche of older colleagues retires or leaves the profession. Smithers and Robinson (1999) remind us that the secondary school population is set to rise by 300,000 over the next six years and this will intensify the problem. They emphasise the relationship between graduate recruitment to teaching and graduate employment in other spheres; and this in turn depends upon the general demand for graduate skills, which is likely to increase; and also depends upon the future state of the economy. The Consultation Paper itself acknowledges the recruitment problem as 'fierce' with 'a shortfall of 25 per cent on overall recruitment targets at secondary level' (para. 17, p.14). The ICM poll in February 2000 found that over 50 per cent of teachers were planning to leave the profession within the next ten years and this was not just confined to older teachers as more than a third of those under thirty-five planned to leave within the same timespan. Similar findings were presented by the joint TTA/ NUT study in six London boroughs.

At issue is how distinctive are the strategies proposed in the Consultation Paper under the banner of modernisation from those of the previous conservative administrations, and whether they will lead to solutions to the problems of recruitment and retention. The previous government was also committed to a radical overhaul of education in the interests of the economy in order to enable the UK to compete more effectively in international markets. Propelled by the philosophy of the New Right, there was a sustained attempt to introduce new reforms into education and to restructure the economy, employment and the 'culture of dependence'. As Gamble (1983) argues, the New Right in Britain was an uneven coalition of neo-liberal thinking on the free market and competition with a neo-conservative emphasis on tradition, authority and national identity. The neo-liberals saw enterprise, individual choice and the market as the driving forces for economic improvement together with the reduction of social overheads such as welfare costs. They welcomed these forces as contributing to the efficiency of the public services, including education. To such changes in education were added the agenda demanded by the neo-conservatives: state control of the curriculum and qualifications, and greater regulation of the teaching profession and its training (Whitty, 1988).

New Right policies were one social and economic response to global competition; however it is argued that there is an alternative as modelled in Clinton economics. Brown and Lauder (1994) label this group as 'left modernisers'. The fundamental principles on which their policies are based are:

- investment in human capital;
- strategic investment in the economy as a way of moving forward towards a high-skill, high-wages magnet economy (magnet here used in the sense of attracting inward investment and employment);
- a vision of a society permeated by a culture of learning. For it is the knowledge, skills and insights of the population that provide the key to future prosperity.

Such a position clearly establishes education and training at the centre of economic strategy and to this extent New Labour claims to be adopting the left modernising agenda but it also borrows generously, as will be argued, from the established legacy of the New Right.

There is continuity of policies with the previous government in the reduction and targeting of welfare costs subsumed under the banner of the reform of the welfare state; there is also the firm grip on public expenditure with consequences for those benefiting from public services and the regulation of public sector; the public sector, as an entity is not popular with many in the new administration. It is claimed that such control over the public sector serves to maintain the UK as a haven within Europe of relatively low taxation and attractive to inward investment. However, there have been small steps towards redressing some of the unbalanced legislation of the past decades with the reconsideration of rights for individuals at work, including the national minimum wage; collective rights, such as the re-recognition of trades unions; and some family-friendly policies such as the implementation of the 'European Working Time Directive' (DTI, 1998). Such policies distinguish this administration from those before and simulate what is referred to as the 'third way'.

The legacy of the New Right

It can be argued that the Consultation Paper embodies such a mixture of principles that on the one hand it is offering additional funding for the education service, while on the other it is making demands for increased productivity with the tighter regulation of teachers. The Consultation Paper seeks to address the policy tasks by a combination of 'improvements' for teachers – better leadership, better rewards, better training and better support, but the paper clearly rests on assumptions which are critical of the teaching profession and which obviously embody elements of the New Right philosophy. There is much that will be welcomed in the paper and that is intended to prove attractive to those already serving and leading the profession, and those considering a career in teaching. The proposals are claimed to parallel the best practice in other fields of modern employment: the improvement of working conditions, the provision of appropriate and modern equipment, the recruitment and training of support staff, the removal of inappropriate chores which divert the productive work of teachers, the commitment to the investment in the initial and ongoing human capital of teachers. However, the assumption is that many teachers are not working hard enough, their work is not focused, they are not keeping up; the key words of individualism, enterprise, competition and ambition, the shibboleths of the New Right, reveal the dominant thinking in the paper.

With one exception, the School Performance Award Scheme, the policies promoted in the paper tend to concentrate on the achievements or failings of the individual teacher as the key to success. Individual teachers will be identified as having the appropriate skills and achievements for promotion through the performance threshold to enhanced salaries. Other teachers will be identified as having the appropriate skills for 'fast track' professional development to senior positions. The remainder of the teaching force will carry on much as now but with closer monitoring by management, their salaries and conditions being the subject of annual cost of living reviews by the STRB.

The shift to this competitive individualism will accomplish three things. It will significantly increase competition between individuals, very much in the established tradition of the New Right. It will weaken the notion of the school as a collective enterprise, of one teacher being very dependent on another as the children come with their skills and knowledge enhanced by contributions from a variety of colleagues. It will also weaken any base for pluralism in schools, as there will be no obvious loci for teachers to congregate; departments and similar structures may well be significantly diluted so that they provide no obvious base for association. Furthermore, as Hextall and Mahony (1999) argue, 'the individualising orientation also drives directly to the heart of collective models of organising and protecting teachers, their rights, conditions of service and rewards'. Again the weakening of collective bargaining and collective action was central to the political agenda of the New Right.

Like many apparent modernisation proposals, their justification lies in an interpretation of past practices being dismissed as part of a cultural aberration, the individual teacher is now to be judged and rewarded on the basis of his or her assessed skill. This is presented as a new departure:

> The main reason why the system has rewarded experience and responsibility but not performance is cultural. Heads and teachers have been more reluctant than comparable groups to distinguish the performance of some teachers from others, except through the reward of responsibility points.
>
> (DfEE, 1998a p.32)

Interestingly the assertion presented is that performance had little to do with being offered posts of responsibility and that experience did not count. Such assertions will strike many teachers as somewhat novel.

The notion of individual competition is closely linked with ambition, a new virtue extolled in the paper. Traditional structures, such as length of service and positions of responsibility, are to become less important and the teacher will have to make career choices much more located on individual grounds. Teachers will choose whether to attempt to cross the performance threshold, what kind of further training to embark upon and whether to engage in advanced and more demanding contracts, with the associated risks.

There is then an attempt to change the culture of the school as an organisation from what might be described as a mechanistic institution with transparent hierarchical structures to an organic form with a more fluid, flexible structure. Yet there are contradictions in the proposals, and there is to be a well-rewarded management structure with substantially increased powers of surveillance and regulation.

The tradition of teacher criticism

The Consultation Paper at one level tries to provide a basis for making the teaching profession more attractive and solve the problem of poor recruitment to, and poor retention and motivation in, the profession; yet at another fails to disguise itself from being firmly cast in the recent tradition of teacher criticism. This may be to satisfy the large audience in Britain which has now come to expect, as part of the current cultural heritage, the vilification of its teachers with the help of the state and the media.

State criticism of the teaching profession, orchestrated with the 'Great Debate' twenty-five years ago, has been vigorously sustained and developed by the subsequent conservative administrations, providing a strong basis for a sequence of interventions into the control of the educational system with the marginalisation of the other partners, namely the teachers themselves and the local education authorities. Such criticism has, until recently, been used conveniently to explain Britain's relative economic decline (Merson, 1995). Teachers were criticised for not trans-mitting the basic skills and failing to prepare young people for employment (DES, 1977); for failing to encourage appropriate attitudes to enterprise and wealth creation (DES, 1985); and for not having experience of busi-ness and industry themselves and for promoting an anti-industrial culture (DTI, 1988). Such a sustained and comprehensive litany of criticism has legitimised the grounds for the state to intervene into all phases and aspects of education and to achieve substantial limits to the status and scope of the teaching profession (Esland, 1996). Both the Literacy and the Numeracy Strategies (DfEE, 1997 and 1998b) can be interpreted in this tradition and based on the assumption that primary teachers were still failing to transmit basic skills effectively and needed prescriptions on both pedagogy and content to remedy this. In the Consultation Paper, the structure and culture of the profession is the most recent focus for criticism. It is con-sidered out-of-date: 'the status quo is not an option' and 'we can only realise the full potential of our schools if we recruit and motivate teachers and other staff with ambition' (foreword, DfEE, 1998a).

In the Consultation Paper there are both explicit and implicit criticisms of the profession. The explicit criticisms are that teachers are not achieving the 'high standards' expected for a modern society, they are 'reluctant to change', are 'poorly led and managed' and are 'poorly trained'. 'Teachers too often seem to be afraid of change and therefore resist it' (p.16); and now they must 'anticipate change and innovation' (p.14) (DfEE, 1998a). Many teachers would find such a claim difficult to recognise after a period of uninterrupted, substantial and often inconsistent change in cur-riculum and assessment arrangements and provision for its own account-ability over the last twenty years.

As has been argued, one response to greater international economic competition, common to the New Right and the modernisers, has been to look for gains in efficiency and productivity amongst workers. This has led to intensification of workload, which has been seen amongst manual and non-manual workers by Larson (1980) and, in the case of teachers, by Apple (1986). Interpretations of intensification vary with author but common themes emerge: more of the teacher's time devoted to the task of teaching, the scope of administrative duties extending, and less time for collegial relations, relaxation and private life. Evidence emer-ging from monitoring the implementation of the national curriculum suggests that intensification of work was marked for many teachers, parti-cularly primary teachers (Campbell and Neill, 1994) – this was explained in part by the poor central management of the initiative. It now appears that the Consultation Paper seeks to further intensify teachers' workloads.

There is an assumption throughout the paper that teachers in general are not working to the limits of their capacity, despite studies and claims to the contrary. It is teachers who cross the performance threshold who are going to bear the brunt of the intensification. The work of a promoted teacher is to be extended:

> Successful teachers would be expected to make a much fuller professional contribution to teaching and to learning in the school, including more time to their own professional growth and development and extending learning opportunities for pupils in addition to, as a matter of course, continuing to teach to a high standard.
>
> (DfEE, 1998a p.36)

And:

> There would be higher professional expectations for all teachers above the threshold . . . We will consult on whether this requires a different more demanding contract for this group of teachers.
>
> (DfEE, 1998a p.38)

For those new and serving teachers recruited to the fast track:

> . . . fast-track entrants would be asked to accept supplementary contracts, which entailed a longer working year and greater mobility.
>
> (DfEE, 1998a p.47)

A further contribution to teacher productivity is that, apart from those in leadership roles, teachers will be allowed to be more focused on the principal task of teaching. Qualified teaching assistants will free teachers of some of their 'administrative chores', there will be extensive use of ICT (Information and Communications Technology) and there will be a general improvement in the capital stock of schools, allowing teachers, like other workers in a modern economy, to make more effective use of their skills.

However, the distinction between teaching and 'administrative chores' may not be as simple as it appears. The task of teaching has a range of moral and pastoral dimensions and duties and these are particularly evident and of high profile in the primary phase. Envisaging the teacher as exclusively involved in teaching and assessment may be to adopt too specialised a function and too limited a profile of skills and might not accurately reflect the moral scope of the work of teachers. This is another occasion where the Consultation Paper departs from the modernising features of best practice in contemporary employment where workers are increasingly expected to be multiskilled and ready to adopt a flexible range of functions as change and demand arises. A truly modern perspective might envisage teachers becoming more productive by having access to a wider range of skills and able to change roles, dealing with different age-phases, different packages of curriculum materials and different pastoral and leadership functions as demand arises; but no such analysis is provided by the paper.

There is a culture of mediocrity where:

> The tradition to which adherence remains powerful is to treat all teachers as if their performance was similar, even though teachers themselves know that this is not the case. The effects have been to limit incentives for teachers to improve their performance and to make teaching much less attractive to talented and ambitious people than it should be.
>
> (DfEE, 1998a p.32)

This paragraph, more than any other, reveals the assumptions made about what motivates teachers and others in contemporary society and locates its philosophy firmly in competitive individualism.

As for teachers and change: 'Teachers too often seem afraid of change and therefore to resist it' (DfEE, 1998a p.16). However, there is an attempt to widen the blame and allocate some of it to the previous administration:

> Poorly managed change, conflict in the 1980s and early 1990s and uncertain funding for education over many years have also made their contribution to this state of affairs. Worst of all, there has been a widespread sense among many teachers and their leaders that nothing can be done to change it.
>
> (DfEE, 1998a p.16)

But the impact of the changes in the last twenty years on teachers and their work is not to be underestimated. Ball (1990) classifies the reforms as the 'privatisation' of parts of educational assets and provision, the 'marketisation' of schools through competition, the 'differentiation' of institutions to offer apparent diversity and choice, and intermittent 'vocationalisation' of elements of the curriculum. He sees all these as significant developments in restructuring the educational service and bringing it into greater congruence with commerce and business. To the list, Ball adds the 'proletarianisation' of teachers; as the national curriculum essentially removed a large measure of choice and creativity from teachers' work with the separation of policy decisions from their execution; and an increasing gulf is opening up between teachers and their managers caused by the new initiatives. It is to the further proletarianistaion of teachers that the Consultation Paper will contribute more fully.

The myth of the modern

Although the paper seeks to present itself as being about the modernisation of the profession, there is very little that is truly modern in the proposals. The claims to be modern are pivoted on three areas: the adoption of new management regimes, new conditions and structures of work, and the promotion of ICT.

New management regimes

Throughout the paper, 'improved management' in skills, processes and structures can be seen as a central strategy for the modernising of the profession. Commentators see this as the performance management model, which in turn is embedded in the ideology of managerialism borrowed from the private sector and other professions, not necessarily from the latest *high-trust* practice. The government's commitment to the model was trailed in the White Paper 'Excellence in Schools' (DfEE, 1997b), where the preoccupations of 'improving appraisal, tackling poor performance and improving support for teachers' were flagged. A characteristic of this model of management is that it appears to be transferable from one employment context to another without reference to the particulars of the relationships and purposes of the work. It is offered as value-free and 'technicist' and hence unproblematic; so there are no problems anticipated in transferring this model of management from, say, a building society to a primary school.

As is argued by Esland *et al.* (1999), much of the discourse of managerialism has been part of the New Right political agenda which rests on a management practice which is driven by an overarching requirement for control and compliance amongst employees. This in turn, it is argued, has seen a series of regulations and methodologies which has exerted powerful constraints over the identities, responsibilities and workloads of professional workers in the public sector who formerly regarded their working relationships as founded on collegiality and high levels of trust. The discourse of new managerialism is set within assumptions about the inevitable logic of ever-increased efficiency and productivity. Managers are to have more power to manage and new techniques are embraced to secure not only compliance but also a redefinition of professionalism.

Reeves (1995) argues that many of these management processes have already been trailed in further and higher education institutions since incorporation. The purposes of further education have been exclusively redirected to 'modernise the country's forces of production' and the former social and political and cultural aims of education have been displaced. The reconstruction of colleges is likely to emulate the organisa-tional features found in the business sector, transforming former profes-sionals into managers and workers. An older concept of the independent professional lecturer individually responsible for the success of his or her own class of students is no longer viable: personal professional values are formally restructured at national and institutional level. The model that further education presents for schools is a salutary one, with a narrowed competence-based curriculum and teachers whose work has been deprofes-sionalised, intensified and marginalised.

Much of the discourse in the Consultation Paper follows in this tradi-tion. There is promotion of a range of regulating devices of management; the language frequently used is that of assessment, observation, target-setting, monitoring and annual appraisal together with rewards dependent on performance.

> At the heart of all good performance management must be a thorough annual assessment of the performance of every member of staff which should result in the setting of targets for improvement and develop-ment over the next year. In the case of teachers, appraisal must include assessment of classroom performance through observation and analysis of the progress their pupils have made.
>
> (DfEE, 1998a p.35)

Some other examples of the new management tasks appear neither overly modern nor sophisticated:

> By the same token we look to heads to tackle management problems squarely. Heads and senior managers should mange the performance of teachers on a day-to-day basis and should be aware of any emerging problems. The new capability procedures which schools have in place by the end of 1998 provide for rapid action – leading to dismissal if appropriate – where teachers fall below acceptable standards of compe-tence. The Government is also concerned about rates of absenteeism across the public sector. We will set targets to reduce levels of sickness

absence in schools – as the Government is doing across the public sector as a whole.

(DfEE 1998a p.39)

It is interesting and revealing to see how the problem of absenteeism is framed – that there cannot be good grounds for absenteeism such as sickness or bereavement and that it is only a matter of setting the appropriate targets. There is no reflection of the modern policies of more family-friendly conditions of employment being sought by other government departments such as the DTI, which take into account the broader location of work in the modern world and in the family context.

Modern conditions

There is an assumption running through the paper that other professions and types of work have modernised and teachers have somehow been left behind:

> Teachers too often seem to be afraid of change and therefore to resist it. Many seem to believe they are unique victims of the process of constant change, although the reality is that in many other sectors change has been more revolutionary and had greater impact on pay, conditions and styles of work.

(DfEE, 1998a p.16)

When attempting to characterise developments that are modern in the sphere of the organisation of work and production, commentators such as Murray (1989) have adopted the analysis of fordism and post-fordism. The characteristics of fordism were the production of standardised products with product-specific machinery using semi-skilled workers who were heavily and scientifically regulated in their tasks by what has become known as Taylorism. Fordism relied on the provision of mass-produced goods and services for large-scale and relatively stable patterns of consumption. There are those who argue that such an approach to production of goods and services has changed since the seventies. Piore and Sable (1984) cite two important factors, which encouraged a shift towards more flexible strategies of production, described as post-fordism: the industrial unrest of the late sixties and early seventies and the changing nature of market demand. The industrial unrest from 1968 onwards, itself one reaction to the rigid and unvaried regimes of fordist production, was met by some companies in an innovative fashion with decentralised and geographically dispersed production, the use of sub-contracting and the adoption of new flexible technologies. Some markets, it was argued, became saturated in terms of demand for mass-produced goods, there was increased competition from the newly industrialised countries, some of which were advanced technologically, this in turn forced cost-cutting and innovation on home producers. Consumers' tastes, once their basic needs had been satisfied, became more diverse leading to the development of niche markets, encouraging the production of low-volume, high-quality goods in contrast to the fordist, high-volume, and low-quality products. The analysis can equally be applied to services as to goods, and to services in the public sector.

Post-fordism is described as the response to the above factors, encouraged and enabled in some cases by new technology and by more responsive forms of flexible production of goods and services. It is claimed that there has been a move from large mass production strategies to smaller, more innovative companies with highly skilled workers working in teams with new technology able to change production and tasks swiftly, to cater for changes in consumer demand: a shift from production of scale, to production of scope. Such apparent changes were optimistically interpreted as providing opportunities for high trust relations between managers and employees, more discretion for employees and collective participation. Such changes are very partial and often held up by some management gurus as ideals to pursue. Such changes have been encouraged in the service sector and in the public sector.

It appears that the current government sees teachers as redolent of the fordist workers of the public sector, reluctant to change and develop. Teachers are seen as concerned with reducing class size, with improving teacher–pupil ratios, and keeping the three-term year. All these are interpreted as traditional features limiting teacher 'productivity'. Now teachers are to be encouraged to alter the nature of their productivity through greater flexibility, and responsiveness with the help of new technology, all three concepts are used frequently throughout the paper.

> Schools are using technology and more flexible staffing to vary group sizes, to provide additional support for particular groups who need it and to enhance the quality of lessons.
>
> (DfEE, 1998a p.60)

However, there are those who claim the changes in the organisation of work and productivity of the last thirty years are not represented by the optimistic shift from fordism to post-fordism but rather from fordism to neo-fordism, particularly in the USA and the UK. Avis (1996) draws our attention to the contradiction between the discourse of modernisation,

with the implications of high trust and innovative work relations characteristic of post-fordism, and the reality of the new managerialism and its
increased surveillance and regulation of workers. Neo-fordism harnesses
new technology and new developments in management to increasingly
regulate workers. Managers have increased power to manage and the
gulf between manager and worker is increased with work being fragmented, for example between conception and execution. There is
increased surveillance of workers and low-trust management regimes.
Flexibility is applied to pay and conditions, with part-time work, short-
term contracts, contracts dependent on performance; there is increased
insecurity. Many of the recommendations of the Consultation Paper can
be interpreted as fitting the neo-fordist model.

Behind the rhetoric of modern management lies the architecture of
hierarchical management adopting processes that are redolent of very
traditional, authoritarian and Taylorist regimes. As Murray (1989) argues,
'the contractual core of Taylorism – higher wages in return for managerial
control of production': this equation seems to be at the heart of the
Consultation Paper.

Flexibility

Notions of being flexible and of flexibility are used throughout the paper
and, as has been argued above, there are two important spheres of interpretation for these concepts; flexibility of skills and flexibility of conditions.
Flexibility of skills refers to the repertoire of skills an employee has and is
able to exercise so that he or she can engage in a range of different tasks
as and when changes in demand require. Flexibility of conditions is primarily concerned with the conditions, patterns and rewards of employment
and ensuring that the numerical workforce supply can be readily altered to
match changes in demand or task. In the rhetoric of modernisation, only
the positive image of flexibility is allowed to emerge; its darker side, that
of insecurity and periodic exclusion from the labour market, is carefully
obscured.

In terms of the important principle of flexibility of skills, little is said in
the Consultation Paper hence distancing it from any truly modern conception of work. There is the notion of ongoing and improved training
throughout the career of the teacher in order that their skills and knowledge can be updated to adapt to curricular and other changes, although
this is not clearly developed in the paper. As argued above, if anything,
the conception of teaching is to become a more narrow activity with
teachers doing little of anything else. There is the notion of flexibility of
function which implies a wider range of skills but this is mainly for the

cadre of high-flying teachers, some 5 per cent of the force, who will wish, or be required, to change roles, from teacher to manager, to advisor, to inspector.

But most of the paper is devoted to flexibility in conditions; there is the notion of flexibility of contracts, which introduces a considerable degree of uncertainty and perhaps insecurity into the system. Those on promoted contracts will only enjoy the rewards while their contracts are conducted proficiently subject to annual reviews and while demand for their particular role remains. Such flexible contracts will apply to those in management and leadership roles with increments only awarded when targets are met. Finally, there is the local flexibility of rewards; schools will have much more discretion in how they financially reward the performance and skills of individual teachers in order to meet local problems and challenges. This will allow leeway to depart from the whole notion of national pay-scales and *de facto* introduce local pay bargaining. The emphasis in the paper is then on flexible conditions, most of which will represent a deterioration from the *status quo* with, for some teachers, improvement of pay as compensation for loss of conditions: so much for modernisation.

Infatuation with information technology

The present government has demonstrated its unqualified infatuation with technology, whether in the case of genetically modified crops or in the introduction of new, but demonstrably unsuccessful, information technology systems, in its attempts to modernise the Passport Agency, the Immigration Service and the National Health Service. In the Consultation Paper, all ICT is presented as enhancing and liberating. ICT will give schools access to the worldwide web, it will enable the networking of pupils' homes, and it will provide improved access for special needs pupils to learning. Teachers will be liberated from the bureaucratic chores of registration and enabled to get on with their core function of teaching. But not all is liberating: for pupils there may well be little that does not come under the surveillance of ICT. There will be electronic registers; assessment and recording will be aided by technology; all aspects of pupils' performance will be monitored and recorded in a 1984 ethos – one aspect of the modern. The impact on the teacher and serious learning has yet to be carefully considered. It may be that the speedy adoption of ICT in education will be very different from that in other forms of work and enterprise. Aronwitz and Difazio (1994), in their account of the introduction of computer technology at work in the USA, claim that for the vast majority of workers, computerisation has resulted in further subordination, displacement or irrelevance. But to raise such warnings in the face of modernisation is to be instantly decried as luddite, even though we are faced daily with evidence of the social failure of the computer in terms of its powers to deskill and regulate the work place.

Conclusions

Under the guise of modernising the teaching profession, to make it superficially attractive to new recruits and to stave off some of the current wastage from the profession, the government has offered incentives of pay associated with a new career structure for the 'ambitious'. At the same time it has taken the opportunity to set in place a new apparatus for control and regulation. Managers are to be given enhanced powers of surveillance and control to ensure teachers' compliance and increased productivity. There is to be a reduction of security of employment for many teachers. The teacher's task is to become increasingly narrowed. Individual teachers will be encouraged to compete with each other for the rewards of such compliance. The traditions of cooperation and collegiality will be hard to sustain. This social model will not be lost upon the children nor on society.

References

Apple, M. (1986), *Teachers and Texts*, New York: Routledge & Kegan Paul.

Aronwitz, S. and Difazio, W. (1994), *The Jobless Future*, Minneapolis: University of Minnesota Press.

Avis, J. (1996), 'The Myth of Post-Fordist Society' in J. Avis *et al.*, *Knowledge and Nationhood*, London: Cassell.

Ball, S. (1990), 'Industrial Training Or New Vocationalism? Structures And Discourses', in S. Ball (ed.), *Politics and Policy Making in Education*, London: Routledge.

Brown, P. and Lauder, H. (1996), 'Education, globalisation and economic development', in *Journal Of Education Policy*, Vol. 11, No. 1, pp.1–25.

Campbell, R. J. (1985), *Developing The Primary School Curriculum*, London: Holt, Rinehart & Winston.

Campbell, R. J. and Neill, S. R. St. J. (1994), *Primary Teachers at Work*, London: Routledge.

DES (1977), *Education In Schools: A Consultative Document*, Cmnd. 6869, London: HMSO.

DES (1985), *Better Schools*, Cmnd. 9469, London: HMSO.

DfEE (1997), *The Implementation of the National Literacy Strategy*, Suffolk: DfEE.

DfEE (1997b), *Excellence In Schools*, Cmnd. 3681, London: TSO.

DfEE (1998a) *Teachers Meeting the Challenge of Change*, London: TSO.

DfEE (1998b), *The National Numeracy Strategy: Final Report of the Numeracy Task Force*, Suffolk: DfEE.

DTI (1988), *DTI – The Department For Enterprise*, London: HMSO.

DTI (1998), *Fairness At Work*, Cmnd. 3968, London, TSO.

Esland, G. (1996), 'Education, Training And Nation-State Capitalism: Britain's Failing Strategy', in J. Avis, M. Bloomer, G. Esland, D. Gleeson and P. Hodkinson, *Knowledge and Nationhood*, London: Cassell.

Esland, G., Esland, K., Murphy, M. and Yarrow, K. (1999), 'Managerializing Organizational Culture', in J. Ahier and G. Esland (eds), *Education, Training and the Future of Work*, Vol. 1, London: Routledge.

Finegold, D. (1991), 'Education Training And Economic Performance in Comparative Perspective', in D. Phillips (ed.), *Oxford Studies in Comparative Education*, Wallingford: Triangle Books.

Gamble, A. (1983), 'Thatcherism And Conservative Politics', in S. Hall and M. Jaques (eds), *The Politics Of Thatcherism*, London: Lawrence & Wishart.

Hextall, I. and Mahony, P. (1999), 'Modernising the Teacher', paper presented at The European Conference Of Educational Research, Lahti, Finland.

House Of Commons (1997), *Education and Employment Committee Sixth Report: The Professional Status, Recruitment And Training Of Teachers*, London, TSO.

Larson, S. M. (1980), 'Proletarianisation And Educated Labour', in *Theory and Society*, Vol. 9 (1), pp.131–75.

Lindblom, C. E. (1968), *The Policy Making Process*, New Jersey: Prentice Hall.

Merson, M. (1995), 'Political explanations for economic decline in Britain and their relationship to policies for education and training', in *Journal of Education Policy*, Vol. 10 (3), pp.303–16.

Murray, R. (1989), 'Fordism And Post-Fordism', in S. Hall and M. Jaques (eds), *New Times*, London: Lawrence & Wishart.

Phillimore, A. J. (1989), 'Flexible Specialisation, Work Organisation and Skills: Approaching the "Second Industrial Divide"', *New Technology, Work and Employment*, pp.79–91.

Piore M. J. and Sable, C. F. (1984), The *Second Industrial Divide – Possibilities For Prosperity*, New York: Basic Books.

Reeves, F. (1995), 'The Modernity Of Further Education', in *Education Now*, Bilston: College Publications.

Robinson, P. and Smithers, A. (1999), *Teacher Supply 1999: Old Story Or New Chapter*, Liverpool: Centre for Education and Employment Research, University of Liverpool.

Whitty, G. (1989), 'The New Right and The National Curriculum: State Control or Market Forces?', in *Journal of Educational Policy*, Vol. 4, pp.329–41.

6 Teachers' lives and teaching performance

Pat Sikes

Introduction

As well as being an educational researcher with a particular interest in bio-graphical and narrative approaches to teachers' lives and careers, at the time of writing, I am, amongst other things, a PGCE (Postgraduate Certificate in Education) professional tutor, the chair of governors at a Church of England primary school, the mother of children in years three and five and the wife of a deputy-head of an 11–16 secondary school. In all of these roles I come into intimate contact with issues around teachers and teaching, teachers' lives and teaching performance, but each time it is from a different position with different implications for my perspectives, understandings and experiences. In the same way, teachers' perspectives, understandings and experiences of their work are influenced by the various social positions they occupy. In this chapter my intention is to take a holistic, person-focused approach in order to consider the performance management system coming into statutory force in England and Wales in September 2000. I shall be making use of teachers', students', governors', parents', advisors' and trainers' stories and auto/biographical accounts in order to explore the personal meanings and implications of this 'innovation' which, typically, is based on a nomothetic and technicist notion of teachers and their work. In doing this I follow Bullough in believing that 'when seeking to explain why something happened in a class-room, increasingly the road to understanding takes a biographical turn, not a detour' (Bullough, 1998 p.19).

I came to this view during the early 1980s when researching teachers' perceptions and experiences of teaching as a career at a time when falling rolls meant declining promotion prospects (see Sikes, 1986). Now it seems obvious that career motivation, commitment, performance, values and beliefs cannot be considered as discrete aspects of a person's life. How-ever, when I started that research I was looking for neat and tidy answers, for ways of motivating teachers as a homogeneous group. I was forgetting though that some people, for instance, need promotion to finance growing families, whereas others seek it because they want to be in a position to develop their own interests or to have greater opportunity to disseminate particular values, and so on. Thus, no strategy will ever be appropriate for everyone. My later work – amongst other things on TVEI (Technical and Vocational Education Initiative) (Sikes, 1990), the management of in-service training, teacher appraisal, equal opportunities initiatives (Sikes, 1996), and mentoring in initial teacher education (Brooks and Sikes, 1997) – further convinced me that pedagogical, curricular and organisational innovation is always mediated and influenced through and by the biographies of the teachers (and the pupils) it concerns (Sikes, 1992). The management of performance is no exception.

Performance management in schools

The stated purpose of the performance management system is to raise standards of student achievement by supporting and improving teachers' work through a structured programme of monitoring and appraisal. Each teacher is to be set measurable performance objectives that will be systematically reviewed. Official documentation emphasises that teachers will benefit in terms of their job satisfaction, career development and progression (DfEE, 2000).

The system takes the form of a yearly cycle of objective setting, monitoring and review of every teacher's performance which it is the responsibility of each school's governing body to oversee. The process is ostensibly school-centred – with the exception of the DfEE-accredited external adviser, brought in to assist the governors nominated to review the headteacher's performance, and of accredited consultants providing performance management training for heads, teachers and governors. Responsibility for maintaining what Gill Helsby refers to as the 'ubiquitous mantra of raising standards' (Helsby, 1999 p.99), and for reculturing schools is laid firmly at the door of governors and headteachers – the managers. Thus teachers are marginalised, their professional knowledge and expertise is given little value and, as various commentators have noted, education is commodified, marketised, conceptualised as a product to be delivered by personnel, i.e. teachers, who must be managed (Ball, 1994; Dale, 1989; Hatcher, 1994; Helsby, 1999; and Robertson, 1996). As Sharon Gewirtz has pointed out, the language used to describe such innovations is not neutral but, rather, forms part of discourses which 'function as powerful disciplinary mechanisms for transforming teacher subjectivities and the culture and values of classroom practice' (Gewirtz, 1997 p.219).

   Whilst such discourses may well impact upon, even 'transform', teachers' perceptions and experiences of their work, there is little evidence to suggest that top–down, imposed innovations and so-called reforms do lead to raised standards (Acker, 1997; Barber, 2000; Fullan, 1993; Helsby, 1999; Sikes, 1992; and Smyth, 1991). Ironically, perhaps, this seems to be largely because teaching is so much about subjectivities, about interactive relationships with the various parties involved and about how individual teachers perceive themselves and their role in the whole innovation/reform 'enterprise'. Ivor Goodson once wrote, 'in understanding something so intensely personal as teaching it is critical we know about the person the teacher is' (Goodson, 1981 p.69). Elaborating on this, Nias has claimed that 'the self is a crucial element in the way teachers themselves construe the nature of their job' (Nias, 1989 p.13). A technicist approach, such as that represented by policy imposition and 'performance management cycles' is unlikely, indeed will probably be unable, to take such factors into account.
   And then there is the underlying assumption that something is very wrong in order to warrant imposition, legislation and surveillance. Teacher morale is known to be low and government criticism and intervention is commonly accepted as a major root cause of this. Constant criticism and the eroding of autonomy may well have a negative effect on how teachers perceive themselves: it certainly has significant implications for the content and nature of their work. Perhaps this pain is all the greater because teachers themselves, as parents as well as professionals, are keen to provide the best education possible. They want (appropriate and relevant) standards to be high – for their own children as well as for their pupils (Sikes, 1997). It is, therefore, particularly galling to be cast as the problem, or at least a major part of the problem. Of course, focusing on the teachers and their performance deflects attention from the social, economic, technological, moral factors which, in combination, make their contribution to the challenges facing teachers. But, as has so often been noted, as a result of their obvious and highly visible role in preparing the next generation and being relatively powerless in the wider context, teachers, viewed as a group of workers, provide a convenient scapegoat for a multitude of structural problems. And yet, as the (English and Welsh) advert for teaching as a career says, 'everyone remembers a good teacher'. It is at the personal level, in interactions with individual pupils, colleagues and local settings, that the power lies; and there, at the same time, the capacity for damage (of all kinds and to all involved) is the greatest. To have meaningful effectiveness, performance management systems, it is suggested, need to acknowledge and value the personal. And, perhaps, they also should be introduced and framed in a way that makes it explicit that the

desire to develop and improve professional practice need not inevitably be grounded in any confession of personal 'failure'.

Acknowledging and valuing the personal: a brief methodological note

In England and Wales, those involved in doing research in educational settings began the new millennium with the government-endorsed exhortation to produce evidence-based research which:

> [firstly] demonstrates conclusively that if teachers change their practice from x to y there will be significant and enduring improvement in teaching and learning; and [secondly] has developed an effective method of convincing teachers of the benefits of, and means to, changing from x to y.
>
> (Hargreaves, 1996 p.5)

And, from the current Secretary of State:

> One of our prime needs is to be able to measure the size of the effect of A on B. . . . We're not interested in worthless correlations based on small samples from which it is impossible to draw generalisable conclusions. We welcome studies which combine large-scale, quantitative information on sizes which will allow us to generalise, with in-depth case studies which provide insight into how processes work . . . [although] researchers [should be] more open and balanced about the strengths and potential weaknesses of their data . . . [they] should make sure they are not seduced . . . into reducing complex and qualified conclusions into a set of simplistic and misleading messages which can do much harm.
>
> (Blunkett, 2000)

In this chapter in this particular book it is unnecessary to revisit and rehearse ontological, epistemological and methodological arguments about the relative value of different positions. Fitness for purpose has been taken as the key criteria for choosing specific research approaches and forms of writing. Since the purpose is to explore the personal meanings and implications of performance management systems, to consider the ways in which life histories, personal, subjective idiosyncrasies and circumstances affect perceptions and experiences – and outcomes and responses – personal accounts and stories are appropriate. Of course, they do not easily lead to generalisations except, perhaps, the most obvious one, which is teachers are people with private lives and that:

> it is difficult to separate, convincingly and reliably, self from profes-sional persona. It seems . . . to be in the nature of teaching, that the mask of the role player is likely to slip.
>
> (Thomas, 1993 p.239)

Given this, I will follow Bill Tierney's injunction to:

> refrain from the temptation of either placing [my] work in relation to traditions or offering a defensive response. I increase my capacity neither for understanding nor originality by a defensive posture. To seek new epistemological and methodological avenues demands that we chart new paths rather than constantly return to well-worn roads and point out that they will not take us where we want to go.
>
> (Tierney, 1998 p.68)

Where I do want to go, is into making sense of personal meaning using personal accounts and stories. Like Peter Clough:

> when I try to make sense of 'data', I (almost involuntarily) situate them in contexts of realization which owe more to the processes of making art – however flawed – than to those of 'social science'.
>
> (Clough, 1999 p.444)

This may make for a 'messy text' (Marcus, 1994); but then, that is a characteristic of the crisis of representation affecting research (Denzin and Lincoln, 1994 p.2) occasioned by an awareness of the difficulties of demonstrating conclusively that x can lead to y and that it is possible to measure the effect of A and B, as Hargreaves and Blunkett, quoted at the start of this section, would have us attempt.

And so, here are some of the stories relating to, and about, performance management that I have collected. They are not particularly exciting or sensational or action packed but they are important because it is through the construction, telling and retelling of our personal stories, to ourselves and to others, that we attempt to make sense of our lives and give them meaning. They are about, and represent different perspectives on, making sense of performance management. For personal narratives have a status as personal, as well as research, data. As Rapport (1999) puts it, personal narrative is a means by which individuals existentially appre-hend their own lives (Rapport, 1999 p.4) (see also Bruner, 1990; and

Polkinghorne, 1988). Nor are these stories exceptional in any other sense than that they are unique to the people they belong to but, given the intrinsic value of each individual, given the importance of the individual in a teaching context, and given the line taken in this chapter, this is sufficient. I acknowledge that there are many questions around personal stories and 'truth' but will not address them here (although I would add that such questions apply to all forms of research and reporting, see Clough, 1992 p.2) (readers are referred to: Goodson and Sikes, 2001; Rosie, 1993; and Sikes, 2000, for further discussion).

Stories and accounts of performance management

Managing performance management: a headteacher's story

'We had a staff meeting on Monday night about performance management so I could report back on the heads' training day. It really was very good so I've booked the bloke for our staff training in September at the Moat House and we're going to do it with Sheila's school. But anyway, I asked them to think about being team leader but nobody wanted to take it on because they didn't want to have anything to do with something that might affect people's pay. I did say it was up to the individual teacher as to whether they brought performance management observations as data for threshold payments but they still weren't happy about it. I'm not going to say any more at the moment because it's the end of term, people are knackered and you can't expect them to think about taking anything else on. Perhaps in September they'll come back refreshed and might be more prepared to consider it then. But at the end of the day, if no-one volunteers I'm just going to have to ask Veronica and Mary to do it, on top of everything else. Oh yeh, Tom asked whether there'd be any extra money for being a team leader and I said I didn't think so.'

(Rob, primary school head, in interview)

Mrs Patel got used to us: a pupil's story

'Mr Richards was very poorly. He'd been falling over in the classroom and getting bad headaches and we'd had to take the emergency card to the office to get Mrs Smith to come. So he had to go to hospital and Mrs Patel came to take us. She was a supply teacher but she taught us for about two months. When she first came it wasn't very good because people kept throwing pencils and rubbers at everybody else. I went under the table to get out of the way. Mrs Patel didn't do anything but she did get upset. She tried to shout but she couldn't because she wasn't used to shouting. The next day the children started to behave better because Mrs Patel had got used to us.'

(Year three pupil, in interview)

Becoming a 'better' teacher?: A mother-teacher's story

'When I had Becci it all changed. I'd always loved my children, the kids in the class I mean, but when I went back after the maternity leave, I was fierce. Like a mother tiger! There's that thing about mother-teachers having only half an eye on the job because their primary commitment is to their family. Well, of course it is but that doesn't mean you slack up at school. With me it was the opposite because now I wanted the best for all the kids because I wanted Becci's teachers to give her the best when she went to school. It was almost a superstitious thing really, a sort of silly insurance policy. I work so much harder on planning and preparation and actual teaching in the classroom. I'm totally bushed when I get home at night. I'd say that my 'performance' has got better and better – and it's not just because I'm more experienced, it's because of Becci. I'm not saying it will last, mind you, but that's how it is now.'

(Hannah, primary school teacher, in interview)

Special needs, a special case?: A SENCO's story

'As a SENCO [Special Needs Coordinator] I worry about performance management and performance-related pay and all that stuff. I know that they've made all sorts of noises about acknowledging the sort of work that we do, and so on and so forth but, on one level, that almost makes the whole thing meaningless. It's certainly patronising in my view. Because we can work and work and work with a kid and at the end of the period of time, whatever it is, a lesson, a week, a month, a term, a year, years, whatever, there's no discernable change. 'Performance management' is an insulting term. I'm not keen on behavioural objectives, even though I know that they can lead to results for some kids, but so much of teaching is about relationships and there's something almost pathological about managing relationships; I think there is anyway. And what sort of things can you measure? By and large things which don't matter – and I think that is particularly true with some of the kids that people I know work with.'

(SENCO, special school, in interview)

'11:55 *(and we haven't even started work): a pupil's story*

'We all ambled in from play. Fast-moving games outside had set our spirits alive but now all that happiness had gone for it was time for another literacy hour with Mr Legge. The very thought of such things could suck your very soul out of you and into a muddy puddle.

Our teacher was not cruel (if anything, he was a nice man). He just didn't have the power to get a class's concentration and keep it for more than a few minutes at a time. He couldn't interest or amaze you like a good book can. In fact, he was plain boring.

Eventually the noises of an excited class subsided with the entrance of a visitor. Usually the aim of certain members of the class was to talk and mess around in the cloakroom to try and waste time. Today we knew to behave when the visitor was in the room for he was an OfSTED Inspector.

Sadly, even with the Inspector we couldn't expect much change with the quality of the next hour. Most teachers would try their utmost hardest to ensure a good lesson with an Inspector. Not Mr Legge. So far, nothing had changed this week. If anything, yesterday's history lesson had been the worst this year!

We all took our seats and the lesson began. Our text was Chapter 17 of the *December Rose* (the class reader). Everyone hated the book except me. I had become deaf to the lack of expression and let myself be thrown in to a world of imagination containing murder and foreign gentlemen. My imaginary world was stronger than the rest of the class's put together.

Chapter 17 was the longest in the book and it was the whole 20 odd pages we were reading, not just part of it. Our teacher stopped now and then to get us to read. I read a lot more than anyone else did.

It got worse and worse. A fake cough saved the Inspector from falling to sleep and we still hadn't started work. My friend nudged me and pointed to the clock. 11:55 it read. Little did I know that I soon would not be sitting next to my friend for in his attempt to get our attention our teacher moved our places and put us girl, boy. Boys on the right, girls on the left.

11:57. The text was finished and writing books were handed out. Just then the dinner bell rang and we went to dinner, not having done a spot of work. Bored but relieved.'

(Year five pupil, written account)

Losing the spark: Sam's story

'Sam had always known that he wasn't the most inspiring of teachers but he did his best and by and large, he enjoyed his job and most of his kids seemed to like him. Then he got the virus. They'd thought at first that it was cancer, cancer of the liver. At least he hadn't died and he could remember the relief in Sarah's eyes when the consultant told them both that he'd get over it. He had, 'got over it'. But it changed him. When he went back to work, after six months off, it was different. Sure, at first he got tired easily, but that got better and within a month he was back to football coaching – and enjoying it. The classroom was a different matter. Different classes, different sets of kids. This happened. It was normal. But it wasn't that. He had lost something. He'd lost his spark, his interest, his motivation. He couldn't get excited in the same way and some days seemed to drag by. He felt that he was going through the motions. When the information about the threshold came out he thought long and hard about whether to apply. Could he justifiably do so? Wasn't he one of those boring, useless teachers the government was always on about? And yet his exam results continued to be OK. So why not? He ought to take what he was entitled to. But performance management? That was a laugh! He'd do what he was told. Of course he would. But he couldn't see that the gaping hole that used to be his love for the job could ever be filled now.'

(From an account told to me by one of Sam's colleagues)

A distinctive approach to performance management: a diocesan advisor's story

'It's important that we remember that, in schools, no-one is more important than anyone else. That should be generally true but it's not. There's so much injustice around, at all levels. At the diocesan level you perhaps get a better overview because we cross different LEAs [Local Education Authorities] and you can see how heads get paid differently – there can be thousands of pounds in it, depending on the LEA or on how well individuals can twist arms. I went to a head's retirement last night and worked out that, if she'd been in the same size school in the neighbouring authority she'd be retiring £100,000 better off – £100,000! And I want to ensure that there is justice all through. We've called our model policy [for performance management] "A Model Policy for the Affirmation, Celebration and Management of Performance" because we believe that performance management must be rooted within our distinctive vision of Christian education. Everything we do has to be rooted within our distinctive nature otherwise why should we exist? We endeavour to ensure that all our work, all our policies are explicitly Christian. In our behaviour policies, for example, we work towards reconciliation. I believe that education is about helping people to become more fully human and under that there are obvious implications for performance management.

We're not just talking about standards of performance, things that can be measured. You don't fatten the pig by weighing it. So we've taken the DfEE documents and done nothing illegal with them. All the bits that have to be there by law are there but we believe that raising standards has to be within the distinctive nature of Christian education and in that the individual has to be accounted for as a crucial part of the whole. The whole can't be healthy if the bits aren't. Think about how you feel when you've got toothache, and that's what I mean. And you have to think about the teacher and their life and what's going on in it and celebrate their essential humanity.'

(Diocesan education adviser, in interview)

An alternative – and affirming – approach to performance management

What follows is not a story in the same way as the previous ones are, being extracts from a model policy suggested for Roman Catholic and Church of England schools in a number of northern dioceses. It can, nevertheless, be considered as a narrative in its own right and as a narrative framework for shaping the stories of the individuals who will be working in the schools which adopt it (N.B. Sections in bold are those suggested by the DfEE):

'Our vision of Christian education calls our school to be a Christ-centered community. We believe that God is incarnate in the 'day to day' life of our school. Our understanding of Christian spirituality is therefore as much about dealing with each other as it is about meeting God.

We believe that each member of our community has a divine origin and an eternal destiny.

We believe that through his Incarnation Jesus affirmed us as whole people and redeemed us through his resurrection.

We believe therefore that the intrinsic dignity of each member of our school community is to be honoured in spirit, in word, in deed and in law . . .

From our Christian perspective, committed to the ongoing search for excellence, we seek to consolidate and improve school performance by developing the effectiveness of teachers, both as individuals and as teams. We recognise that this requires our teachers to maintain a healthy balance between work and home life and appreciate that over-work can be destructive to self and to school. **The evidence** from Ofsted and other sources **is that standards rise when schools and individual teachers** have an agreed, shared vision and **are clear about what they expect pupils to achieve. This is why** we believe affirmation and **performance management is** (are) **important** . . . **Performance management** will be **an ongoing cycle, not an event, involving three stages of planning, monitoring performance and reviewing performance. The end of year review and Stage 1 may happen at the same time.** However, we believe this to be a very narrow view. Therefore challenge, evaluation, consolidation, celebration and prayerful reflection will be important characteristics to our approach in this school and will be an accepted part of the process.'

(Diocese of Sheffield, 2000)

Intersecting stories

As time passes, stories about the introduction of the performance manage-ment system are likely to proliferate and get longer and increasingly intri-cate as there is more and more to tell. There will be numerous stories, whose plots and storylines will differ depending upon the perspective and position of the narrator. As I write, the official DfEE 'plot' concerns an innovation which will raise standards (of teaching and pupil achieve-ment) whilst benefiting teachers in terms of their career development and job satisfaction. The underlying question of this chapter is: how will the official story articulate with the individual stories of the teachers, governors, pupils, parents and others who are caught up in the narrative. The stories I have recounted give some indication of the complexity of the matter: a complexity which arises from the nature of teaching and learning as interactive and thereby narrative, relationship-based, subjec-tively experienced and perceived activities.

Finally

The central themes of this chapter are that:

- teachers are people who happen to be teachers: individuals whose perceptions and experiences are influenced by who and what they are, rather than a homogeneous group;
- what happens in one area of life has implications for other areas: it is not possible to compartmentalise lives into the professional and private;
- teaching is based on relationships – with pupils, colleagues, parents, governors etc; and
- within schools, teachers are differently positioned because of who and what they are, the area they specialise in, their geographical location, and so on. Blanket systems do not serve all equally.

The performance management system being introduced into English and Welsh schools is, basically, technicist, managerialist and mechanistic. The discourses and approaches associated with it are, essentially, antithetical to the essence of life as lived insofar as they neglect the various and complex nature of humanity. Those concerned with social justice have long pointed out the ways in which mechanistic and technicist approaches to management tend to privilege hierarchical, hegemonic values to the detriment of those who are not male, white, middle-class, able-bodied heterosexuals. Readers are likely to be well aware of the vast and ever-growing body of literature relating to educational policy, management and equality issues and of the need to consider the teacher as a person whose social positioning and life outside of work has implications for their professional performance. Indeed, this very volume makes a contribution to this canon.

The key message coming out of all of this work would seem to be that, in order to understand, and thereby develop, teaching performance, we need '"thick" descriptions of teaching where the values, cultural significance and meaning of teaching experiences are paramount' (Smyth, 1991 p.10). Following on from this we need 'thick' approaches to performance management which are people-friendly, which acknowledge that (a) teachers have lives, and (b) teaching is relationship-based. Such approaches would, it seems, be far more likely to have a positive effect than those which apparently deny the humanity of teachers in regarding them as operatives with production targets/objectives to meet.

The model policy quoted in this chapter does appear to have gone a considerable way towards accommodating the human element whilst staying within the requirements of the legislation. Of course, the Christian emphasis is inappropriate in any other than a Christian school context, but relatively little rewording could make this an approach which anyone with a concern for social justice and a commitment to developing and improving schools and schooling, teachers and teaching, could be happy with. To repeat what the diocesan advisor quoted earlier said, 'you don't fatten the pig by weighing it', and nor can you develop teachers by regarding them as one-dimensional automatons.

Acknowledgements

I would like to thank Robyn and Joby Sikes-Sheard, Frank McDermott, Peter Clough, Malcolm Robinson, Alan Parkinson and OLW for their help in writing this paper.

References

Acker, S. (1997), 'Primary School Teachers' Work: The Response to Educational Reform', in G. Helsby and G. McCulloch (eds), *Teachers and the National Curriculum*, London: Cassell, pp.34–51.

Ball, S. (1994), *Education Reform: A Critical and Post-Structural Approach*, Buckingham: Open University.

Barber, M. (2000), 'Washington Speech', reported in *Times Educational Supplement*, 7 July 2000.

Blunkett, D. (2000), 'Influence or Irrelevance: Can Social Science Improve Government?', speech at an ESRC meeting, 2 February 2000, reported in *Research Intelligence*, No. 71, pp.12–21.

Brooks, V. and Sikes, P. (1997), *The Good Mentor Guide*, Buckingham: Open University.

Bruner, J. (1986), *Actual Minds, Possible Worlds*, Cambridge MA: Harvard University Press.

Bullough, R. (1998), 'Musings on Life Writings: Biography and Case Study in Teacher Education', in C. Kridel (ed.), *Writing Educational Biography*, New York: Garland, pp.19–32.

Clough, P. (1992), *The End(s) of Ethnography*, London: Sage.

Clough, P. (1999), 'Crises of Schooling and the "Crisis of Representation": The Story of Rob', in *Qualitative Inquiry*, Vol. 5, 3, pp. 428–44.

Dale, R. (1989), *The State and Education Policy*, Buckingham: Open University.

Denzin, N. and Lincoln, N. (1994), 'Introduction: Entering the Field of Qualitative Research', in N. Denzin and Y. Lincoln (eds), *Handbook of Qualitative Research*, London: Sage, pp.1–17.

DfEE (2000), *Performance Management: Guidance for Governors*, London: DfEE.

Fullan, M. (1993), *Change Forces: Probing the Depths of Educational Reform*, London: Falmer Press.

Gewirtz, S. (1997), 'Post-Welfarism and the Reconstruction of Teachers' Work in the UK', in *Journal of Education Policy*, Vol. 12, 4, pp.217–31.

Goodson, I. (1981), 'Life History and the Study of Schooling', in *Interchange*, Vol. 11, 4, pp.62–76.

Goodson, I. and Sikes, P. (2001), *Developing Life Histories*, Buckingham: Open University.

Hargreaves, D. (1996), 'Teaching as a Research-Based Profession: Possibilities and Prospects', Teacher Training Agency Annual Lecture, London: TTA.

Hatcher, R. (1994), 'Market Relationships and the Management of Teachers', in *British Journal of Sociology of Education*, Vol. 15, 1, pp.41–61.

Helsby, G. (1999), *Changing Teachers' Work*, Buckingham: Open University.

Marcus, G. (1994), 'What Comes (Just) After "Post"? The Case of Ethnography', in N. Denzin and Y. Lincoln (eds), *Handbook of Qualitative Research*, London: Sage, pp.563–74.

McDermott, F. and Robinson, M. (2000), *A Model Policy for the Affirmation, Celebration and Management of Performance*, Sheffield: Diocese of Hallam and Diocese of Sheffield.

Measor, L. and Sikes, P. (1992), *Gender and Schools*, London: Cassell.

Nias, J. (1989), *Primary Teachers Talking: A Study of Teaching as Work*, London: Routledge.

Polkinghorne, D. (1988), *Narrative Knowing and the Human Sciences*, Albany: State University of New York Press.

Rapport, N. (1999), 'Life With a Hole, Howl, Hill, Hull in it: Philip Larkin at Life's Crossroads', *Auto/Biography*, Vol. 7, Nos 1 and 2, pp.3–12.

Robertson, S. (1996), 'Teachers' Work, Restructuring and Post-Fordism: Constructing the New "Professionalism"', in I. Goodson and A. Hargreaves (eds), *Teachers' Professional Lives*, London: Falmer Press, pp.28–55.

Rosie, A. (1993), '"He's A Liar, I'm Afraid": Truth and Lies in a Narrative Account', in *Sociology: Special Edition Auto/Biography in Sociology*, Vol. 27, 1, pp.144–52.

Sheffield Hallam Pastoral Centre (2000), 'Model Policy for Roman Catholic Schools in the Diocese of Hallam and Church of England Schools in the Diocese of Sheffield', Sheffield: Diocese of Sheffield.

Sikes, P. (1986), 'The Mid-Career Teacher: Adaptation and Motivation in a Contracting Secondary School System', University of Leeds: Unpublished PhD.

Sikes, P. (1990), 'Teacher in TVEI', in R. Dale, P. Sikes, *et al. The TVEI Story: Policy, Practice and Preparation for the Workforce*, Buckingham: Open University, pp.82–98.

Sikes, P. (1992), 'Imposed Change and the Experienced Teacher' in M. Fullan and A. Hargreaves (eds), *Teacher Development and Educational Change*, London: Falmer Press, pp.36–55.

Sikes, P. (1997), *Parents Who Teach: Stories From Home and From School*, London: Cassell.

Sikes, P. (2000), 'Truth and "Lies" Revisited', in *British Educational Research Journal*, Vol. 26, No. 2, pp.257–70.

Smyth, J. (1991), *Teachers As Collaborative Learners*, Buckingham: Open University.

Thomas, D. (1993), 'Treasonable or Trustworthy text: Reflections on Teacher Narrative Studies', in *Journal of Education for Teaching*, Vol. 19, 3, pp.214–21.

Tierney, W. (1998), 'Life History's History: Subjects Foretold', in *Qualitative Inquiry*, Vol. 4, 1, pp.49–70.

7 Developing teachers in a performance culture

Is performance-related pay the answer?

Linda Evans

Introduction

There was once a teacher, working in an English primary school in the early 1980s, who worked out a way of increasing her salary by £1,000. If she were to become a graduate – more specifically, a 'good honours' graduate – she would immediately advance through five points on the salary scale. So she undertook a part-time B.Ed degree course and became both a good honours graduate and £1,000 per annum better off.

Does this brief tale illustrate that teacher development may be achieved by financial incentive? Answering this would, of course, require much more information than has been provided; such as whether or not the teacher in question did actually develop after undertaking a degree course – which would require a clear idea of what is meant by teacher development; whether any development manifested by the teacher may be attributable to the influence of the degree course; and just how potent and enduring an incentive was the £1,000 anticipated salary rise. Such questions and issues are addressed in this chapter.

The underlying issue – of whether or not teacher development may be achieved by means of financial incentive – is pertinent because in the UK the teaching profession is poised, at the beginning of the twenty-first century, on the brink of change. In the 1998 Green Paper (DfEE, 1998) the government presented its new vision of the teaching profession, reflecting its concern to raise standards in education. The bywords are 'modernisation of the profession', 'a new professionalism' and 'a first-class profession'. There is reference to 'performance management', 'a career of learning', and to rewarding 'excellent teaching'. Clearly, this government wants to get the best out of its teachers.

One of the key mechanisms aimed at bringing about the realisation of this 'new vision of the teaching profession' is the performance-related pay initiative, applicable to headteachers and classroom teachers, and announced in the Green Paper:

> We propose two pay ranges for classroom teachers, with a performance threshold giving access to a new, higher range for high performing teachers with a track record of consistently strong performance.
>
> We therefore propose a pay system with the following objectives:
> • It should attract, retain and motivate all staff . . .
>
> (DfEE, 1998, paras 65 and 71)

But how likely is it that a policy of performance-related pay will help to modernise the profession and get the best out of teachers? Does it have the potential to motivate towards better performance and make a significant contribution to teacher development? The government clearly thinks so, despite opposition from some teachers' unions on the grounds that performance-related pay is divisive (Woodward, 2000). In the furore following the high court's ruling in 2000 that the performance-related pay initiative's assessment procedure was illegal, the Secretary of State for Education, David Blunkett, is reported to have commented: 'I'm not embarrassed about the performance-related promotion, the prospects for paying good teachers well, giving them entirely new scales which they can aspire to as good teachers' (Woodward, 2000). Certainly, judging from the profession's response to the initiative when it was introduced in 2000 – (more than 197,000 teachers applied for the £2,000 pay rise that would, dependent on evaluations of the quality of their practice, take them over the standard pay threshold) – Mr Blunkett had every reason to be optimistic. But this high take-up rate is no guarantee that 'a first-class profession' will follow.

The performance-related pay policy is an integral part of the performance culture that the UK government has introduced as a key item on its agenda for raising standards in education. Clearly, then, it must be considered to be an important teacher development tool. But this consideration is very likely to be based on the premise that giving people monetary rewards for high performance will ensure that high performance is perpetuated and sustained. In reality, the issue is not as simple and straightforward as that.

The motivational potential of pay: the story so far

Outside the academic community there has in the past been an apparently commonly-held assumption that motivation is pay-related. In relation to teachers in the UK, for example, the media and the teachers' unions have promulgated the notion that pay is an important determinant of three aspects of motivation: recruitment, retention and improvement. In response to the report of the interim advisory committee on teachers' pay and conditions, it was suggested in the *Times Educational Supplement* (TES) that, in relation first to recruitment and, second, to improvement, pay could be a key motivator:

'If our teaching force is to be recruited from among the brightest and best of our graduates, the money must come first. Then there is every chance that quality will follow. But the graduate in question needs to be attracted by a competitive starting salary, and confident of a career progression that will reward ability and application.'

(TES, 1991 p.23)

Pay is also assumed to be an effective motivator in relation to improving job performance. Indeed, it is this assumption that underlies the practice of performance-related pay, or merit pay. This is predicated on acceptance of the expectancy theory of motivation and productivity, which posits that individuals are more likely to put effort into their work if there is an anticipated reward that they value. Supporters of this view contend that the ultimate goal, improved quality, can only be achieved at a price:

. . . this government will one day have to pay its teaching force sufficiently highly to achieve the quality of education to which it has so far merely paid lip service.

(Andain, 1990)

And:

Teachers work hard and standards are improving in some aspects of school work. But they are not good enough, nor are they improving fast enough, because teachers are not being paid for high quality performance.

(Tomlinson, 1990)

Similarly, pay is often perceived as a retention factor. For example, the allowances paid to schools in designated social priority areas in the UK, in accordance with the recommendations of the Plowden Committee, and published in the Plowden Report of 1967 (CACE, 1967), were intended to retain staff in these schools. The idea that paying employees enough money will ensure that they do not leave the job stems, in part, from the equity theory of motivation and productivity (see Mowday,

1996 pp.53–71). This theory holds that individuals are satisfied if they feel justly compensated for their efforts and accomplishments.

In relation to performance-related pay specifically, research has revealed the practice generally to be flawed. Johnson (1986) highlights the failure of a number of merit pay schemes introduced in the United States during the twentieth century and points out that some were even found to demotivate. Chandler's (1959) research in the United States compared morale levels in schools where merit pay policies were operational and schools where they were not. His findings revealed no significant difference in morale levels. Mathis' (1959) research findings corroborate Chandler's. Mayston (1992), moreover, concludes that performance-related pay is an over-simplistic approach to tackling problems of teacher motivation, that its potential for success is questionable, and that it may even demotivate. The story so far is that the evidence available does not present a particularly promising picture of the potential of performance-related pay to transform the teaching profession.

The notion that people will work harder, and to higher standards, in return for financial reward is based on common-sense reasoning. Ask anyone in the street how to raise morale amongst teachers, or how to motivate them better, and almost certainly he or she will suggest paying them more. Yet, research – quite apart from that referred to above, which examined performance-related pay – has demonstrated that motivation, morale and job satisfaction are not dependent upon pay (Chapman, 1983; Sergiovanni, 1968).

My own research into factors influencing morale, job satisfaction and motivation amongst teachers, carried out between 1988 and 1993 (see Evans 1998, pp.46–56, for full details of the research design), revealed conditions of service, within which category I include salary, to have only limited influence on teachers' attitudes to their work. The comment of one of my teacher interviewees reflects, in general, the attitudes of most of my sample:

> 'I haven't looked at my pay slip for the last 12 months . . . and I don't know why – it's not a driving force any more. At one stage I used to long for pay day and look carefully at how much I'd got . . . but it doesn't bother me any more.'
>
> (Teacher interviewee, 1989)

One of the key studies to reveal that motivation and job satisfaction are not pay-related is that of Herzberg (1968), whose research into the job satisfaction of engineers and accountants in Pittsburgh led to his formulating the motivation–hygiene, or two-factor, theory. Herzberg's research findings revealed two distinct sets of factors; one set which motivates, or satisfies, employees, and one set which may demotivate or create dissatisfaction. He labels these motivation and hygiene factors respectively. Pay is listed as a hygiene factor.

The essential point of Herzberg's theory is that hygiene factors are not capable of motivating or satisfying people, even though they may be sources of dissatisfaction. Removing hygiene factors that are creating dissatisfaction does not – indeed, cannot – create job satisfaction. So, for example, if employees are dissatisfied with their salary, giving them a pay rise will not motivate or satisfy them; it will merely remove their dissatisfaction. Herzberg, in fact, likens a pay rise to 'a shot in the arm', which may offer a temporary boost, but whose effects are short-lived.

Yet, although research findings dismiss pay as a motivator, experiential evidence might appear to present a different picture. We all know that an attractive salary often encourages job applications, and that promotion is often sought because it brings remuneration. The fact that nearly 200,000 teachers in England and Wales applied for performance-related pay when it was introduced in 2000 indicates that pay does have some motivational potential. Consider, too, the case of the primary school teacher, presented at the beginning of the chapter, who embarked on a degree course in order to earn more money. Clearly, people may be motivated by money. That being the case, is it reasonable to expect a performance-related pay policy to make some contribution towards developing the teaching profession? In order to address this question it is important, first, to examine what is meant by 'teacher development'.

Understanding teacher development

If we want to know how to get the best out of teachers we need to understand teacher development. Essentially, we need to understand the teacher development process; what must happen in order for teachers to develop. Yet, this process is far from clear, as Russell and Munby point out:

> Ask any teacher or professor, 'How did you learn to teach?' As likely as not, the response will be 'by teaching' or 'by experience', and little more will follow, as though the answer were obvious and unproblematic. While there is an implicit acknowledgement that actions and performances can be learned through or by experience, there is little understanding of how this comes about.
>
> (Russell and Munby, 1991 p.164)

One of the main reasons why the teacher development process is unclear is probably that so much of it involves teachers' learning, and the process whereby people learn is by no means clear. Another reason is, I suggest, is that teacher development research and literature have neglected consideration of conceptual issues. As a result, the concept of teacher development is unclear; very few definitions of it are available and many key writers in the field do not even make explicit their interpretations of it. Yet, this neglect has impacted upon identification of what the teacher development process involves because it is difficult to identify the process of something that is not clearly conceptualised. As Freidson writes, in relation to professionalisation:

> We cannot develop theory if we are not certain what we are talking about . . . To speak about the process of professionalisation requires one to define the direction of the process, and the end-state of professionalism toward which an occupation may be moving. Without *some* definition of profession the concept of professionalisation is virtually meaningless, as is the intention to study process rather than structure. One cannot study process without a definition guiding one's focus any more fruitfully than one can study structure without a definition.
>
> (Freidson, 1994 p.15)

Even if this could be achieved, without clear conceptualisation dissemination of the process would be susceptible to unreliability arising out of misunderstanding and misinterpretation, because construct validity would be threatened. Definitional precision is integral to meaningful dissemination. It is also an important part of identifying processes.

What do we mean by 'teacher development'?

My response to the conceptual imprecision prevalent in the field of teacher development has been to formulate my own interpretation and definition of the concept, which is explained in greater detail elsewhere (Evans, 2000), and which I apply to the examination of issues in this chapter. In defining teacher development I have been influenced by Hoyle's (1975) identification of two distinct aspects of teachers' professional lives: professionalism and professionality. Hoyle does not define these two terms, but he explains his distinction as being between status-related elements of teachers' work, which he categorises as professionalism, and those elements of the job that constitute the knowledge, skills and procedures that teachers use in their work, and which he categorises as professionality.

Professionality is neither a widely-known, nor a widely-used term and, after extensive consideration and analysis, I have defined it as: an ideologically-, attitudinally-, intellectually-, and epistemologically-based stance on the part of an individual, in relation to the practice of the profession to which he or she belongs, and which influences his or her professional practice.

My interpretation of teacher development reflects my view that it may enhance the status of the profession as a whole, exemplified by the evolution of an all-graduate profession, and it may improve teachers' knowledge, skills, and practice. This interpretation is outlined below. Since it is my own interpretation, rather than a consensually accepted one, my description and explanation of it necessitate much use of the words 'I' and 'my'. This should not be misconstrued as a reflection of egocentricity, rather it is intended to reflect the subjectivity – and, hence, speculative status – of the interpretation.

I define teacher development as the process whereby teachers' professionality and/or professionalism may be considered to be enhanced. My interpretation of teacher development incorporates consideration of its having a range of applicability that extends from an individual to a profession-wide level. It may be applied to variously formed professional groups or units, such as: the staff of an institution, or a department in an institution; teachers who hold a common role (e.g. primary headteachers, mathematics teachers, further education teachers); and the profession as a whole.

Within my definition, I currently identify two constituent elements of teacher development that relate fundamentally to individual teacher development: attitudinal development and functional development. Each element reflects specific foci of change. I define attitudinal development as: the process whereby teachers' attitudes to their work are modified. I currently perceive attitudinal development as incorporating three constituent change features, or foci of change: intellectual, ideological and motivational. These respectively refer to teachers' development in relation to their intellect, their ideologies and their motivation.

I define functional development as: the process whereby teachers' professional performance may be improved. I currently perceive functional development as incorporating three constituent change features or focuses of change: procedural, purposive and productive. These respectively refer to teachers' development in relation to the procedures that they utilise, the purpose(s) underpinning their work, and what and/or how much they produce or do at work.

These change foci are not mutually exclusive. It is quite feasible – in some cases, quite likely – that teachers may, at any one time, develop in relation to more than one of them. Indeed, some (such as intellectual and ideological) are so interrelated that it would be difficult for teachers to develop in relation to one and not the other. It is also worth emphasising, as I point out above, that the two constituent elements of teacher development that I identify lie within my definition of teacher development. This means that they, and the foci of change that relate to each of them – if they are to constitute teacher development – must effect what may be considered to be the enhancement of teachers' professionalism and/or professionality. Change that may be considered detrimental to teachers' professionalism and/or professionality would not therefore constitute teacher development. So the teacher who becomes demotivated, for example, or whose output falls, would be manifesting motivational and productive change, but not development. Of course, not all cases would be as clear-cut as these two examples. My inclusion within my definition of teacher development of the words 'may be considered to be' is deliberate, to incorporate consideration of subjectivity in relation to views about what actually constitutes development. What the government, for example, may consider to be teacher development may be quite different from teachers' own views, which may also conflict with parents' or school governors' views.

I also identify two dimensions, or forms, of teacher development which represent a combination of range of applicability, to which I refer above, and either, or both, of the constituent elements. These are: role development and cultural development. Once again, within my over-arching definition of teacher development, I define each of these. Role development is: the process whereby the accepted parameters, remits and responsibilities of specific recognised specialist professional roles may be redefined and/or modified. And I define cultural development as: the process whereby teachers' professional culture is redefined and/or modified.

Applying this precise and involved interpretation of teacher development, the potential of performance-related pay to develop the teaching profession is not straightforward to calculate, estimate or even conjecture. The reason for this is that it sheds little light on *how* teachers develop. Yet, whilst the teacher development process remains unclear, understanding teachers' attitudes to their work – in particular, what affects teacher morale, job satisfaction and motivation – does offer valuable clues about which elements and dimensions of teacher development (as I identify them) are likely to be affected by performance-related pay.

Understanding teachers' job-related attitudes

There is no shortage of anecdotal evidence that pay is an important factor in the retention of teachers. Blackbourne, for example, reported on a huge turnout of teachers at an alternative jobs fair:

> And who can blame them? A spokesman for the Bacteriostatic Water Systems stall said two of the company's top earners were ex-teachers with salaries per month – not per year – of more than £25,000.
>
> (Blackbourne, 1990)

However, such evidence tends to identify pay as a demotivator, rather than a motivator. It is important to recognise that the factors that demotivate may not necessarily be those that motivate; indeed, Herzberg's (1968) two-factor theory makes a clear distinction between the two. But, if, despite experiential evidence to the contrary, pay is *not* an effective motivator – as research evidence suggests – why is it not? And what factors do motivate teachers, give them job satisfaction and raise their morale?

It is necessary to answer the second question before being able to tackle the first. Evidence of what motivates teachers is, for the most part, confined to more general studies of employee motivation or, reflecting the neglect in recent years of a conceptual rigour which might distinguish between morale, motivation and job satisfaction (an issue that I discuss in detail elsewhere; Evans, 1997; 1998 pp.6–12) to studies of teachers' overall attitudes to their work. Research evidence tends broadly to corroborate Herzberg's (1968) findings that the five specific motivation factors – those capable of providing job satisfaction – are achievement, recognition (for achievement), advancement, responsibility and the work itself. In his classic study of American teachers' working lives, Lortie (1975) categorises factors such as these as psychic rewards and, as a category, psychic rewards were identified by his sample as the greatest source of job satisfaction. In particular, the reward of feeling that they had 'reached' students, and that students had learned, was identified as a source of satisfaction by the greatest number of Lortie's teachers.

Chapman's (1983) study, which focused on 437 college graduates who had entered the teaching profession and were still teaching, revealed recognition and approval to be key motivational factors. Chapman and Hutcheson (1982) found a distinction, in relation to the kinds of factors that motivated them, between teachers and ex-teachers. Those who had left teaching were more extrinsically motivated than those remaining in it. Similarly, of Kasten's (1984 p.4) sample of 138 American elementary classroom teachers, the 64 per cent whose responses to a questionnaire item indicated that they would choose teaching as a career again 'overwhelmingly focused on the delights and satisfactions of working with children. Other reasons given were the importance of the job, personal rewards, variety in the work, and a feeling of competence'.

Intrinsic rewards were identified as important retainers in a qualitative study of the motivation of American secondary school teachers:

> The most powerful motivational forces which attract, maintain, and keep successful teachers in the classroom are a complex of intrinsic rewards which come together in the ideal occupational combination of working with students, seeing students learn and succeed, believing one's job in service to others is valuable, and being able to grow personally and professionally.
>
> (Bredeson, Fruth and Kasten, 1983 p.57)

McLaughlin *et al.*'s study of teachers' incentives, rewards and working environments revealed similar motivators:

> We found . . . that the dominant motivation and source of reward for teachers lies in promoting students' growth and development. The thing that makes teaching meaningful and worthwhile is watching students learn and 'working with wonder'. 'If it weren't for the natural responsiveness of children', one teacher said, 'I would have walked away a long time ago, sold stockings at Macey's, and made the same amount of money'.
>
> (McLaughlin *et al.*, 1986 pp.420–1)

Farrugia (1986), Galloway *et al.* (1985) and Nias (1981; 1989) all make explicit reference to a broad consistency between their research findings and Herzberg's two-factor theory. More specifically, Nias (1989) identifies affective and competence-related rewards, both of which she relates to working with children. Furthermore, the importance as motivators of leadership and collegial support, which has been emphasised in several studies (see, for example, ILEA, 1986; Johnson, 1986; Nias, 1980; Nias, Southworth and Yeomans, 1989) is also evidence of the applicability to education contexts of Herzberg's theory, since it is partly the recognition and approbation of leaders and colleagues that motivates teachers.

My own research findings have led me to develop a model of the process whereby individuals experience job fulfilment (Evans, 1998 pp.13–18) and my analyses have led me to identify one fundamental source of job fulfilment: achievement. I have challenged Herzberg's (1968) identification of five factors, arguing that they may all be cancelled down to achievement;

the other four motivation factors being contributors to or/and reinforcers of a sense of achievement. Recognition, for example, is not, in itself a source of job fulfilment; it merely serves to reinforce the individual's sense of achievement and it is this sense of achievement that people find satisfying. What motivates people, therefore, is the opportunity to experience a sense of achievement. Precisely what gives teachers a sense of achievement – and hence motivates them – varies, though, from individual to individual, since teachers are not a homogeneous group. Some will derive a sense of achievement just from teaching a class and feeling that they are making a difference to children's lives, others will not find this as fulfilling as participation in decision- or policy-making, and others will want to lead and manage other adults in order to feel a sense of achievement.

Motivation, as I define it (Evans, 1998 p.34) is concerned with the degree of inclination towards an activity, but that degree of inclination is determined by the pursuit of goals which will satisfy needs. What motivates, therefore, in a work context, is the desire for job satisfaction; individuals are motivated to participate in activities that appear to them to be oriented towards job satisfaction. Morale levels are determined by expectancy of continued job satisfaction, and high morale, resulting from high expectations, motivates individuals towards goal-focused activity which is expected to sustain, and increase, job satisfaction, which, in turn, raises morale.

Yet, whilst I argue that recognition is not a fundamental source of job fulfilment, I do consider it to be a motivator; indeed, my research (Evans, 1999) has revealed it to be a very potent motivator. Although attaining job fulfilment is a subjective process that is determined by the perceptions, views and values of only the individual concerned, it is easy to see how these may be influenced by other people. In particular, recognition of teachers' efforts and achievements has the potential to make a significant contribution at several stages of the job fulfilment process as I describe it (Evans, 1998 pp.13–18). A form of recognition that works extremely well is positive feedback on their work from people whose judgement teachers value and respect; often, respected senior colleagues.

Since performance-related pay is a form of recognition, then, it is reasonable to assume that it is an effective motivator. But this is not the case. Recognition comes in different forms, both explicit and implicit. Pay is one form of recognition, praise is another, recommendation another, and promotion yet another. But, as it stands, none of these has enduring qualities as a motivator, which reduces their effectiveness. The way in which they may be made enduring, and hence more effective, is by constant repetition. In the case of praise, this is possible; in the case of pay, it is not. A school leader or manager may be a persistent – even habitual – 'praiser' who is able to sustain a fairly constant stream of praise directed at his or her colleagues. Provided that the praise were always perceived by the recipient(s) to be genuine and merited, and provided the praiser were respected professionally and considered to have sound judgement, this would very likely motivate effectively. Without such repetition, though, the motivational qualities of recognition are very short-lived. So it is with pay. As a motivator, recognition is not a laurel upon which people are able to rest, and derive lasting fulfilment; it needs constant replenishment. Pay may, therefore, motivate in the sense that it provides the impetus for activity – to apply for a job, to seek promotion, or, as in the case of the teacher presented at the beginning of the chapter, to undertake a course of study that will bring salary enhancements – but, having provided the impetus, its motivational capacity is not sustained. Only if a continual supply were available would pay serve as an effective motivator. Of course, this is why, in one sense, the continual supply of a fairly constant amount of money in the form of a wage or salary motivates people to keep going to work when they may prefer to be doing something else with their time. But this is not sufficient to motivate towards extra effort or better performance since its being available – generally speaking – irrespective of whether extra effort is applied means that it is not perceived as a form of recognition; it is perceived as a right.

Let's return for a moment to consider the primary school teacher whose case I introduced at the beginning of the chapter. Surely – you might think – pay motivated her. But what actually happened was that, having provided the impetus to undertake a degree course, the motivational effect of pay quickly diminished. The teacher became so enthusiastic about and involved in her course that she was motivated by the desire to succeed; she became determined to do her very best to get a good degree. Her aim to increase her salary was eventually replaced by her aim to gain a first class honours degree. So unimportant did financial concerns become that, when her anticipated study leave from her job was threatened at one point, fearing that this would impact upon her examination success, the teacher was quite prepared to resign from her job in order to be able to spend time studying. As a motivator, the desire to feel a sense of achievement had completely eclipsed the desire for more pay.

Will performance-related pay contribute to teacher development?

The UK government's performance-related pay policy is intended to provide the motivation for teachers to participate in school-based performance management which, it is expected, will raise standards both in relation to pupil achievement and teacher development (DfEE, 2000a).

Of the two elements of teacher development that I have identified: functional development and attitudinal development, there is more chance of performance-related pay bringing about the former than the latter – at least, initially. This is because attitudinal development is difficult to achieve, and when it does occur it often does so gradually, over time, and imperceptibly. But functional development – the process whereby teachers' professional performance may be improved – is precisely what the UK government wants to achieve; attitudinal development would probably be considered a very desirable bonus, but not an essential outcome.

There is every chance that the performance-related pay policy in the UK will bring about procedural, purposive and productive change in many teachers and, in doing so, make a contribution to teacher development. The threshold standards required of teachers qualifying for performance-related pay (DfEE, 2000b pp.3–6) all clearly relate to functional development and its three change foci. They relate to it, but they do not equate with it. The reason for this is that, according to my interpretation and definition, only if change occurs that may be considered to constitute an enhancement to teachers' professionality and/or professionalism can teacher development be considered to have taken place. What this means is that, if their meeting the threshold standards does not constitute change for teachers – that is, if they have for some time been teaching in a way that meets the standards – then there is no evidence of development. And for those teachers applying for performance-related pay, their cases do rest upon their having met the standards for some time. In this sense, then – at least initially – the performance-related pay policy does not make any contribution to teacher development. It is simply being used as a reward for what the government considers to be consistently good practice.

Yet, performance-related pay could make a contribution to teacher development by encouraging and enticing teachers who do not yet do so to develop their practice in order to qualify for it, just as the lure of an extra £1,000 salary prompted the primary school teacher to whom I have referred to undertake a degree course. Indeed, it is quite likely that this will occur. But, having lured teachers to higher levels of performance, this pay rise will not sustain their efforts; its effects will be very short-lived. What will sustain teachers' high levels of performance is, depending on the individual teacher, either or both of two things. First, teachers' own self-motivation, and second, challenging, respected leadership that gives high-quality teachers recognition for their efforts. Leadership of this kind was revealed in my own research (Evans, 1998; 1999) to be particularly effective at developing teachers – and, moreover, at bringing about attitudinal development. It was also effective in motivating teachers, developing them intellectually, and changing their ideologies, as my teacher interviewees commented:

> 'Well, at one school, Littlefield, we had a head who was a very good motivator and was very free with his praise . . . and he would come into your room and say, "Oh, it looks lovely in here; oh, you *are* working hard!" . . . It was the praise business . . . *and* he worked hard himself . . . you knew where you stood with him . . . But . . . er . . . he was a good motivator, and I think it was just that one little word of thanks every now and again that did it.'
>
> (Ann)

> 'I don't know what it is about her (the headteacher), but she made you want to do your best – and not just for her, but for yourself . . . You weren't working to please *her*, but she suddenly made you realise what was possible, and you, kind of, raised your game all the time . . . She had a very strong educational vision . . . Now, up until that time – I mean, I'm a much slower learner – I was piecing together my educational philosophy and, a lot of the time, just . . . you know, struggling to get by . . . er . . . and she really just turned me round like nobody else ever has done. . . . She was very, very challenging on a direct level . . . So she, kind of, developed . . . er . . . you know, what you were doing, and asked questions.'
>
> (Helen)

Carried out effectively by senior staff of this calibre, performance management of the kind that the UK government wants to promote in schools (DfEE, 2000a) will make a significant contribution to teacher development. But – let us make no mistake – it will be the effective performance management, not the performance-related pay introduced as an integral component of it, that will make the difference.

Finally, let us return to the case of the primary school teacher whom I introduced at the beginning of the chapter. Having been lured by financial incentive to step out on the teacher development path she continued on and on relentlessly. Achieving a first-class honours degree she went on to gain an MA degree and a doctorate. When she first became a teacher she had been very much what Hoyle (1975) describes as a restricted professional. She was conscientious and hard working, thoroughly enjoyed her work, and had a high level of commitment to it. She was generally considered by colleagues to be an extremely competent practitioner; but, being a 'restricted' professional, she operated mainly at an intuitive level, with very little rationality underpinning her work. She considered educational theory to be entirely irrelevant to classroom practice, attended in-service courses – but only those of a practical nature – and was not in the least bit interested in undertaking long, award-bearing courses, even though she had left college with only a teacher's certificate. The prospect of earning an extra £1,000 changed that.

Fifteen years later she left teaching to become an academic. In her final teaching post her practice had become so innovative that teachers from neighbouring schools came to see her classroom and watch her working. She chose to become an academic so that she could continue, as part of her job, to do what she had enjoyed so much on her degree courses – research. She left teaching because she felt frustrated and constrained by the irrationality which underpinned most of the decision-making in the schools where she worked and because the values and educational ideologies that she held were seldom shared by her colleagues; particularly senior colleagues. She is, of course, the author of this chapter.

Although it is not an enduring motivator, pay may serve to spark off an initial interest in treading a path that leads to professional development on a grand scale. Without the right environment, though, the path could easily trail off to a dead end. The right environment is one that continually encourages and motivates teachers by affording them recognition for their efforts; one that challenges them, but does not overface them with un-realistic demands that create stress; one that provides intelligent, effective leadership. The 'performing school' needs to provide such an environment for teachers if it is to succeed within the performance culture that now shapes education in the twenty-first century. Although they certainly deserve it, paying teachers more will not, in the long term, ensure their continued high performance. That will be secured at an institutional, not national, level by school cultures that provide teachers with opportunities to achieve, and that afford them recognition for their achievement.

References

Andain, I. (1990), 'Protest of the undervalued', in *The Guardian*, 17 April 1990.
Anon (1991), 'Which comes first, money or quality?' in *The Times Educational Supplement*, 8 February 1991, p.23.
Blackbourne, L. (1990), 'All's fair in the hunt for better jobs', in *The Times Educational Supplement*, 11 May 1990, p.A4.

Bredeson, P., Fruth, M. and Kasten, K. (1983), 'Organizational incentives and secondary school teaching', in *Journal of Research and Development in Education*, Vol. 16, No. 4, pp.52–8.

CACE (The Plowden Report) (1967), *Children and their Primary Schools*, Vol. 1, London: HMSO.

Chandler, B. J. (1959), 'Salary policies and teacher morale', in *Educational Administration and Supervision*, Vol. 45, pp.107–10.

Chapman, D. W. (1983), 'Career satisfaction of teachers', in *Educational Research Quarterly*, Vol. 7, No. 3, pp.40–50.

Chapman, D. W. and Hutcheson, S. (1982), 'Attrition from teaching careers: a discriminant analysis', in *American Educational Research Journal*, Vol. 19, No. 1, pp.93–105.

DfEE (1998), *Teachers Meeting the Challenge of Change*, London: DfEE.

DfEE (2000a), *Performance Management in Schools; performance management framework*, London: DfEE.

DfEE (2000b), *Threshold Assessment: guidance on completing the application form*, London: DfEE.

Evans, L. (1997), 'Addressing problems of conceptualisation and construct validity in researching teachers' job satisfaction', in *Educational Research*, Vol. 39, No. 3, pp.319–31.

Evans, L. (1998), *Teacher Morale, Job Satisfaction and Motivation*, London: Paul Chapman.

Evans, L. (1999), *Managing to Motivate: a guide for school leaders*, London: Cassell.

Evans, L. (2000), *Examining Teacher Development*, paper presented at the CEDAR International Conference, University of Warwick, March, 2000.

Farrugia, C. (1986), 'Career-choice and sources of occupational satisfaction and frustration among teachers in Malta', in *Comparative Education*, Vol. 22, No. 3, pp.221–31.

Freidson, E. (1994), *Professionalism Reborn: theory, prophecy and policy*, Cambridge: Polity Press.

Galloway, D., Boswell, K., Panckhurst, F., Boswell, C. and Green, K. (1985), 'Sources of satisfaction and dissatisfaction for New Zealand primary school teachers', in *Educational Research*, Vol. 27, No. 1, pp.44–92.

Herzberg, F. (1968), *Work and the Nature of Man*, London: Staples Press.

Hoyle, E. (1975), 'Professionality, professionalism and control in teaching', in V. Houghton, R. McHugh and C. Morgan (eds), *Management in Education: the management of organisations and individuals*, London: Ward Lock.

ILEA (1986), *The Junior School Project*, London: ILEA Research and Statistics Branch.

Johnson, S. M. (1986), 'Incentives for teachers: what motivates, what matters', in *Educational Administration Quarterly*, Vol. 22, No. 3, pp.54–79.

Kasten, K. L. (1984), 'The efficacy of institutionally dispensed rewards in elementary school teaching', in *Journal of Research and Development in Education*, Vol. 17, No. 4, pp.1–13.

Lortie, D. C. (1975), *Schoolteacher: A Sociological Study*, Chicago: University of Chicago Press.

Mathis, C. (1959), 'The relationship between salary policies and teacher morale', in *Journal of Educational Psychology*, Vol. 50, No. 6, pp. 275–79.

Mayston, D. (1992), *School Performance Indicators and Performance-Related Pay*, London: The Assistant Masters and Mistresses Association.

McLaughlin, M., Pfeifer, R., Swanson-Owens, D. and Yee, S. (1986), 'Why teachers won't teach', in *Phi Delta Kappan*, February, pp.420–26.

Mowday, R. T. (1996), 'Equity Theory Predictions of Behavior in Organizations, in R. M. Steers, L. W. Porter and G. A. Bigley (eds), *Motivation and Leadership at Work*, 6th edition, New York: McGraw-Hill.

Nias, J. (1981), 'Teacher satisfaction and dissatisfaction: Herzberg's "Two-Factor" hypothesis revisited', in *British Journal of Sociology of Education*, Vol. 2, No. 3, pp.235–46.

Nias, J. (1989), *Primary Teachers Talking: A Study of Teaching as Work*, London: Routledge.

Nias, J., Southworth, G., and Yeomans, R. (1989), *Staff Relationships in the Primary School: a study of organisational cultures*, London: Cassell.

Russell, T. and Munby, H. (1991), 'Reframing: the role of experience in developing teachers' professional knowledge', in D. Schön (ed.), *The Reflective Turn*, New York: Teachers College Press.

Sergiovanni, T. J. (1968), 'New evidence on teacher morale: a proposal for staff differentiation', in *North Central Association Quarterly*, No. 42, pp.259–66.

Tomlinson, H. (1990), 'Performance rights?' in *The Times Educational Supplement*, 9 November 1990, p.11.

Woodward, W. (2000), 'Blunkett humiliated in pay row', in *The Guardian*, 15 July 2000, p.2.

8 A culture of teaching 'under new management'[1]

John Smyth

In this chapter I want to start out by invoking what I am calling the category of the 'preferred teacher', but equally I could have chosen the label 'performing teacher', or some other equally ambiguous term. My intention, after that, is to try and render something of the confusion that is coming to characterise the work of teachers worldwide in these increasingly fractured, managerialised and marketised times. The reason I have chosen a category capable of multiple and contested meanings depending upon the vantage point taken, is precisely because it captures so well the shifting terrain around current policy moves designed to weld schools on to fast capitalism (Smyth *et al.*, 2000). Secondly, I want to explore what a rejuvenated view of teaching might look like – one that is embedded in a reconstituted and reinvigorated professionalism that has the culture of teaching and learning at its centre (Hattam *et al.*, 1995), and that draws it sustenance from a wider democratic politics of schooling. Ball speaks about what I have in mind in terms of the 'authentic' teacher, one 'whose practice is based upon the values of "service" and a shared moral language which provides for reflection, dialogue and debate' (Ball, 1999 p.1).

What I have not spelled out, of course, in my notion of the preferred teacher are elusive questions like: preferred by who, for what purpose, under what conditions, and with what set of ultimate aims in mind? Central to any process of preferring is the act of attaching comparative worth or value to some attributes or things, ahead of others. In other words, there is a ranking or holding out of particular entities as worthy of being given priority over others. I can best capture the dominant policy position prevailing at the moment around recent school reforms, in and across a variety of countries, by using a rather long citation from a recent work of mine, where I was pursuing an emerging cameo of the preferred teacher – one that comes from the vantage point of governments bent on attaching schools to the economy:

Within the kind of educational reform context described here teaching is increasingly being constructed as work in which there needs to be maximum opportunity for a flexible response to customer needs and where the teacher is hired and dispensed with as demand and fashion dictates. This ethos of schools as marketplaces also means a differentiated mix of teachers, some of whom are fully qualified, others who are cheaper to employ for short periods of time and who can rapidly be moved around within auxiliary and support roles to help satisfy growing niche markets. Coupled with this is a mindset in which the teacher is required to act as a kind of pedagogical entrepreneur continually having regard to selling the best points of the school, promoting image and impression, and generally seeking to maximise the school's market share by ensuring that it ranks high in competitive league tables. A crucial element of this educational commodity approach to teachers' work is the attention to calculable and measurable aspects of the work, especially educational outputs, for without that kind of information the capacity of the school to successfully promote itself will be severely circumscribed. There will be a need for the teacher to be a team member within the corporate culture of the school always mindful that anything she may do will impact in some way on the schools' outside image. However, team membership which will sometimes be glorified with terms like 'collegiality', 'partnerships' and 'collaboration' will reside very much at the operational and implementation level, for to incorporate strategic decision making, might be to threaten the wider mission of the school. Interactions with students will occur within an overall framework of 'value added' in which students are 'stakeholders', continually deserving of receiving educational value for money. Teaching will be increasingly managerial in nature, both as teachers are managed and themselves manage others – there will be clear line management arrangements with each layer providing appropriate performance indicator information to the level above about the performance of individual students against objectives, and the success of the teacher herself in meeting school targets and performance outcomes. The remuneration of both the teacher and the school will be based on attaining these agreed performance targets.

(Smyth and Shacklock, 1998 pp.122–3)

What this official picture of the preferred teacher does is render invisible the much wider 'hidden injuries of schooling' (Furlong, 1991) that are concealed within a naturalised economic view of teachers' work. The essence of the work of teaching is, therefore, stifled and not 'allowed to breathe', to borrow a phrase from George Marcus (1998), because of the way it is continuously framed within a narrow economic policy paradigm. When teachers themselves try and step out and take a principled professional stand against the increasing incursion of alien agenda into their work, as they did recently in New South Wales where high school teachers resisted the introduction of a testing regime they believed was damaging to students, they are labelled as 'self-interested'. Even sections of the media who appear to be somewhat sympathetic to the teachers' cause, argue that the problem lies in an image of teaching that needs to be fixed up. But, this is to very largely miss the mark.

Symptomatic of this view is the recent claim in the Australian press (but it could equally have been in almost any other country, because it is just as appropriate), that 'teachers need a makeover' (Bantick, 2000 p.18). The implication is that teachers need to fix up the perception held of them by the wider community, notwithstanding that they appear to be 'caught on a cleft stick. They want to be seen as a profession, yet the means of drawing attention to themselves is harmful and alienating' (Bantick, 2000 p.18). The counter view is that 'when teachers take a stand, they are seen as being militant. Yet this is usually at the end of a great deal of frustration' (Bantick, 2000 p.18). But still the individualistic 'victim blaming' argument continues to be put:

> Teachers alone can improve their own image. If they want to be treated seriously, teachers will need to give more thought to how they represent and promote themselves. Teachers are sharply aware that the public perception of them is generally not positive.
>
> (Bantick, 2000 p.18)

The article goes on to point out that in Britain a high profile Oscar-winning film director has been engaged by the British GTC to lift the image of teachers.

What fails to be properly understood in this push towards surface, image and impression management, is that there are some deep and fundamental changes happening in teachers' work, and most of them coalesce around the discursive shift in how the work of teaching is increasingly being managed (Gunter, 1997; Shain and Gleeson, 1999).

Hartley (1999) casts some helpful light here on what is happening. His argument is that what we are experiencing at the moment is a 're-enchantment' with school management, after a couple of decades of being dazzled (but not necessarily informed) by the possibilities of structural reform – market-driven initiatives, consumer sovereignty, the self-managing school, and the like (Troman, 1997). There seems to be wind of a more sobering realisation that what has to change is the 'culture' of what occurs in teaching; in particular, a 'reculturing' of the management relationships between head teachers/principals and teachers. Now, while this shift might not start out from a vantage point that is necessarily to teachers' liking, nor have an agenda of working in teachers' interests, the fact that the terrain has begun to shift back in the direction of classrooms is not altogether a bad sign on the heels of a couple of fairly gloomy decades (see Power *et al.*, 1997; and Whitty *et al.*, 1998 on the role of the school manager, the state and the market). Teachers might (at least at the level of individual schools and their communities), be able to reposition themselves (as many politically astute teachers have already done) back into the debates about the nature of their work and their substantial role in it.

For Hartley (1999), the re-enchantment with school management hinges around two notions of 'marketing' – 'relationship marketing' and 'internal marketing':

> . . . relationship marketing refers to the ways in which schools seek to manage the new key 'player' in the educational market, namely the parent; and internal marketing refers to the ways in which head teachers may come to manage teachers within schools.
>
> (Hartley, 1999 p.311)

The genesis of this apparent re-enchantment of educational management with matters educative and pedagogical lies in the alleged pursuit of the 'search for meaning' which could possibly herald 'the new legitimatory rhetoric in the management of teachers' (Hartley, 1999 p.317). This supposedly softer image of management brings with it, Hartley argues, 'a litany of "soul values" that distinguishes leadership from management' (cited in Bleach, 1998). As Hartley puts it:

> Emotions are to be recognised, not suppressed, in the management of organisations. The worker/teacher may now come to be regarded as an internal customer, a customer who is perhaps 'delighted' by management, and who will in turn 'delight' the pupil.
>
> (Bleach, 1998 p.318)

Teachers at the centre of an 'emergent professionalism'

However, before we can grapple properly with the claim of deprofessionalisation of teaching – for that is what it is (see Bottery, 1997; Bottery and Wright, 1996; 1997; Helsby, 1995; 1999; and Troman, 1996) – my argument is that teachers first need to better understand their work in order to be able to defend that work.

The writings of Nixon, Ranson and colleagues (Nixon and Ranson, 1997; Nixon, Martin, McKeown and Ranson, 1997a; 1997b) are informative here in showing how teachers might recapture some of the lost space, through what is being described as the notion of 'emergent professionalism'.

Over a number of years this group of researchers has worked at articulating what this reworked professionalism might look like; first, by focusing upon examining the construction of educational failure through an analysis of the impact of disadvantage on learning, while looking at institutional responses to failure. Second, they have built up a set of explanations that take account of the wider cultural shifts in power and control. And, third, they highlight the considerable tensions still existing within the 'new' (but still dominant) evolving form of professionalism (Nixon *et al.*, 1997a). Finally, they draw attention to the features of what they term a 'pedagogy of recognition' as a basis for a process of 'community-based regeneration' (Nixon *et al.*, 1997a p.139).

Nixon *et al.* (1997a) put their central argument very succinctly:

> . . . that schools must, as a matter of survival, reach out to the local community in order to establish an alternative power base from which to reclaim their professional legitimacy and authority. This requires both institutional restructuring and professional reorientation – away from school-led change towards community-based action.
>
> (Nixon *et al.*, 1997a p.122)

What is especially interesting about their work is the way they pursue 'constructions of failure' through studying schools located in contexts of extreme disadvantage in the UK, by trying to better understand 'how disadvantage impacts upon learning, and . . . how culture both reinforces and resists that impact' (Nixon *et al.*, 1997a p.123). Pursuing how disadvantage operates to set communities apart, means conceiving of educational failure quite differently – as part of a much wider 'failure of democratic will' in which the '"social rights" of citizenship have, for a significant proportion of the population, never been addressed' (Nixon *et al.*, 1997a p.124). In other words, there has been a persistent, deliberate and prolonged lack of community consultation and participation. It is the case, at least in the UK as described by Nixon *et al.* (1997a), that the consequences of institutional failure have largely been excluded from the analysis of damaged communities, a situation that would not be tolerated by the middle classes.

By focusing on the responses to forms of institutional failure, Nixon *et al.* (1997a) are able to demonstrate how an important precursor to turning around such experience of failure, is to first acknowledge 'the complex, cultural aspects of "failure"' (Nixon *et al.*, 1997a p.127), and then to work with the community to recognise cultural identity, personal agency, and the ways in which schools can succeed.

The result for Nixon *et al.* (1997a) has been the identification of significant differences in schools in terms of their responses to wider institutional failure, in which a number of school regimes might be identified and summarised thus (Nixon *et al.*, 1997a pp.128–30):

(a) *Non-reforming*: little evidence of restructuring by these schools; failure is ascribed by the school as being 'out there'; the school is regarded as a temporary refuge or sanctuary from the debilitating conditions; a lot of emphasis is on 'care' by teachers, but there is no attempt to change the conditions of learning; blame is attributed to cultural deficits; and schools are locked into accommodation rather than challenge through structural change.

(b) *Community-passive*: schools are actively restructuring, but this is being led by professionals; breakdowns are seen as a failure of communication between teachers and students; failure is ascribed to student under-achievement; there is a compensatory view of failure; and a lack of community support leaves these schools vulnerable for their survival.

(c) *Community-active*: restructuring is actively occurring; there is community support for a programme of community regeneration; failure is a shared responsibility between school, students and parents – with all having to change; learning is seen as an entitlement and as a shared responsibility; and such schools are likely to survive because of their action around community-based regeneration.

Nixon *et al.*'s (1997a) analysis bears some striking similarities to our own schema (McInerney *et al.*, 1999 p.31), where we identify the following types of school and their differing characteristics:

(a) *'Stuck' schools:*
   • low levels of teacher reflection;
   • deficit view of students;
   • teacher privatism;
   • little or no debate.
(b) *Collaborative schools:*
   • coherent school planning;

- student-centred;
- curriculum development;
- collaborative teaching and learning.

(c) *Socially critical schools:*
- social justice emphasis;
- critically reflective teachers;
- promoting critical literacy;
- celebrating difference.

While our own conceptualisation was similarly developed from working with disadvantaged schools, the community regeneration aspect – while increasingly present in moving from stuck to socially critical schools – was not as central, although we would argue that socially critical teachers are strong community activists in the ways they reflect and act on/with wider groups, how they frame the structural causes of poverty, and how they envisage critical literacy as promoting improved life chances for students. So, our own conceptualisation is certainly about the politics of recognition, albeit starting from a similar but somewhat different position.[2]

Nixon and Ranson claim that many schools have effectively broken down in the 'fragmentation, compression and complexity of contemporary culture' (Nixon and Ranson, 1997 p.208) as traditional interpretations about professionalism around ideas of autonomy and status no longer have currency. Instead, in the way Nixon and Ranson put it, the issue hinges around the reworking of an agreement:

> Many traditional 'agreements' – between teachers, between pupils and teachers, and between parents and teachers – have already broken down. Teachers, therefore, are having to become adept at achieving new agreements regarding the purposes and processes of learning. The need to 'reach' agreement, then, is a defining feature of the emergent professionalism.
>
> (Nixon and Ranson, 1997 p.197)

A central aspect of the trajectory of this new professionalism is the notion of 'agreement as integrative action' – action that 'involves a consideration of both ends and means' (Nixon and Ranson, 1997 p.199). Emergent professionalism will fail, they say, if it does not extend to students and parents, working with the former 'as agents of their own learning', and the latter 'as complementary educators' even if 'the deep and underlying "codes" of the emergent professionalism are as yet unsettled' (Nixon and Ranson, 1997 p.197). Teachers cannot stand apart from but must instead 'engage with the different and sometimes conflicting values of communities' (Nixon and Ranson, 1997 p.203). This will essentially amount to a structural and institutional regeneration in which schools will become the vanguards for a reformed civil society. But this will mean dissolving traditional distinctions and forging new coalitions and alliances capable of achieving the new agreements. Put another way, continuing reliance on an inward looking style of teacher professionalism will not enable teachers to exert a strong influence necessary to reshape public education against the new management of education. What is required is for teachers to reorder and mediate their own professional interests beyond their own institutional boundaries.

Where the work of teaching becomes 'fractured', to use Nixon *et al.*'s terminology, is around 'competing notions of what constitutes professional authority and the right to exercise professional judgement' (Nixon *et al.*, 1997a p.131). In those situations where teachers are treated in 'low trust' (Sullivan, 1994) ways, and where the work of teaching is framed by a 'deluge of directives' (Webb and Vulliamy, 1996) in terms of frameworks, policies, appraisal mechanisms, testing regimes, etc., it is not hard to see how teachers might keep 'harking back to residual notions of the teacher as expert . . . based upon principles of closure and exclusion' (Nixon *et al.*, 1997a p.131). On the other hand, when teachers are 'committed to a professional identity and a set of professional values that accord with the notion of teacher as learner' (Nixon *et al.*, 1997a p.132), then teacher professionalism is much more committed to principles of 'openness and integration' and 'a radical pluralism of outlook' (Nixon *et al.*, 1997a pp.131, 135).

There is always a danger, in discussions of this type, of either going around in circles of mutually reinforcing despair, or equally unhelpful circuits of unwarranted optimism. There is a need to try and peg the terrain down somewhat more concretely, and I want to do that by exploring an idea originally posited by Connell (1995) of teaching as a 'social practice' – a notion carried further more recently by Ozga in terms of what she calls 'policy stories about teachers' or 'teachers as a policy case' (Ozga, 2000 p.13).

Teaching as a social practice

To speak of teaching in terms of having 'a capacity for social practice' (Connell, 1995 p.98) is to regard teaching as having an inherent capacity to render learning outcomes of a particular kind. But more is involved than a simple ability to frame educational outcomes. For example, to speak of teachers' capacity to labour in purely technical terms could, in Connell's terms, amount to a disproportionate emphasis being placed upon the need for students' 'ability to spell' – something teachers might desire, but for quite different reasons to those of employers. The symbolic meaning accompanying such an externally imposed view of the importance of the ability to spell, can bring with it an equally invisible view of a capacity to labour that emphasises qualities of 'diligence, orderliness, and obedience to rules' (Connell, 1995 p.98).

Clearly, such instrumental views of teaching and its attendant relationships to learning, rest decidedly uneasily with views of teaching as being primarily about socialisation and for interaction. In other words, where the terrain is that of 'culture, identity formation, and communication' (Connell, 1995 p.99). Views of this kind are more akin to 'education as a cultural process' in which social interaction amounts to a capacity for creativity and a tolerance for an 'open-ended difference, with final determinations of meaning always deferred' (Connell, 1995 p.100).

At yet another level, Connell (1995) argues that teaching is about 'a capacity for power', not necessarily in an authoritarian sense, but rather in terms of 'a collective capacity to exercise political responsibility' (Connell, 1995 p.100). Teachers do not have the option to choose to be non-political because the nature of the work is such that they are continually involved in making decisions that affect 'the social distribution of resources' (Connell, 1995 p.101). At the most immediate level this is 'the curriculum-as-realised in the classroom' (Connell, 1995 p.102), particularly through the competitive academic curriculum.

Another way to come at this is through the imagery of Popkewitz (1998) of 'struggling for the soul' in the politics of schooling and the construction of the teacher. The essence of his argument is that in order to understand, and therefore to change, contemporary schooling, we need a different scaffolding (a term he borrows from Foucault) 'making visible the roles through which difference and diversity are normalised in teaching' (Popkewitz, 1998 p.6).

The reason we need this different scaffolding is that common sense does not have the capacity to 'open up a potential space for alternative acts and alternative intentions' (Popkewitz, 1998 p.6); what is required instead are acts of resistance that permit a 'moving against the grain', challenging the 'assumptions behind much contemporary discourse about teaching . . . that there are rational paths to salvation – the efficient school, the effective teacher, the authentic teacher' (Popkewitz, 1998 p.7).

Behind the practices of such policy-making 'we find no moral, political [or] cultural certitude' (Popkewitz, 1998 p.7). Instead, Popkewitz argues for an approach to educational reform that aims:

> . . . to destabilise reigning forms of reasoning through inquiring into how the objects of schooling are constructed – to understand how

particular forms of knowledge inscribe power in ways that qualify and disqualify students from action and participation.

(Popkewitz, 1998 p.7)

Popkewitz is arguing that it is the forms of knowledge we hold that in the end blind us and cause us to be selective in what we see, think, feel and say about teaching. The need is for a scaffolding of ideas with which to dislodge 'the repressive elements that prevent children from participating' (Popkewitz, 1998 p.135) – which is to say, the conventional ideas, motives and purposes that underpin our current ideologies and practices.

I want to turn now to a scaffolding that might permit the kind of educative restoration that I am arguing for.

Sustaining a culture of debate about teaching and learning

Over the past decade, myself and colleagues have been working with teachers to find ways of subverting the toxic practices of managerialism (see also Hatcher, 1994; 1998a; 1998b) that have been allowed free reign in schools, and replacing them with approaches that have a more educative and pedagogical agenda. We have done this from a position of working with groups of schools that face some of the most severe forms of disadvantage and disfigurement, mostly due to poverty. Our experience has been that fundamental change is only possible at the level of the school, when school culture is considered the key to school reform (Smyth *et al.*, 1999). There are a number of quite complex interconnecting aspects to this, but I will come to these shortly.

We have extremely serious misgivings about whether the permeation of market forces into schools will in the long run serve the interests of students, schools or the wider society. We agree with Power and Whitty (1999) that the infiltration of the ideology and practices of the market into schools has done untold 'damage [to] the cultural work of the school' (Power and Whitty, 1999 p.19) as the values of consumption and individual 'material gratification' have been allowed to trivialise what schools are about through processes like the 'glossification of school imagery' (Gewirtz *et al.*, 1995 p.127). The likely outcome, if uninterrupted, will be the 'complete structural disarticulation' (Power and Whitty, 1999 p.25) of educational systems from the wider social contexts they are supposed to be serving. We can already see this clearly in the case of higher education:

. . . it is possible to see a commodification of learning packages, a drive towards 'pick and mix' courses which have been described as a 'cafeteria curriculum' and a degree of de-institutionalisation with the growth of distance learning through new technologies.

(Power and Whitty, 1999 p.25)

The position I want to adopt here is that re-articulation or reclamation is only possible at the level of the school, for it is there, notwithstanding official misgivings, that the most profound understandings of schools exist. It is among teachers, students and parents that the re-assertion of what is essential to schools will have to be most vociferously and robustly debated.

My experience has been that when schools find the courage and the space within which to push back into what I label the 'efficiency reforms' (Smyth, 2000), then they are able to create a culture and a reform agenda for themselves that cascades across elements of:

- critical reflection on teaching and learning;
- the promotion of student voice in the life and curriculum of the school;
- school/community dialogue;
- working to make a curriculum for social justice;
- engaging with strategies for information technology/media culture.

There are a number of defining moments or elements of school culture here that constitute what Bernstein (1992) would refer to as a 'constellation', that are important to highlight in the educative restoration that constitutes the most likely antidote to the managerialist ideological onslaught. The following diagram summarises these aspects:

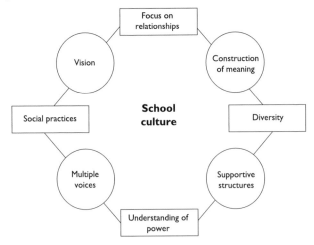

Figure 8.1 A constellation of school culture.
Source: Smyth, McInerney, Lawson and Hattam, 1999 p.11.

To explain each of these briefly, and to take the boxes first:

Social practices

It is in the nature of schools that they thrive on social interaction, but of a kind that has within it a capacity for creativity along with a tolerance for ambiguity, contestation and open-ended difference.

Focus on relationships

This is how people give expression to the way they value one another and is something of a signifier of the way in which the school is trying to grow and develop through setting a positive example. A shorthand way of putting this might be in terms of 'teaching democracy democratically' (Worsfold, 1997).

Diversity

This is where there is a preparedness to acknowledge multiple perspectives and differences of viewpoint and is indicative of a school that has developed a maturity of outlook about itself and what it is attempting.

Understanding power

Acknowledging that there are a variety of hierarchies in schools – gender, race and class in particular – and being willing to confront them at the level of understanding how they operate institutionally, is a crucial step in moving towards a more equitable distribution of power. In this context, disadvantage is not seen simply in terms of something imposed on schools from outside, but it is often reproduced through the concrete practices that operate in schools and that are reinforced daily.

Multiple voices

This is another way of talking about participatory decision-making involving a preparedness by those who have ultimate authority in schools to listen to the variety of ways in which all groups in schools give expression to their often quite divergent aspirations. This is in contrast to schools where discussion and debate are sparse, and where the only voices heard are the ones in ascendant positions.

Supportive structures

The kind of organisational practices and processes put in place in schools that enable and permit dialogue and debate around teaching and learning are an important endorsement of what is considered to be of paramount importance in the school. Where these are absent, even though there might be fine sounding rhetoric about schools as learning organisations, such claims ring hollow.

Vision

This amounts to having an issue or a clearly articulated focus and direction around which energy and effort can be creatively and productively harnessed to move the school forward. This needs to be something to which everyone in the school can relate, and not be limited to the aspirations of a small dominant elite.

Construction of meaning

Schools are places, above all, in which people are continually trailing, testing out and reformulating ideas on how they understand the world, and their role as active agents in trying to change it. There needs to be ongoing affirmation that this is a desirable thing to do.

What this constellation of elements of school culture amounts to is a set of framing or boundary conditions that might be regarded as indispensable to teacher learning. They are very much at odds with the kind of conditions and their attendant emphases that prevail under conditions of managerialism. For example:

- a low level of teacher trust;
- a fetish for bench-marking and measurement of outcomes;
- a persistent and harping rhetoric about accountability;
- an emphasis on competition and market solutions;
- the (re)construction of hierarchies;
- requirements for high levels of compliance;
- deprofessionalisation of the work of teaching;
- heavy reliance on directives and policy to fix problems;
- regarding teaching as being essentially technical in nature;
- getting 'line management functions' right;
- arguing that teaching is an apolitical activity; and
- teamwork, but only to implement other people's agenda.

As Morley and Rassool (1999) put it, a decade after the major reform act of 1988 that changed the face of education in England and Wales:

> . . . we find teachers not as cultural workers able to engage freely in critique and self-definition, creating new spaces within which the parameters of educational debate and pedagogical possibility could be redefined. Instead, we find them rigidly locked into the technicism of school effectiveness taxonomies focused on quality control which, in turn, are subjected to a myriad of external and internal bureaucratic forms of control. [The] emphasis has shifted qualitatively towards concerns about the *effectiveness* of schools and the *performativity* of teachers . . . [characterised by]:
> - narrowly defined professional competencies;
> - the regulation of task-oriented institutional practices and processes, systems monitoring and the management of, largely attitudinal and behavioural change within organisations.
>
> (Morley and Rassool, 1999 p.33)

As these commentators argue, 'school *performance* now represents the central concern within education' in a context that increasingly forbids 'analysis of societal relations and asymmetries of power within the educational system' (Morley and Rassool, 1999 p.34). In other words, there is a denial of 'education as a socio-cultural practice', with the culture of management now strongly 'fram[ing] educational policy and practice, and the predominant focus on the monitoring of work practices and processes, dislocat[ing] education from its socio-cultural base' (Morley and Rassool, 1999 p.34).

The argument presented in this chapter has been that we need a new 'critical professionality' of teaching that is informed by a robust culture of debate around issues of teaching and learning – as an alternative to the toxic practices of managerialism alluded to earlier in the chapter. This antidote is necessary in order to refashion school reform worldwide so that it is more cognisant and respectful of those who have the largest repositories of knowledge about teaching – classroom teachers. The argument (see Smyth, 2000a for further detail) is essentially double-sided and reciprocal, in which the reclamation of teaching from the prevailing managerialist discourses has to be pedagogically inspired. In other words, the wider set of relationships within which teaching is being constructed between schools and society, needs to be problematised. Similarly, whether and in what ways teachers accept, or resist, current dominant views of their work, is a matter of wider public concern that has implications for civil society, civic virtue, and the prospects for a vibrant democracy.

Allowing a stunted view of teacher professionality to prevail, in which the construction of what constitutes a teacher is totally derivative either of market or government inspired forces, cannot be allowed to go unheeded or unchallenged. The alternative conceptualisation being offered in this chapter is one that has as its centrepiece a passionate concern for and reinvigoration of the tradition of 'teacher-as-intellectual', engaged in critical forms of teaching against the grain and for social and democratic responsibility (Smyth, 2000b). The point was well made recently by Bottery and Wright (2000) that regardless of the genesis of current official efforts to reform teaching, a matter of paramount international significance is that teachers themselves must reassert the importance of professional spaces within which to construct and debate what it means to be a teacher. In Bottery and Wright's terms:

> Wherever on a spectrum from 'market led' to 'government directed' a particular government takes a stand, however, the result appears to be the same – one in which governments control and direct the activities of the teaching profession, and in which the teaching profession apparently acquiesces.
>
> (Bottery and Wright, 2000 p.3)

Having the courage to push back through debate about the centrality of pedagogy in the school reform debate, would enable classroom teachers to situate what they do in schools and classrooms within the wider set of social, political, cultural and economic changes. This is not to deny that there are still large unanswered questions about where their unions stand in this. And, clearly, this will be no small task, but if taken seriously it could result in the injection of a much-needed moral, political and ethical set of perspectives into what it means to be a teacher. How prepared teachers are to speak out in the wider public debate about the nature of schooling, through their words as well as their actions, has crucial implications for the wider 'public good and a stable civil society' (Bottery and Wright, 2000 p.5).

Conclusion

The kind of reinvigorated democratic politics of teachers' work that I am arguing for in this chapter is one that moves considerably beyond managerialist notions, or what Bottery calls 'the convergence of management codes' (Bottery, 1994 p.329); and that also supplants the views of the 'new modernisers' (see Brown and Lauder, 1997; Bottery, 1999). That is, those who argue that it is possible to put a human face on capitalism

(Latham, 1998) by reconfiguring the relationship between the economy, society and government. They look more progressive than the free marketeers they seek to replace, because they champion notions like 'communitarianism' and 'character education', as Bottery (1999) has shown. But even so, the three visions – the economic (high skills, high tech); the societal (a culture of learning); and the governmental (more direction) – are fundamentally flawed because they are likely to lead to even further centralisation of decision-making, an increase in illiberalism towards minority groups, and even further neglect of the underprivileged (Bottery, 1999 p.103).

What I am offering as an alternative, are the constituent elements of a theorisation of school change that is different both from the vision of the market, and the perspective of the reformers who would merely tinker with that viewpoint without fundamentally challenging its efficacy. I am much more inclined to be forthright about the need for schools to be unapologetically democratic institutions, where knowledge, contestation and debate prevail, and where authority is vested in expertise based on the power of argument and persuasion.

Notes

1 After I had drafted this chapter, and during the revisions, I encountered Shain and Gleeson's (1999) use of the term 'under new management'. I wish to acknowledge their use of this term which is similar to the way in which I am using it. I also explore this in more detail in 'Teaching under (re-)construction' in Smyth and Shacklock (1998), pp.42–76.
2 There is clearly no space in which to provide the detail of this work, but readers are referred to: Hattam, McInerney, Lawson and Smyth, 1999; McInerney, Hattam, Smyth and Lawson, 1999; McInerney, Smyth, Lawson and Hattam, 1999; Smyth, McInerney, Hattam and Lawson, 1999a; 1999b. This research was supported by a grant from the Australian Research Council and was conducted jointly with the Department of Education, Training and Employment, South Australia.

References

Ball, S. (1999), *Educational reform and the struggle for the soul of the teacher* (Education Policy Studies Series No.17). Hong Kong: Hong Kong Institute of Educational Research, The Chinese University of Hong Kong.

Bantick, C. (2000), 'Teachers need a makeover', in *The Australian*, p.18, 22 March 2000.

Bernstein, R. (1992), *The New Constellation: the Ethical-Political Horizons of Modernity/Post-Modernity*, Cambridge: Polity Press.

Bottery, M. (1994), 'Education and the convergence of management codes', in *Educational Studies*, Vol. 20 (3), pp.329–43.

Bottery, M. (1997), 'Teacher professionalisation through action research – possibility or pipe-dream', in *Teachers and Teaching: Theory and Practice*, Vol. 3 (2), pp.273–92.

Bottery, M. (1999), 'Education under the new modernisers: an agenda for centralisation, illiberalism and inequality', in *Cambridge Journal of Education*, Vol. 29 (1), pp.103–20.

Bottery, M. and Wright, N. (1996), 'Cooperating in their own deprofessionalisation? On the need to recognise the "Public" and "Ecological" roles of the teaching profession', in *British Journal of Educational Studies*, Vol. 44 (1), pp.82–98.

Bottery, M. and Wright, N. (1997), 'Impoverishing a sense of professionalism: who's to blame?', in *Educational Management and Administration*, Vol. 25 (1), pp.7–24.

Bottery, M. and Wright, N. (2000), *Teachers and the State: Towards a Directed Profession*, London and New York: Routledge.

Brown, P. and Lauder, H. (1997), 'Education, globalization and economic development', in A. Halsey, H. Lauder, P. Brown and W. Wells (eds), *Education: Culture, Economy and Society*, Oxford and New York: Oxford University Press (Vol. 172–92).

Connell, R. (1995), 'Transformative labour: theorizing the politics of teachers' work', in M. Ginsburg (ed.), *The Politics of Educators' Work and Lives*, New York and London: Garland, pp.91–114.

Furlong, J. (1991), 'Disaffected pupils: reconstructing the sociological perspective', in *British Journal of Sociology of Education*, Vol. 12, pp.293–307.

Gewirtz, S., Ball, S. and Bowe, R. (1995), *Markets, Choice and Equity in Education*, Buckingham: Open University Press.

Gunter, H. (1997), *Rethinking Education: the Consequences of Jurassic Management*, London: Cassell.

Hartley, D. (1999), 'Marketing and the "re-enchantment" of school management', in *British Journal of Sociology of Education*, Vol. 20 (3), pp.309–23.

Hatcher, R. (1994), 'Market relationships and the management of teachers', in *British Journal of Sociology of Education*, Vol. 15 (1), pp.41–62.

Hatcher, R. (1998a), 'Profiting from schools: business and the Education Action Zones', in *Education and Social Justice*, Vol. 1, pp.9–16.

Hatcher, R. (1998b), 'Labour, official school improvement and equality', in *Journal of Education Policy*, Vol. 13 (4), pp.485–99.

Hattam, R., Brown, K. and Smyth, J. (1995), *Sustaining a Culture of Debate About Teaching and Learning*, Adelaide: Flinders Institute for the Study of Teaching.

Hattam, R., McInerney, P., Lawson, M. and Smyth, J. (1999) *A school as a learning community: Hackham West Schools* (Case Study Series: Teachers' Learning Project), Adelaide: Flinders Institute for the Study of Teaching and Department of Education Training and Employment.

Helsby, G. (1995), 'Teachers' construction of professionalism in England in the 1990s', in *Journal of Education for Teaching*, Vol. 21 (3), pp.317–32.

Helsby, G. (1999) *Changing Teachers' Work: the 'Reform' of Secondary Schooling*, Buckingham: Open University Press.

Latham, M. (1998), *Civilising Global Capital*, Sydney: Allen & Unwin.

Marcus, G. (1998), *Ethnography through Thick and Thin*, Princeton, NJ: Princeton University Press.

McInerney, P., Hattam, R., Lawson, M. and Smyth, J. (1999), *Developing Middle Schooling Practices* (Investigation Series: Teachers' Learning Project), Adelaide: Flinders Institute for the Study of Teaching.

McInerney, P., Hattam, R., Smyth, J. and Lawson, M. (1998), *Middle Schooling from the Ground Up: Teachers' Learning at Seaford 6–12 School* (Case Study No. 5), Adelaide: Flinders Institute for the Study of Teaching.

McInerney, P., Smyth, J., Lawson, M. and Hattam, R. (1999), *A rigorous curriculum in an isolated community: Indulkana Aboriginal School* (Case Study Series: Teachers' Learning Project), Adelaide: Flinders Institute for the Study of Teaching.

Morley, L. and Rassool, N. (1999), *School Effectiveness: Fracturing the Discourse*, London and New York: Falmer Press.

Nixon, J., Martin, J., McKeown, P. and Ranson, S. (1997a), 'Confronting "failure": towards a pedagogy of recognition', in *International Journal of Inclusive Education*, Vol. 1 (2), pp.121–41.

Nixon, J., Martin, P., McKeown, P. and Ranson, S. (1997b), 'Towards a learning profession: changing codes of occupational practice within the new management of education', in *British Journal of Sociology of Education*, Vol. 18 (1), pp.5–28.

Nixon, J. and Ranson, S. (1997), 'Theorising agreement: the moral base of the emergent professionalism within the "new" management of education', in *Discourse*, Vol. 18 (2), pp.197–214.

Ozga, J. (2000), *Policy Research in Educational Settings: Contested Terrain*, Buckingham: Open University Press.

Popkewitz, T. (1998), *Struggling for the Soul: the Politics of Schooling and the Construction of the Teacher*, New York: Teachers College Press.

Power, S., Halpin, D. and Whitty, G. (1997), 'Managing the state and the market: "new" educational management in five countries', in *British Journal of Educational Studies*, Vol. 45 (4), pp.342–62.

Power, S. and Whitty, G. (1999), 'Market forces and school cultures', in J. Prosser (ed.), *School Culture*, London: Paul Chapman, pp.15–29.

Shain, F. and Gleeson, D. (1999), 'Under new management: changing conceptions of teacher professionalism in the further education sector', in *Journal of Education Policy*, Vol. 14 (4), pp.445–62.

Smyth, J. (2000a), 'The self-managing school: the reform we had to have?', Adelaide: Flinders Institute for the Study of Teaching.

Smyth, J. (2000b), 'Reclaiming social captial through critical teaching', *Elementary School Journal*, Vol. 100 (5), pp.491–511.

Smyth, J., Dow, A., Hattam, R., Reid, A. and Shacklock, G. (2000), *Teachers' Work in a Globalising Economy*, London and New York: Falmer Press.

Smyth, J., Hattam, R., McInerney, P. and Lawson, M. (1999), *School Culture: the Key to School Reform* (Investigation Series, Teachers' Learning Project), Adelaide: Flinders Institute for the Study of Teaching.

Smyth, J., McInerney, P., Hattam, R. and Lawson, M. (1999a), *Placing girls at the centre of curriculum: Gepps Cross Girls High School* (Case Study Series: Teachers' Learning Project), Adelaide: Flinders Institute for the Study of Teaching.

Smyth, J., McInerney, P., Hattam, R. and Lawson, M. (1999b), *A culture of reform for social justice: the Pines School* (Case Study Series: Teachers' Learning Project), Adelaide: Flinders Institute for the Study of Teaching.

Smyth, J. and Shacklock, G. (1998), *Re-making Teaching: Ideology, Policy and Practice*, London: Routledge.

Sullivan, K. (1994), 'The impact of educational reform on teachers' professional ideologies', in *New Zealand Journal of Educational Studies*, Vol. 29 (1), pp.3–20.

Troman, G. (1996), 'The rise of the new professionals? The restructuring of primary teachers' work and professionalism' in *British Journal of Sociology of Education*, Vol. 14 (4), pp.472–87.

Troman, G. (1997), 'Self-management and school inspection: complementary forms of surveillance and control in the primary school', in *Oxford Review of Education*, Vol. 23, pp.345–64.

Webb, R. and Vulliamy, G. (1996), 'A deluge of directives: conflict between collegiality and managerialism in the post-ERA primary school', in *British Educational Research Journal*, Vol. 22 (4), pp.441–58.

Whitty, G., Power, S. and Halpin, D. (1998), *Devolution and Choice in Education: the State School and the Market*, Buckingham: Open University Press.

Worsfold, V. (1997), 'Teaching democracy democratically', in *Educational Theory*, Vol. 47 (3), pp.395–410.

Part III
Ringmasters and big tops?
Performance and performativity in policy frameworks

The final section of this book widens the focus of the debate: we move from the examination of schools and professional cultures to the examination of policy and policy frameworks. In the 'big top' of the performance culture, contributors explore the assumed relationships between schooling and society, between education and the economy; in this section contributors explore the macro-educational framework within which our performing schools will thrive or fail.

Gleeson and Gunter explore the balance between 'carrot and stick' in performance management. Based on experience in other educational sectors, they are sceptical about the long-term ability of performance-related pay to sustain a high status profession. For Gleeson and Gunter the 'modernisation' of teachers is fundamentally about the exercise of power, its location and deployment. Geoff Whitty extends this analysis. For Whitty, 'professionalism' is always socially constructed, an amalgam of workplace-derived practices, social expectations and legislative forms. He wonders whether the current policy-models on offer – effectively state control or professional self-governance – are the only valid models and considers whether the politics of a redefinition of professionalism will resolve long-lasting disputes between the state-based advocates of managed professionality and the voices of dissent which look to self-governance. Whitty sees no easy resolution, but urges new modes of governance which escape current forms of defensive thinking.

Pat Mahony and Ian Hextall explore some further tensions around the concept of 'performance' in an educational setting where government is making increasingly explicit demands on teachers, but also where, increasingly, the boundaries between public and private sectors are, in Mahony and Hextall's phrase, 'porous'. As a result, the professional culture of teaching is in the process of redefinition, but the final form of this redefinition is far from clear. The challenge is implicitly taken up in the final two contributions. John Elliott and Stephen Ball explore some of the dimensions of the culture of 'performativity'. For Elliott, the imposition of the culture of performance indicators and performance management is a characteristic of an audit society, which at best neglects the organisational and cultural processes by which excellence is developed and at worst denies them. A renewed professional culture demands a different policy mix. The final contribution is a wide-ranging and theoretical examination by Stephen Ball of what he calls 'performativities and fabrications'. In Ball's analysis, the Green Paper is, in the last resort, a sideshow in the grand circus of the performing school in a performing society. As performance becomes an icon in education, social and economic policy, and professional identity must become increasingly fabricated.

9 The performing school and the modernisation of teachers

Denis Gleeson and Helen Gunter

Introduction

In the past decade, attempts to introduce performance criteria into secondary education, as part of a wider restructuring and deregulation of state education, have been both controversial and contested. Ostensibly concerned with increasing efficiency and raising standards, such reform has been contingent upon changing professional and managerial cultures away from a developmental and policy narrative to one based on enterprise and market principles. This chapter examines the process of such change from the Education Reform Act (ERA) (1988) to the Green Paper (DfEE, 1998), and beyond. It argues that the reconfiguration of professionalism has more to do with a political realignment of teachers and the state, than with improved teaching and learning. At the same time, we recognise that this process is not new (Grace, 1995) and is part of a continuous historical process of contestation and renewal. In providing a critical analysis of the politics of modernisation, the chapter goes on to examine its likely impact on changing conditions of secondary education. A key argument is that the Green Paper (DfEE, 1998) is primarily concerned with imposing performance procedures rather than with identifying successful principles of teaching, learning and management which might drive those procedures.

The Green Paper (DfEE, 1998) sets out plans for the introduction of performance-related pay, the introduction of a pay threshold, new models of professional development, a new role in managing performance for head teachers and a series of other changes. These include threshold payments and the introduction of a fast-track route through the teaching profession for able entrants, the creation of a national college for school leadership and the development of training schools. The proposals have been described as the most thorough-going reform of the teaching profession since the introduction of compulsory schooling in 1870 (Blair, 1999), and are closely linked with wider market reforms in the public sector. As successive governments have increasingly articulated the global requirements of a 'knowledge economy', traditional educational cultures and organisational structures for teaching are found to be wanting. The drive to improve indicators of educational performance, and to ensure that teachers are equipped and able to operate in rapidly changing commercial environments, is influencing attempts to reorganise, reskill and reculture teaching. A common thread running through this process is the increasing focus on new forms of schools and new kinds of teachers, and on measuring their performance through inspection and league tables, and on holding teachers more directly accountable through both rewards and sanctions.

Modernising teachers

The recent policy assumption that, once put in place, managerial procedures will promote the desired learning outcomes that follow is not new, and ignores periodic shifts in the nature of teacher control. In the immediate post-war period (1945–1975), teachers enjoyed a high degree of autonomy and trust in knowing what was best for the pupils in their care, and the state did not strongly intervene in defining teachers' work. In the 1980s and 1990s, following Jim Callaghan's Ruskin Speech (1976) and with conservatives taking office in 1979, new management procedures became the preferred alternative to the informal and voluntaristic modes of professionalism associated with the 1960s. Concern over declining educational standards associated with alleged abuse of teachers' licensed autonomy led, at that time, to widespread reforms culminating in the Education Reform Act of 1988. By identifying teachers as 'part of the problem' of a low-skill, low-wage, low-productivity economy, the pendulum of license swung in favour of exposing teachers and other public sector workers to market realism, accountability and the tightening ratchet of state control (Esland, 1996). In the conditions now prevailing under New Labour, following nearly two decades of New Right reform, the restructuring of teacher professionalism has resurfaced in a 'third way' of linking target-setting, performance and financial rewards. As Grace (1995) and others have noted (Whitty *et al.*, 1995), the struggle over teacher relations with the state is part of a continuous historical process involving not only recurring debate over what schools are for, but also what teachers do. From Callaghan to Thatcher and, more recently Blair, the pursuit by government for control over the means and ends of education reveals more about shifts in the regulation of teachers than about the specific content of education itself. Such historical shifts, for illustration purposes, may be described as shown in Table 9.1 (see over page).

Though not clear-cut, these dispositional shifts find expression in broader historical, political and economic changes. These changes characterise the transition from a high- to a low-trust economy, and the consequent implications for the management of the education system. There was a brief historical moment in the 1960s and 1970s, when state teachers challenged government policies over tripartism, selection and differentiation; but this short-lived relative autonomy has since been clawed back by successive governments. That period of teacher politicisation provoked various policy responses in the 1980s and 1990s in terms of who controlled 'the secret garden of the curriculum', and whose right it was to manage schools, beyond the self-seeking interests of professionals. Most recently, in the 1990s, the promotion of neo-taylorist scientific management styles is evident in the use of rational and linear development planning, in which the teacher is the object to be integrated and managed. This approach found expression in the rhetoric of intolerance of 'incompetent' teachers or of 'new-wave' managerial vision; of 'teamwork, empowerment, and fitness for purpose'. Central to this has been the importance of teacher appraisal which is explicitly recognised in the 1991 Education (School Teachers Appraisal) Regulations (DES, 1991a), designed to help teachers realise their full potential and to carry out their duties more effectively (Regulation 4(2)). In January 1995, the then School's Minister, Robin Squire, spoke to the Fourth British Appraisal Conference where he highlighted the importance of appraisal, its integration into the management of the school, and its need to continue after the end of GEST (Grants for Educational Support and Training) funding:

> Appraisal is a vital tool helping teachers to realise their potential and carry out their duties more effectively. In turn this serves the ultimate goal of improving the quality of education for pupils.
>
> (DfEE Newsletter, 31/1/95)

Official review of teacher appraisal and its contribution to educational outcomes concluded that:

> Overall, this evaluation provides convincing evidence that appraisal has been implemented with skill, commitment and energy at both LEA and school level. It shows that for many teachers and schools appraisal has already brought considerable benefits, some of which have had a direct impact on teachers.
>
> (Barber *et al.*, 1995 p.i)

Table 9.1 Shifts in the performance control of teachers and their work

Modes of regulation	1960s–mid-1980s *Relative autonomy* *Development*	1980s–1990s *Controlled autonomy* *Performance management*	2000 onwards *Productive autonomy* *Performativity*
Teacher accountability	Accountability to self through informal reflection. External accountability through peer review.	Accountability to self through formal review. External accountability through line manager. Senior management surveillance of process.	Internal accountability to self and the organisation through formal audit of student learning outcomes. Senior management control over the process.
Control over teacher performance	The teacher works within the structures and curriculum established by the headteachers. Some voluntary appraisal systems in schools.	Performance controlled through use of line management system overseen by headteacher and senior management. Mandatory appraisal operationalised from 1991. Local agreements are allowed and the link with performance-related pay not usually made.	Teacher and organisational targets are now assimilated into the national curriculum and performance framework. Performance-related pay integrated into audit, appraisal and target procedures.

Evidence about performance	Informal evidence collection.	Formalised qualitative evidence, e.g. classroom observation.	Formalised quantitative evidence based on pupil outcomes, and qualitative evidence based on personal statements and classroom evaluation.
Measurement of performance	The meaning and the interpretation of performance is based on and determined by ongoing professional relationships and reference groups.	Development targets are generated from a professional development discussion based on data from self-review, and formal classroom observation.	Performance is measured through transparent, statistical calculations about the value added by the teacher to pupil outcomes.
Teacher orientation towards children	Professional emphasis on ethical commitment to children.	Children are customers to be attracted to the school through high learning outcomes.	Children are objects and targets to be assessed and counted.
Head and Senior Manager orientation towards teachers	Headteacher has a traditional and professional legitimacy and status.	Headteacher and senior managers have a surveillance role over the performance management process.	Headteacher and senior managers are 'middle managers' between the government and teachers, and are publicly accountable for performance outcomes.

However, a year later, a report by OfSTED, based on school inspection visits and OfSTED Section 9 Inspection Reports, observed that teacher performance had not been well supported through appraisal (OfSTED, 1996). In particular, the report raised concerns that performance-related pay and its reputed link with appraisal needed further review. OfSTED noted that while Circular 12/91 (DES, 1991b) identified that such a link was 'legitimate and desirable', schools tended to follow the appraising body's (LEA or the governors for a grant-maintained school) recommendation not to make any link between appraisal, pay and promotion. The report concludes that appraisal was 'functioning below its full potential' and justified its call for a review based on a shift away from ethical accountability to the student, discipline and profession, towards the accountability of the school in the market. In June 1996, OfSTED and the TTA produced a report (TTA/OfSTED, 1996) summarising responses to the OfSTED report (OfSTED, 1996), emphasising management improvements required for a more effectively designed and operationalised system. The emphasis is not just on the link between targets and development planning, but on how appraisal is integral to the cost-cutting function of the self-managing school:

> In those schools where appraisal is a part of normal management strategies, is consistent with a school's culture and style, dovetailed into its administrative structures and integrated with the other functions carried out in the school, it works without any extra resource requirements other than those normally necessary to secure well managed schools. This includes training for aspiring and existing Headteachers and for subject leaders, on how to monitor and improve standards in schools.
>
> (OfSTED, 1996, paragraph 3.4, p.6)

What is consistent in the views of government over the last decade is that appraisal is about performance, and professional development is conceptualised as the teacher meeting the developmental needs of the school. Individual professional development is acknowledged but the emphasis is on the efficient and effective deployment of teachers as resources in raising levels of achievement (Gunter, 1999). Teaching and learning is identified as an organisational outcome to which the effective installation of management processes and tasks, such as appraisal, will lead. The review by OfSTED and the TTA of appraisal during 1996 reaches the conclusion that the failure to deliver outcomes in teacher performance can be explained largely in terms of problems with implementation in schools and by LEAs, not the concept itself. Our critical reading of these policy texts leads us to conclude that the evidence about what does and does not work in teacher appraisal and PRP systems was not allowed to inform the political goals of the Conservative government of the day or those of the incoming new Labour government.

The change of government in May 1997 continued the policy trend with teacher development being defined by Morris (1998) as performance driven rather than a morally committed process. This is followed through in the Green Paper of 1998 in which appraisal is strongly criticised for not being fully integrated into effective management. In taking forward the implementation of annual performance appraisal and performance-related pay, the performance management proposals (DfEE, 1999) appear to be a reinvention of the previous appraisal requirement, but with strings. While much of this will be familiar to teachers, such as classroom obser-vation, the tone and content of the package is more closely tied around managed performance and effectiveness. This Taylorist tendency is evident through the performance management cycle (plan, do, monitor and review) combined with human resource management in which teachers' work is tied more closely with externally imposed standards and targets. While the label remains the same a different version of appraisal and man-agement is emerging. This involves a noticeable shift away from prioritising site-based change strategies to that of data gatherers and analysts who inform and measure their own and others' teaching.

Barber and Sebba (1999) relate such restructuring to the global require-ments of a 'world class education system' and argue that the current government's policy is to reform and use funding mechanisms to 'motivate and increase the professionalism of teachers and encourage risk and ambi-tion'. The government is emphatic that there is little choice in the matter (DfEE, 1998) or, as Merson (in this volume), states: 'the status quo is not an option'. One implication of such thinking is that the modernisation of the teacher requires new forms of incentive that will promote greater enter-prise in the teaching profession (Tooley, 1999). A prevailing view is that teachers resist change and that there is a need to reward successful teachers if there is to be an eradication of the 'culture of excuses' which affect some parts of the teaching profession (Blair, 1999).

In contemporary discourse the term 'modernisation' has become synon-ymous with such restructuring in the most stubborn areas of the public sector (education, health, local government) considered least amenable to change. The restructuring of the public sector through privatisation, competitive tendering and decentralisation of operational functions to agencies has led to significant changes in the public sector workforce (Farnham and Horton 1992), with an increasing emphasis on a core staff supported by part-/full-time fixed-term contract staff as consultants.

Embedded within this is a move away from fixed pay scales based on national agreements to individualised agreements based upon performance. Furthermore there has been a trend away from the public sector professional reflected in the civilianisation of aspects of police and social work, through to private sector business managers becoming chief executives or governors of public sector institutions. Finally, the nature of the work has changed with an increase in the management function. Public sector workers are now more actively managed and they themselves are more directly involved in self-regulatory management tasks such as planning, target-setting, monitoring and evaluating.

Performance management is, according to White (1999), premised on the desire to replace municipal public values associated with sound and fair management, 'the legacy of Victorian reforms in government which wiped out patronage and corruption', with a more inquisitive style of operational management. Overlain on top of earlier market and user–provider reforms, associated with Thatcherism, New Labour's 'third way' has sought to produce 'social entrepreneurship' as a means of converting teachers and students to cultural and behavioural change. PRP, targeted outcomes for individuals and institutions, and fast-tracking for professionals, signal a shift to a business narrative, based on doing 'what works'. In creating devolved political and institutional powers to support this shift governments world-wide have opted to 'steer not row' expensive public bureaucracies (White, 1999). Yet despite recent evidence of poor performance in both public and private sectors demonstrating failure to meet consumer needs (arising in fraud, misselling or, in some cases, death and injury), this has not led to questions about whether private sector solutions constitute the best way of challenging public sector conservatism. Nevertheless, as Fielding (1999) argues, there is a strong psychological need to act and be seen to act through target-setting:

> It is, in one sense, the viagra of economic and educational under-performance: set some targets and you'll feel better, be seen to get something done and satisfy the prurience of an increasingly promiscuous accountability.
>
> (Fielding, 1999 p.277)

If, in theory, the basis of such control is premised on efficiency and rational economic principles it has, in practice, created a considerable bureaucracy of regulatory bodies, (OfSTED; QCA; TTA), often larger and more unwieldy than those they were designed to replace. With ever more invention the new managerialism has sought to marry economic (value for money) with quality criteria (raised levels of educational achievement).

However, professionals in such areas as health and education have not fully identified with performance management, and their cooperation is now being enlisted through incentives increasingly designed to connect pay and performance with quality, testing, targets and outcome indicators. This is now having considerable consequences in the education workplace and what it means to be a professional in education.

Allied to such an imperative the championing of performance management from private to public sector has been transformed into a virtuous discourse, synonymous with efficiency itself. Three factors explain the central ingredients of this process: tight control over public spending, manpower and cash limits; decentralisation of budgets and managerial responsiveness to consumer demand at local level; and quality assurance systems that connect target-setting, inspection and assessment with outcomes tied to appraisal and performance-related pay. Such changes are part of a shift towards human resource management in which employees must be efficiently and effectively deployed in order to meet targets. Employees are required, therefore, to be committed to the organisation through self-management strategies such as recruitment policies, appraisal schemes, performance-related pay, training and communication. The line manager takes prime responsibility for the employee's commitment and performance and communication is with the individual rather than through collegial or professional networks. Fuelled by recession, unemployment and global competition, the New Right with its emphasis on 'management's right to manage' and, more recently, New Labour with its focus on 'third-way' modernisation, share much in common. Though the latter is not an automatic extension of the former, both adhere to forms of managerialism which regulate teachers through centralised and devolved powers simultaneously. In this respect the dispositional shifts we referred to earlier are policy-connected rather than a contrast between ERA (1988) and the Green Paper (DfEE, 1998).

In drawing attention to this continuum diagramatically (Fig. 9.1), we emphasise ways in which performance management seeks to add value to earlier incremental, and often contradictory, procedural reforms initiated by ERA (the Education Reform Act) (1988). Crudely stated, the model describes the quality cycle that has framed education policy in the past decade and which looks set to define the next. ERA alone was unable to fulfil its policy objectives due more to the absence of a policy mechanism to deliver its objectives than simply the oppressive mix of prescription, tests and inspections characterising its legacy. Whilst ERA's emphasis on externality and control did much to redefine teachers' work it failed to win their professional commitment to the reform process. In recognising this policy failure the Green Paper (DfEE, 1998) represents a strategic

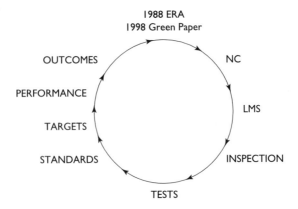

Figure 9.1 Completing the quality cycle through performance mechanisms.

intervention in 'squaring the quality circle' by harnessing pay and performance to national curricular requirements at institutional level. Thus by incentivising the teaching profession, performance management serves a number of functions both in rewarding performance around standards and targets and, at the same time, introducing a management mechanism that promotes enterprise within nationally prescribed limits, and so closes down the spaces for alternative models to develop and thrive.

Performance management is, therefore, not just concerned with teacher pay, recruitment and education improvements and neither is it a straightforward faustian pact of rewarding teachers for accepting new conditions of service. It has further implications which connect managerial procedures with desired outcomes and behaviour which may have little to do with learning, or professional development. Recent critical research of public sector administration stresses, for example, that generalised commercial and business values are being adapted to form what has been labelled the 'new public sector management' (Dunleavy and Hood, 1994; Exworthy and Halford, 1999; and Pollitt, 1993). This process is closely associated with developing a 'contractual capacity' to be entrepreneurial (Yeatman, 1997); and, as others have noted (Kenway, 1994), this 'economising of education' brings with it both the discipline of the market and the legitimising discourse and practice that goes with it (e.g. 'playing the game', dress, language, marketing, decor, etc.) in terms of the ways in which professionals present themselves. We return to this issue later in the paper.

It is worth noting first that the timetable for implementing the Green Paper proposals was not negotiated with trades unions, local authorities, headteachers' or governors' associations (Cutler and Waine, 2000).

Despite the government's expressed commitment to evidence informed policy, there is little indication that the consultation exercise acted on, or took notice of, research critical of performance-related pay (Marsden, 2000). While the consultation process reveals a growing need to better reward teachers, in professional and financial terms, there is no widespread agreement in support of rewarding individual performance. The likelihood is, however, that the implementation of performance management will vary at school level and focus primarily on pupil achievement. This type of variation of approach is not consistent with greater flexibility and space to negotiate the terms of performance management as might appear. According to Gerwitz (1995) and Ball (1997), the prevailing influence of market reforms in schools has already generated strong competitive and market tendencies which performance management techniques (such as total quality management or human resources management – HRM) have simply anticipated and overlain. In practice, Ball (in this volume) refers to a kind of 'schizophrenia' emerging between teamwork and individualisation; self-management and compliance; and professional development and performance, as they become ever more polarised:

> . . . commitment, judgement and authenticity with practice are sacrificed for impression and performance. There is a 'splitting' between the teacher's own judgement and 'good practice' and students' 'needs' on the one hand and the rigours of performance on the other.
>
> (Ball, 2000)

Ball associates such traits with 'fabrication' in which everyday preoccupations with inspection, annual reviews, data compilation and development planning find expression in the behaviour of professionals and those who judge them. From 'playing the game' to strategic compliance, professionals have become adept at distancing themselves from the values they believe in to those which require manipulation in order to get through the wide range of internally and externally imposed targets (Gleeson and Shain, 1999). This tension resides in many areas of work in which red tape (workload and administration) is cut through in order to get the job done. Increasingly, this is becoming more difficult in education where the synthetic demands of performativity close down possibilities for discretion and professional judgement emerging. The panoply of competitive funding, tests, targets and inspection have so regularised conditions of education that learning has become driven by short-term modes of measurement and assessment that now lead the curriculum. This volte-face has not been without its consequences in reconstructing values in education, encouraging schools and universities to manage and to manufacture their performances in overt ways. This includes publicising teaching and test scores, recruitment, inspection and examination results, research achievements, publications and rankings and income generation.

What is new about the new education economy is not just image and presentation, or what Gleeson and Shain (1999) call 'management by carpet', but also a synergy being sought between the corporate and self-image of those working and studying in competitive education environments. Increasingly, presentation of self, notably by teachers and academics in terms of dress, style, behaviour and entrepreneurship, is becoming synonymous with corporate behaviourism. Hartley, 1999 refers to the process going on in schools to achieve this as 're-culturing' (p.311), in which the dichotomy between postholders and teachers is bridged by the internal market where the management 'sells' and the teacher 'buys into' the vision and mission. The emotional work involved is central to mandated models of leadership being used to train senior managers (Gunter, 1999). In this, leadership becomes a form of seduction and, as Burrell argues, pleasure 'is seen as a reservoir of potential energy to be channelled, shaped and directed in the service of corporate goals' (Burrell, 1992 p.66). While much is made of the opportunities unleashed by the empowerment of site-based performance management, the drive for the 'preferred teacher' (Smyth and Shacklock, 1998) masks the endurance of structures that continue to limit teacher commitment to wider educational and participation enhancing values. As Blackmore argues:

> It has meant the remaking of hegemonic masculinity away from the image of the rational bureaucrat to the multiskilled, flexible, service oriented, facilitative and entrepreneurial manager. Whereas the old modernist performance principles of the gender-neutral bureaucrat were about delayed gratification and the denial of pleasure for work, which separated preference from fact, human feeling from the intellect, the new performativities of postmodern 'greedy' organizations exploit the pleasure of the win and getting the job done, as well as the intimacy of social relations to achieve organizational goals. Strategic management seeks to exploit diversity (gender, multiculturalism) to channel individual desires, passion and energy for organizational ends. In so doing, however, interpersonal relations are supplanted by depersonalized or contrived forms of intimacy, which produce new forms of self-regulation such as team work. Management thus manipulates intimacy within social relations and reconstitutes it into purposive-rational action, and in so doing reworks gender relations.
>
> (Blackmore, 1999 pp.37–8)

The personal and professional tension here is for staff to act strategically in dealing with external agendas (fabrication) whilst, at the same time, maintaining a sense of professionality (value) which drew them into teaching in the first place. As Ball argues, such fabrications cut back on the lives of teachers, since performativity demands that staff need to be noticed if they are to make their mark, have influence or gain promotion. This process of making oneself different within a collegial environment is also a process of self-management commensurate with changing conditions of marketisation and modernisation, both central ingredients of new definitions of professional self-control 'from within' the individual him- or herself.

As performance management supplants developmental systems, the role of headteachers has changed from that of leading professionals, working with teachers, to that of chief executives with responsibilities for monitoring efficiency and effectiveness. Overlain on top of this, and somewhat confusing to the entrepreneurial logic of site-based management, is the view of the head as a middle-manager brokering directly the state–school directives. At the same time, whilst heads are being trained for leadership with a vision and mission for the school, they are simultaneously in receipt of education policies that are extremely instrumental and interrupt their own agency as heads. Certainly in their present form, the NPQH and the national standards are not in tune with this technology of leadership, despite the emphasis on charisma and the cult of the personality. Alongside all this, heads have to perform as well, with their performance contingent on their teachers', pupils' and school's achievements. At root here are contradictory messages of the head's role as both transformational, leading staff through vision and mission; and bureaucratic, ensuring the effective patrolling of the parameters of performance through targets and standards (see Mahony and Hextall, in this volume). Yet, despite the limitations of measuring school performance in this way, those institutions most likely to succeed will be those in possession of policy-enhanced skills or those predisposed to 'playing the standards game'. Performance management, based on such criteria, is likely to have two effects: the first is to reward outcomes that are not grounded in authentic learning or professional practice; and the second is likely to distort values of inclusion, favouring those already endowed with cultural capital.

As yet we know little about how performance management is actually working its way through in schools, though impatience with developmental teacher appraisal in the 1990s is indicative of an endemic short-termism in the politics of education that might enable interruptions to the performance management process. Empirical research shows us that the reform process from the 1980s has simultaneously privileged and deprivileged heads, postholders, teachers, pupils and parents in different ways (Whitty *et al.*, 1998). As the reforms are received and reworked at local level, the agency of those involved is central to how performance management will be structured and experienced. Certainly, while heads have felt increasing personal responsibility for school success (and failure) there is evidence of research that illustrates headteacher capacity to exercise agency and respond in different ways to how policy is developed in schools (Grace, 1995; Hall, 1996; Strachen, 1999; and Tomlinson *et al.*, 1999). In this way headteachers can and do exercise professional courage in their leadership relationships rather than engage in sterile visioning and intimacy-inducing processes. Such courage enables strategic non-compliance to take place in which priorities and decisions are made in accordance with ethical commitments to children and contextual factors around what can and cannot be realistically done. This is not based on provider capture, in which power systems are used to buttress self interest, but is based on knowledge and knowing about teaching and learning.

There is also evidence from Australia of the enduring commitment of teachers to maintain and use their critical capacities (Seddon, 1999) in which pedagogy is connected to broader issues of equity and justice rather than just the technical delivery of an externally required curriculum. Smyth and Shacklock (1998) argue that teachers have still not assimilated performance management because they observe and live within deep contradictions between the rhetoric of 'good practice' and the reality of working with children and the community. Central to this is a recognition that integral to learning is teacher and student leadership where 'what works', and what is relevant, is located in an open discussion about who decides what is relevant and why. The teacher's voice remains problematic here, not least through the cultures and systems that can and do operate in and outside of schools that amplify noise to marginalise rather than legitimate argument. Political literacy has a long legacy in the realities of organisational experiences (Gronn, 1996), and teachers have professional and personal biographies where they have experienced alternative methods of accountability, and have formed their own beliefs and taken action on those beliefs about the purposes of education, and what is right and proper in their work with children. However, teachers have often been caricatured as whingers and whiners who have no understanding of what real work in the 'outside' world is like; consequently they have not been allowed to rise to the challenge of educational reform or provide alterna-tives to the reforms that have taken place. The authentic voice of the teacher and the day-to-day narrative of work and relationships is a potential space in which alternative accountabilities can be lived inclusive of students and the community (Sykes, in this volume).

Learners, and the community in which they live and develop, are also implicated and integrated into the performance management processes, either as recipients of an inappropriate curriculum delivered by teachers who do not have a stake in it, or by being actively integrated into the data delivery and measurement systems. As Fielding argues:

> Work within the field is now beginning to encounter students expressing doubts about the genuineness of their school's interest in their progress and well-being as persons, as distinct from their contributions to their school's league table position. The overriding instrumentality of conversations makes listening difficult: attentiveness is overdirected; clues for meaning are trodden underfoot in the scramble for performance; dialogue disappears as reciprocity retreats under the sheer weight of external expectation; contract replaces community as the bond of human association.
>
> (Fielding, 1999 p.286)

Again student voice is problematic as it has been associated with progressive teaching styles and views of children who should be in receipt of rather than involved in the production of knowledge. Asking students their views on a subject or the school may have become increasingly fashionable but it is based on conceptualising the pupil as consumer rather than learner. However, recent research indicates both the existence and value of the pupil voice in developing the conditions for learning rather than the technocratic cause-and-effect assumptions about learning often embedded in government prescriptions (Rudduck *et al.*, 1996).

Site-based management was sold in the 1980s to educational professionals and communities on the basis that it would enhance a more democratic and market-sensitive approach to problem identification and resolution. What remains problematic for current macro-policymakers is that this approach has not been quietly forgotten by everyone interested in securing a vibrant and authentic micro-policy context. The opportunity exists through devolved education policies to revitalise community located approaches, such as the 'Learning in Cities' initiative, which is being seized and acted upon to bring about change 'on the ground'. It is, therefore, puzzling that a government which so clearly wishes to improve education by such means and so frequently proclaims itself to be listening, so often fails to hear the voices which caution against the blanket imposition of tests, standards and performance. Recent research evidence indicates that learning and achievement is contextual and requires altogether different forms of trust, flexibility and 'agreement making' than current forms of universal policy prescription allow (Nixon and Ranson, 1997; Lave and

Wenger, 1991). Endless DfEE leafleting of guidelines to schools on the latest moral panic connected to sex, drug and citizenship education, reveals how out of touch government is regarding the timing and context in which schools might respond. How to ensure that policy gives recognition to difference rather than 'other' – to those who do not neatly fit the smooth processes of nationally defined criteria – is a significant challenge to how we interpret debates about performance, values and democracy in education. This is an issue troubling educationalists around the world as to whether universal standards or prescriptions possess a validity or integrity outside the context of the communities they are aimed at or struggled over. One way of looking at this is to see knowledge in the curriculum as constructed through a 'politics of representation', in which questions about 'whose representations prevail . . . who has the authority to represent reality or, "who must be silenced" in order that these representations prevail?' (Yeatman, 1990 p.31), need be asked. In addressing this neglected issue of power, we have sought to examine where the authentic voice of the teacher fits in here, in terms of a creative and more critical form of professionality. This, as we have argued, involves seeing pedagogy as being located in a local polity, in which difference is not articulated through niche marketing, performance or self-interest, but in the context where learning and achievement take place at school, work and community levels. From this perspective 'what works' in education cannot constitute neat franchised packages or slots into which teachers and learners must fit. Instead, what is called for is a more contextual and critcally engaged pedagogic process that reflects the real rather than the fabricated contexts in which cultural and transformative learning takes place (Lave and Wenger, 1991).

Reaching conclusions

So far our purpose in framing the argument in this way is to illustrate two related points. The first is that the preoccupation with performance obscures a discourse of power, masking deeper issues of regulation and control of teachers and learners. If on the surface rationalist concerns with data, performance, inspection, competition and comparison are designed to improve efficiency, productivity and learning, they also reveal a less obvious purpose in steering market exchange relationships (commodification), characterising the position of teachers and learners in society. The politics of managerialism in driving up achievement, through linking pay, performance and standards, has severely limited debate about teacher development to one of professionalism rather than professionality. Elsewhere, Hoyle (1975) refers to the former as concerned with pay, conditions, status and contracts, and the latter with the meaning of being a teacher in the personal and professional sense within the broader context of community and society.

For the past thirty years government and teachers have been locked into short-term battles over the former in terms of system maintenance and survival in the face of an unrelenting flow of initiatives and reforms. This has often led to defensive positions being adopted by teacher unions which successive governments have exploited. In the 'discourse of derision' (Ball, 1990) that has since followed parents, pupils, community and employers have become weary of the impasse that has come to characterise national education debate. If the commodification of education through policy, bringing with it a new language and hard-nosed business principles, seemed a good idea at the time, it has since floundered under the weight of managerialism and proceduralism. The weakness of the performance model, whilst strong on reducing conflict, argument and debate, has the effect of limiting professional judgement, intensifying teacher labour and reducing the attractiveness of teaching as a creative profession. In the end, improving education through organisational and employee targets and standards has proved a cheaper though not a more effective option than investing in teachers' professional development or in the active participation of the community in the construction of those standards and targets.

Achieving balance between the legitimate aspirations of the teaching profession whilst, at the same time, ensuring that its professional expertise is trusted and democratically engaged in improving education for all, is long overdue (Whitty, in this volume). The state, as both provider and regulator of education, may have won strategic control over teacher performance, but is finding it managerially difficult to deliver the changes it seeks to promote. This is partly explained by a lack of partnership between government, profession, and community, in constructing standards and targets in the first place. It is also partly explained because teaching, learning and society have developed in complexity since the statutory procedures were introduced. Our argument, in conclusion, is that the introduction of performance management and performance-related pay provides only a restricted vision of education improvement with only limited possibilities of actively involving teachers, pupils and community who have been excluded from the policy process. Wider evidence regarding the influence of performance-related pay in the public sector in the UK and abroad would seem to confirm this (Smyth and Shacklock, 1996). Instead, what is required now is a process of building policy and professional practice from below, rather than reaching down from above, without recourse to managerialism or over-specialisation. This involves breaking the current hold of synthetic discourses in which the authentic voices of teachers are heard alongside those of community and society, as a means of improving the quality of teaching and learning beyond the low trust models of performance which currently prevail

References

Ball, S. J. (1990a), *Politics and Policymaking in Education: explorations in policy sociology*, London: Routledge.

Barber, M., Evans, A. and Johnson, M. (1995), *An Evaluation of the National Scheme of School Teacher Appraisal*, London: HMSO.

Barber, M. and Sebba, J. (1999), 'Reflections on Progress towards a World Class Education System', in *Cambridge Journal of Education*, Vol. 29, No. 2, pp.183–93.

Blackmore, J. (1999), *Troubling Women: Feminism, Leadership and Educational Change*, Buckingham: Open University Press.

Blair, T. (1999), *Speech to the London Conference for new Headteachers*, London: DfEE.

Burrell, G. (1992), 'The Organisation of Pleasure', in M. Alvesson and H. Willmott (eds), *Critical Management Studies*, London: Sage.

Cutler, T. and Waine, B. (2000), 'Mutual Benefits or Managerial Control? The Role of Appraisal in Performance Related Pay for Teachers', in *British Journal of Educational Studies*, Vol. 48, No. 2, pp.170–82.

DES (1991a), *The Education (School Teacher Appraisal) Regulations 1991*, London: HMSO.

DES (1991b), *Circular 12/91 School Teacher Appraisal*, London: HMSO.

DfEE (1995), Squire, R., 'Appraisal – A vital tool in the drive to Raise Standards', in *DfEE News*, 22/95.

DfEE (1998), *Teachers: Meeting the challenge of change*, London: DfEE.

Dunleavy, P. and Hood, C. (1994), 'From old public administration to new public management', in *Public Money and Management*, July–September, pp.9–16.

Esland, G. (1996), 'Knowledge and Nationhood: The new right, Education and the global market', in J. Avis, M. Bloomer, G. Esland, D. Gleeson and P. Hodkinson (eds), *Knowledge and Nationhood*, London: Cassell.

Exworthy, M. and Halford, S. (1999), *Professionalism and the New Managerialism in the Public Sector*, Buckingham: Open University Press.

Farnham, D. and Horton, S. (eds), (1992), *Managing the New Public Services*, Basingstoke: Macmillan Press.

Fielding, M. (1999), 'Target setting, Policy Pathology and Student Perspectives: Learning to labour in new times', in *Cambridge Journal of Education*, Vol. 29, No. 2, pp.277–87.

Gerwitz, S., Ball, S. J. and Bowe, R. (1995), *Markets, choice and equity in education*, Buckingham: Open University Press.

Gleeson, D. and Shain, F. (1999), 'Managing Ambiguity: Between Markets and Managerialism. A case study of middle managers in FE', in *The Sociological Review*, Vol. 47, No. 3, pp.461–90.

Grace, G. (1995), *School Leadership: Beyond Education Management. An essay in Policy Scholarship*, London: Falmer Press.

Gronn, P. (1996), 'From Transactions to Transformations', in *Educational Management and Administration*, Vol. 24, pp.7–30.

Gunter, H. (1999), 'Contracting Headteachers as leaders: An analysis of the NPQH', in *Cambridge Journal of Education*, Vol. 29, No. 2, pp.249–62.

Hall, V. (1996), *Dancing on the Ceiling*, London: Paul Chapman.

Hartley, D. (1999), 'Marketing and the Re-enchantment of School Management', in *British Journal of Sociology*, Vol. 20, No. 3, pp.309–23.

Hoyle, E. (1975), 'Professionality, Professionalism and Control in Teaching', in V. Houghton, R. McHugh and C. Morgan (eds), *Management in Education: The Management of Organisation and Individuals*, London: Ward Lock.

Hoyle, E. (1982), 'Micropolitics of Educational Organisations', in *Educational Management and Administration*, Vol. 10, pp.87–98.

Hoyle, E. (1999), 'The Two Faces of Micropolitics', in *School Leadership and Management*, Vol. 19, No. 2, pp.213–22.

Kenway, J. (ed.) (1994), *Economising Education: The Post-Fordist Directions*, Deakin University: Deakin University Press.

Lave, J. and Wenger, E. (1991), *Situated Learning*, Cambridge: Cambrige University Press.

Marsden, D. (2000), 'Preparing to Perform', in *Centre Piece*, Vol. 5, Issue 2, Centre for Economic Performance, LSE: London.

Morris, E. (1998), *Speech to the Seventh British Apparisal Conference 26th January, Appraisal, Effective Teachers, Effective School*, London: DfEE.

Nixon, J. and Ranson, S. (1997), 'Theorising Agreement: the moral basis of the emergent professionalism within the new management of education', in *Discourse: Studies in the Cultural Politics of Education*, Vol. 18, No. 2, August.

OfSTED (1996), *The Appraisal of Teachers 1991–1996*, London: OfSTED.

Pollitt, C. (1993), *Managerialism and the Public Services*, Oxford: Basil Blackwell.

Ranson, S. (2000), 'Recognising the Pedagogy of Voice in a Learning Community', in *Educational Management and Administration*, Vol. 28, No. 3, pp.263–79.

Rudduck, J., Chaplain, R. and Wallace, G. (1996a), *School Improvement, What can pupils tell us?*, London: David Fulton Publishers.

Seddon, T. (1999), 'On the Politics of Change: failed alternatives or creeping alternative counter-practices', in *Education and Social Justice*, Vol. 1, No. 3, pp.32–7.

Smyth, J. and Shacklock, G. (1998), *Re-making Teaching: Ideology, Policy and Practice*, London: Routledge.

Strachen, J. (1999), 'Feminist educational leadership in a New Zealand neo-liberal context', in *Journal of Educational Administration*, Vol. 37, No. 2, pp.121–38.

Tomlinson, H., Gunter, H. and Smith, P. (1999), *Living Headship: voices, values and vision*, London: Paul Chapman.

Tooley, J. (1999), *Reclaiming Education*, London: Cassell.

TTA/OfSTED (1996), *Review of Headteacher and Teacher Appraisal: Summary of Evidence*, London: TTA/OfSTED.

White, M. (1999), 'Whitehall Welfare Analysis', *The Guardian*, 12 August 1999.

Whitty, G., Power, S. and Halpin, D. (1998), *Devolution and Choice in Education*, Buckingham: Open University Press.

Yeatman, A. (1994), *Postmodern Revisionings of the Political*, London: Routledge.

Yeatman, A. (1997), 'Contract, Status and Personhood', in G. David, B. Sullivan and A. Yeatman (eds), *The new Contractualism?*, Melbourne: Macmillan Education Australia.

10 Teacher professionalism in new times[1]

Geoff Whitty

This chapter explores how far sociological discourse about professionalism and the state can help us to understand the contemporary condition of teachers as professionals. It then seeks to relate some of the concepts drawn from this discussion to some more specific developments in teacher education in England and Wales over the past decade. Finally, it speculates about the forms of teacher professionalism that might develop as we move into the twenty-first century.

Sociological perspectives on professionalism

Sociologists in the 1950s and 1960s tried to establish what features an occupation should have in order to be termed a profession. Lists were compiled of the characteristics that any group worthy of the label 'professionals' needed to have. A typical list included such items as the use of skills based on theoretical knowledge, education and training in those skills certified by examination, a code of professional conduct oriented towards the 'public good' and a powerful professional organisation (Millerson, 1964). Occupations that did not entirely meet such criteria – and these usually included teaching – were given the title 'quasi-' or 'semi-professions' (Etzioni, 1969). The attempt to gain the characteristics associated with professions was usually called professionalisation – an occupational strategy sometimes termed the 'professional project'. Some aspects of the teachers' professional project have been apparently successful, others less so. Some would say that, for schoolteachers, the arrival of the General Teaching Council (GTC) marks the turning point and that, after a century of striving, teaching in England is on the brink of becoming a bona fide profession.

However, in commonsense terms, we have talked about the teaching profession for a long time. We have not tended to say that teachers in Scotland are professional and those in England are not. And contemporary sociologists have tended to agree, arguing that their forebears were seduced by the models of medicine and the law and have therefore imposed a normative view of what it means to be a professional as *the* essential definition of a profession. Instead, they suggest that a profession is whatever people think it is at any particular time and that can vary. So the fact that we normally talk about the teaching profession means that teaching is a profession, even when we cannot tick off every one of these core characteristics listed earlier.

Gerard Hanlon, whose ideas I shall return to later, argues that 'professionalism is a shifting rather than a concrete phenomenon' and states baldly that 'when I discuss professionals I am talking about groups such as doctors, academics, teachers, accountants, lawyers, engineers, civil servants, etc. that is those groups commonly thought of as professional by the lay public, academics, the professionals themselves and so on' (Hanlon, 1998 p.45). It may then be more productive to explore the characteristic of teaching as an occupation in the here and now, rather than asking whether it lives up to some supposed ideal. Indeed, Eliot Freidson (1983 p.33), probably the dominant American sociologist of professions in recent years, argues for seeing a profession as 'an empirical entity about which there is little ground for generalising'.

This has implications for current debates about teacher professionalism in the twenty-first century. Some critics have argued that teaching is being de-professionalised – as a result of recent education reforms. But the proponents of the reforms might wish to characterise the process as one of *re*-professionalisation – making teacher professionalism more in keeping with the needs of a new era. However, if we are standing back from our own assumptions and preferences, and adopting the stance of sociologist, it is probably best to see all these various positions as *competing* versions of teacher professionalism for the twenty-first century, rather than seeing any one as fitting an essentialist definition of professionalism and others as detracting from it. The particular version different people support in practice will, of course, depend on their values and their broader political perspectives, as well as the way in which they are positioned by the reforms.

So where does the state come into this? Professional status can also depend on the sort of bargain an occupation has struck with the state – what is sometimes called its 'professional mandate'. Traditionally professions were independent and self-governing, and individual professionals have often been self-employed. But in industrial societies today, most professionals are directly employed and/or regulated by the state. As Dale (1989) puts it, some professions have a licensed form of autonomy, others a regulated autonomy. Medicine and law, and arguably even nursing, have to some extent been licensed to manage their own affairs.

The teaching profession in England has hitherto not been formally licensed in this way, but in the 1960s teachers were seen to have a considerable degree of *de facto* autonomy. Indeed, Le Grand (1997) suggests that in England, during the so-called 'golden age of teacher control' from 1944 to the mid-1970s, parents of children in state schools were expected to trust the professionals and accept that teachers knew what was best for their children. The state did not seem to want to intervene, even though effectively it paid teachers' salaries.

However, a view emerged in the 1970s that teachers had abused this licensed autonomy to the detriment of their pupils and society. Public choice theorists argued that the behaviour of public servants and professionals could actually be better understood if they were assumed to be largely self-interested. Many professional groups and particularly the liberal educational establishment of the swollen state of post-war social democracy came to be regarded as ill-adapted to be either agents of the state or entrepreneurial service providers in a marketised civil society. All this supported the shift to regulated autonomy, involving a move away from the notion that the teaching profession should have a professional mandate to act on behalf of the state in the best interests of its citizens to a view that teaching (and other professions) needws to be subjected to the rigours of the market and/or greater control and surveillance on the part of the re-formed state. So, in the 1970s, we had the William Tyndale Inquiry, Jim Callaghan's Ruskin College speech, the so-called Great Debate and, in the 1980s and 1990s, Sir Keith Joseph, Kenneth Baker, John Patten and Gillian Shephard.

Now we have David Blunkett and we have something of a paradox. At one level we have even more regulation of teachers than under Conservative governments. Yet, at the same time, with the GTC, we appear to have a shift back to licensed autonomy, but on a more formal basis than ever before. Or do we? We do not yet know quite what the GTC will turn out to be and, not surprisingly, most teachers probably think it has some positive and some negative features. What does seem clear is that even licensed autonomy is not what it used to be, as even the doctors (if not yet the lawyers) are finding out. This applies both to individual professionals and to the organised profession. Effectively, the state's modality of control has been changing, so that it can be strong even while appearing to devolve power.

Particularly helpful in understanding this is Neave's concept of the 'evaluative state', where what matters most is not the process by which goals or targets are achieved, but the output. In the education system, as elsewhere, there has been 'a rationalisation and wholesale redistribution of functions between centre and periphery such that the centre maintains overall strategic control through fewer, but more precise, policy levers [including] the operationalisation of criteria relating to "output quality"' (Neave, 1988 p.11). Rather than leading to a withering away of the state, the state withdraws 'from the murky plain of overwhelming detail, the better to take refuge in the clear and commanding heights of strategic "profiling"' (Neave, 1998 p.12).

For teachers, this involves much clearer specification of what they are expected to achieve rather than leaving it to professional judgement. But it is not entirely true that, as Neave implies, the state thereby abandons any interest in how they achieve these things. The specification of outputs itself shapes what teachers actually do, so the state uses its levers to influence what we might call the content of teachers' 'professionalism' – or what is sometimes called teachers' professionality. In the days when they had to study such things as sociology of education, generations of trainee teachers used to struggle with the distinction between professionalism and professionality, introduced into the British literature by Eric Hoyle (1974). Hoyle used the term 'professionalism' to refer to 'those strategies and rhetorics employed by members of an occupation in seeking to improve status, salary and conditions'. But he used the term 'professionality' to refer to the 'knowledge, skills and procedures employed by teachers in the process of teaching'. There are now not only struggles over professionalism in the conventional sense, but also struggles over professionality. And the state has taken a proactive part in this, both positively (in the sense of what it should consist of) and negatively (in terms of what should be discouraged if not outlawed).

What does the struggle between the teaching profession (or at least the so-called liberal educational establishment) and the state over the nature of teachers' professionality involve? Partly, it is a struggle between 'restricted' and 'extended' professionality, another distinction that Hoyle (1974) established in the literature – though what might be included under each category has probably changed somewhat since 1974. Andy Hargreaves (1994 p.19) suggests that the conventional notion of professionalism is one 'which is grounded in notions of esoteric knowledge, specialist expertise and public status': and that this is being superseded by one which involves 'the exercise of discretionary judgement within conditions of unavoidable and perpetual uncertainty'. Michael Eraut (1994) similarly emphasises a whole range of 'process knowledge' that involves making judgements as the hallmark of the modern-day professional. Yet some people argue that current moves towards competence or standards-based training for teachers, as sponsored by the government and the Teacher Training Agency (TTA), point in entirely the opposite direction by actually reducing the amount of control and discretion open to teachers, both individually and collectively. Jones and Moore (1993) have argued that such developments serve to undermine the dominant discourse of liberal humanism within the teaching profession and replace it with one of technical rationality, while Adams and Tulasiewicz (1995) have complained that teachers are being turned into technicians rather than reflective professionals.

One way of understanding this apparent contradiction might be to see it as part of the inevitable heterodoxy of postmodernity, though I have counselled elsewhere against exaggerating the extent to which we have moved decisively into such a condition (Whitty and Power, 1999). Perhaps the two approaches reflect the juxtaposition of what Ronald Barnett calls 'two grand readings of our modern age'. On the one hand, there is 'a proliferation of forms of knowledge and experience'; on the other a 'tendency . . . to favour forms of knowledge of a particular – instrumental and operational – kind' (Barnett, 1994 p.17). Barnett himself has suggested that operationalism is a 'super-dominant tendency in higher education, which is reflective of . . . wider social forces' (Barnett, 1994 p.18).

It is also possible that different elements of the profession are developing different forms of professionalism and professionality. Indeed, the state may even be encouraging this, with some members of the profession being given more autonomy and scope for flexibility than others, but only once they have met what might be termed a 'loyalty test'. Hanlon (1998) suggests that virtually all professions are becoming fragmented, with some members enthusiastically adopting the changing agenda of the state and corporate employers while others are resisting it. He argues that, in the period up to about 1980, most professions (and particularly those serving the welfare state in the post-war period) developed a 'social service' form of professionalism in which professional experts were trusted to work in the best interests of everyone and the resources were made available by the state to help them do so. He shows how this is being challenged by what he calls a 'commercialised professionalism' in the public as well as the private sector, which responds more to the needs of profitability and international competitiveness and therefore privileges the needs of some clients over others. Similar developments have been evident within education as a result of policies of marketisation (Whitty *et al.*, 1998). Gewirtz, Ball and Bowe (1995) identify two traditions on the part of education managers, which they term 'bureau–professional' (or welfarist) and 'new managerialist'. The latter relates to the new public management emphasis on such things as explicit standards/measures of performance, greater emphasis on output controls, the breakup of large entities into smaller units, market-type mechanisms, the introduction of competition and a stress on a professionalised commercial-style management (Bottery, 1996).

This shift of emphasis has led to changes in the nature and extent of the trust that is put in professionals in the public sector on the part of the state and, to some extent, the public. Those who are prepared to manage on behalf of their employers may gain enhanced status and rewards, but those pursuing the welfarist agenda are no longer trusted and have to be controlled more directly. Hanlon suggests that the clash between the two traditions will ultimately lead to a split in the professional ranks. Within teaching, there is still a struggle for hegemony in a potentially united profession, but also signs of possible fracturing along various fault lines.

The state is unlikely to be neutral even if the battles are actually fought out in the professional arena, although there are different elements even within the state and probably different views within the government itself. One reading of the dominant tendency is that it is preparing the leading cadres of the profession for leadership in the new marketised culture of schooling, while others have to be prevented from perpetuating an outmoded social service version of professionalism even if they cannot be won to the new agenda. In these circumstances, one would expect that new teachers would be given a rather restricted version of professionalism or professionality, but also opportunities to demonstrate their potential to join the leading cadres. Those continuing teachers who, through lack of competence or will, did not pass through the performance pay threshold would be limited to a restricted and highly regulated mode of professionalism. Those who did progress satisfactorily might be given licensed autonomy and more discretion in defining the nature of their professionality.

In current policies one can see vestiges of virtually all the developments I have referred to here, but it is not yet clear how they will play out in the coming years.

Modes of professionalism in teacher education

So, if these are some of the things that sociologists of the professions and of teaching say that might be relevant to what is happening to the teaching profession, what does empirical research tell us? Although I focus here on my own area of research on initial teacher education, similar questions could usefully be asked about INSET and training for headship. I draw particularly on the Modes of Teacher Education (or MOTE) research (Furlong *et al.*, 2000).[2] This entailed national surveys of all courses conducted in 1990–1991 and 1995–1996 and more detailed fieldwork with fifty courses. The research was undertaken against a background of rapidly changing policy from Circulars 24/89, 9/92, 14/93 onwards. Since its completion in 1996, the pace of reform has not slackened, with ever more demanding forms of inspection, a national curriculum for teacher training and league tables.

The vast majority of these policy initiatives on initial teacher education were framed with the explicit or implicit aspiration of changing the nature of teacher professionalism, even though this had at times to be pursued alongside two other policy concerns that were also significant in influencing the policies actually produced – namely, the imperative of maintaining an adequate supply of well qualified entrants to the teaching profession; and the aspiration on the part of successive Secretaries of State for Education to establish greater accountability for the content and quality of initial teacher education.

Recent governments of both political hues seem to have been convinced by New Right pressure groups that teacher educators are at the heart of a liberal educational establishment, which is wedded to outdated modes of professionalism and professionality. The preferred strategy of the neo-liberal marketisers has been deregulation of the profession to allow schools to go into the market and recruit graduates (or even non-graduates) without professional training and prepare them on an apprenticeship basis in schools (Lawlor, 1990). Deregulation also had some appeal to neo-conservative critics who detected a collectivist (and even crypto-Marxist) ideological bias among teacher educators in higher education. Thus, for example, an editorial in the *Spectator* argued that the removal of 'the statutory bar on state schools hiring those with no teacher training quali-fication . . . would enable head teachers to find people . . . who at the moment are deterred by the prospect of having to waste a year undergoing a period of Marxist indoctrination' (*Spectator*, 27 February 1993). How-ever, neo-conservatives have also been concerned with 'enemies within' the teaching profession as a whole as well as within teacher education, so they have usually supported state prescription of what trainee teachers should learn rather than just leaving it to schools.

Both the neo-liberal and the neo-conservative elements of the New Right seem to have had their influence but government policies have always been something of a compromise between them, as well as with other relevant (and sometimes irrelevant) interest groups. The Conserva-tive government's introduction of new routes into teaching and the strategy of locating more and more elements of training in schools was partly (though not wholly) a reflection of neo-liberal views. However, the government did not pursue a policy of total deregulation or a wholesale devolution of teacher training to the schools, despite significant moves in that direction. Instead, a combination of neo-conservative concerns and a modernising push for greater international competitiveness (Hickox, 1995) brought about an attempt to shape the content of teachers' professional knowledge through the introduction of a common list of competences or standards to be required of beginning teachers, regardless of the nature of the route by which they had achieved them.

These moves gave rise to charges that the government wanted to deprofessionalise teaching. Thus, for example, Stuart Maclure (1993) suggested that the downgrading of university involvement in teacher education represented an attempt to dismantle the traditional defences of teaching as a profession. Other commentators felt that basing training in particular schools could limit the development of broader perspectives on education, and that specifying a limited range of competences would encourage restricted rather than extended professionality. More charitable observers, though, argued that the government was trying to reform teacher education in order to re-professionalise teaching more in line with what it perceived as the needs of the twenty-first century. Indeed, some – including David Hargreaves (1994) from within the teacher education establishment – regarded school-based training as signifying that the profession of school teaching had come of age and was able to take responsibility for training its own. This view was shared by some of those enthusiasts within teaching who organised school-centred initial teacher training (SCITT) schemes (Berrill, 1994).

One of the reasons why it is possible to regard the reforms in these different lights is that they appear to embody different, even contradictory, elements. Just as in education reform more generally, there seems to have been a dual strategy of devolving some responsibilities to schools while at the same time requiring more things from the centre. To some degree, schools and teachers appeared to have been empowered to develop their own local professionalisms. On the other hand, centrally specified competences and standards mean that local professional freedom is actually quite tightly constrained by the demands of the evaluative state. Obviously, the work of the TTA established in 1994 has been particularly significant here (Mahony and Hextall, 1996). Under the leadership of its first chief executive, Anthea Millett, the TTA has assisted the government in the development and codification of the earlier lists of competences into a detailed set of 'standards' for the award of Qualified Teacher Status (QTS), creating a national curriculum for initial teacher education, policed by OfSTED inspection. Although these proposals originated in the last years of the Major government, they were accepted and extended by the new Labour government elected in May 1997.

To some extent, such agencies of the evaluative state represent a shift away from conventional techniques of coordination and control on the part of large-scale bureaucratic state forms and their replacement by a set of 'discursive, legislative, fiscal, organisational and other resources' (Rose and Miller, 1992 p.189). Yet, these apparently postmodern forms not only impact upon organisational subjectivities and professional identities, they also entail some fairly direct modes of control. Furthermore, particularly under New Labour, some TTA and OfSTED activity is reminiscent of the old-style bureaucratic state, rather than the steering-at-a-distance associated with the evaluative state. Indeed, some of the TTA's key functions have now been taken back under the direct control of the DfEE, though others may be devolved to the GTC in the future.

One of the problems of much of the writing about New Right ideology and state projects is that it tends to be based purely on reading the discourse rather than studying the effects and resistances that constitute ideology-in-practice. So, in the MOTE research, we were interested in the extent to which the reforms in initial teacher education were actually bringing about changes in the prevailing view of what it meant to be a professional teacher. Landman and Ozga have suggested that, although successive government circulars have shifted power from higher education institutions to central government and its associated agencies, teacher education has remained open to 'producer capture'. They also argue that, even though there has been a shift from 'open-ended requirements . . . to the rather more technical competences' (Landman and Ozga, 1995 p.32), there has remained 'room for constructive interpretation' (Landman and Ozga, 1995 p.35).

The MOTE findings provide some support for this position. We looked at the extent to which the professional autonomy of teacher educators in both higher education institutions and schools was constrained by the reforms, and the extent to which the government's requirements were serving to reshape the professionality of trainee teachers. Both our national surveys asked course leaders of undergraduate and postgraduate courses whether their courses were designed on the basis of a particular view of teaching. By the time of our second survey, we were particularly interested in the extent to which the existence of an official list of competences, which has often been criticised for embodying technical rationality and neglecting more reflective and critical competences, was actually changing the model of the teacher espoused by teacher educators. In 1995–1996, we found that 46 per cent of courses adhered to the notion of the reflective practitioner compared with 57 per cent at the time of the previous survey in 1990–1991. Meanwhile, those specifically espousing the competency model had doubled, but only to 11 per cent. Thus, even if it was somewhat less dominant than it had been five years previously, reflective practice, rather than technical rationality, was still by far the most popular discourse of professionalism within university- and college-based (and indeed school-centred) courses.

Another question on our second national survey asked respondents to choose three words from a list which would best characterise the sort of teacher their course aimed to produce. Despite some resistance to this question, the responses beyond 'reflective', 'professional' and 'competent', were quite varied. However, it is noteworthy that some of the terms that New Right critics often associate with HEI-based teacher training – such as 'child-centred' and 'critical' – were amongst the least popular choices. Unfortunately, we did not have a similar question on the earlier survey to compare this with. So the answers could either suggest that such aspirations were never as strong as critics suggested, or a recent drift towards the more conservative interpretations of reflective practice (Zeichner and Liston, 1987) or merely a degree of politically-inspired caution in responding to the question!

Despite the continuing adherence to reflective practice, the actual use of competences in course planning, implementation and assessment increased significantly between our two surveys, well beyond the 11 per cent of courses that explicitly espoused a competency model. So how can the use of competences be reconciled with the continuing attachment to the reflective-practitioner model? Our second survey showed that only about 8 per cent of courses restricted themselves to using the competences specified in the government circulars, while over 75 per cent had chosen to supplement the official lists with additional competences of their own. This was consistent with our fieldwork which indicated that there was little continuing objection to the idea of competences among course leaders, but only because they felt that reflective competences could be added to the official list in order to sustain a broader definition of professionality. So course leaders appeared to be able to defend extended notions of teacher professionality while still conforming to government policy.

However, Landman and Ozga (1995) suggest that 'teacher education and training is vulnerable to the combined effects of financial stringency, devolution of budgetary control to individual schools and enhanced managerialism'. Indeed, they suspect that these might succeed where prescription by circular has failed. The MOTE research suggests that, although both forms of control have certainly been in evidence, definitions of professionality more rooted in the traditions of the profession have survived alongside the newer requirements, albeit within limits largely determined by the state.

Towards a democratic professionalism?

Up to this point, I have tried to stand back and examine current developments in teaching and teacher education with the eye of a sociologist. In this final section of the chapter, while still drawing upon sociological insights, I venture some opinions about what might be desirable directions for teacher professionalism and professionality in the new millennium.

As far as initial teacher education is concerned, the combination of school-based training and officially specified standards seems likely to confine the common elements of teacher professionalism increasingly to an officially prescribed national curriculum for teacher education, with a variety of 'local' professionalisms at the margins. At more advanced levels, the profession as a whole may well become more differentiated and stratified. Although such developments might be characterised as having a certain postmodern cachet, it seems to me that a healthy teaching profession will require continuing efforts to maintain a more broadly-defined sense of common professional identity. Perhaps the GTC will be able to deliver that, though not if it merely tries to defend conventional definitions of teacher professionalism. Nor, I would argue, if it merely seeks to mimic the older professionalisms of law and medicine. But any attempt to develop an alternative conception of teacher professionalism will surely require the mobilisation of broadly-based political support and not just professional partnership.

This is because, in recent years, governments and the media have encouraged the development of a 'low-trust' relationship between society and its teachers, while the constant attacks on teacher educators show no sign of abating. In this context, we have to take seriously some of the charges of our critics who argue that we teachers have abused our professional mandate and pursued our own self-interest at the expense of those less powerful than ourselves – and, in so doing, sometimes inadvertently contributed to social exclusion. Furthermore, the profession itself has not always moved to enhance its wider legitimacy. The defence of the education service has too often been conducted within the assumptions of the old politics of education, which involved consultation between government, employers and unions but excluded whole constituencies – notably parents and business – to whom the New Right subsequently successfully appealed (Apple, 1996). We need to ask some fundamental questions about who has a legitimate right to be involved in defining teacher professionalism and to what end.

Conservative governments have tended to see the solution to the problem of 'producer capture' as lying in a combination of state control and market forces. New Labour has increased state regulation, while seeking to 'modernise' the profession and incorporate it into its own project through a new deal for teachers based on managerialist premises and performance-related pay (DfEE, 1998). At the same time, it has given the teaching profession a GTC, but its long-term role and relationship to the TTA, OfSTED and the DfEE has still to be worked out. My own fear is that battle lines will be drawn up around the GTC between defenders of a traditional professional model and a statist one.

However, are state control and professional self-governance (or some combination of the two) the only modes of accountability open to us? Perhaps it is time instead to rethink the nature of the 'professional project' itself. In Australia, Knight *et al.* (1993) have argued that there has always been a tension between the profession's claim to autonomy and a require-ment that it be open to the needs and concerns of other groups in a demo-cratic society. Thus, like Ginsburg (1997) and Apple (1996), they suggest that there is a considerable tension between the professional project as conventionally conceived and the 'democratic project'. However, they feel that changes in modern societies may now make it possible to resolve that tension and avoid both the teaching profession's and the state's forms of closure. Thus, for them, the alternative to state control is not traditional professionalism, but a 'democratic professionalism', which seeks to de-mystify professional work and build alliances between teachers and excluded constituencies of students, parents and members of the com-munity on whose behalf decisions have traditionally been made either by professions or by the state. Celia Davies (1996 p.673) also identifies new professionalism or a democratic professionalism as relevant to a 'changed policy context and as a solution to some of the problems of professional power long identified in the academic literature'.

So, if altruism and public service remain high on our professional agenda, the next re-formation of teacher professionalism will surely need to be one in which we harness teachers' professional expertise to a new democratic project for the twenty-first century. Foucault pointed out that what he called new forms of association, such as trades unions and political parties, emerged in the nineteenth century as a counterbalance to the prerogative of the state, and that they formed a seedbed for the development of new ideas on governance (Kritzman, 1988). We need to consider what modern versions of these collectivist forms of association might now be developed as a counterbalance not only to the prerogative of the state, but also to the prerogative of the market. In general terms, too little serious thinking of this type has yet been done, notwithstanding Giddens' recent espousal of a 'Third Way' that supersedes both social democracy and neo-liberalism (Giddens, 1998). Perhaps, in relation to democratic decision-making in education, the GTC might take a lead in developing new forms of association that can provide a model for future modes of governance.

Throughout the last twenty years or so, teachers and teacher educators have been understandably preoccupied with issues of short-term survival in the face of an unrelenting flow of new initiatives and inspections. It is now time to begin working with others to develop approaches that relate not only to the legitimate aspirations of the profession but also those of the wider society – and that must include those groups within civil society who have hitherto not been well-served either by the profession or by the state. At a rhetorical level, that does not seem a million miles from the thinking of the present-day unions or even New Labour. But, in the light of recent history, my question would be, is either the state or the professional willing to face up to the challenge?

Notes

1 An earlier version of this paper was presented at the Annual Conference of the Standing Committee for the Education and Training of Teachers on 'Teacher Professionalism and the State in the 21st Century', Dunchurch, Rugby, 26–28 November 1999 and published in the *Journal of In-service Education*, Vol. 26 (2), 2000.
2 'Modes of Teacher Education: Towards a Basis for Comparison' (ESRC Project, No. R000232810) and 'Changing Modes of Professionalism? A Case Study of Teacher Education in Transition' (ESRC Project, No. R000234185). The generic title of MOTE was used informally for both projects.

References

Adams, A. and Tulasiewicz, W. (1995), *The Crisis in Teacher Education: A European Concern?*, London: Falmer Press.

Apple, M. (1996), *Cultural Politics and Education*, New York: Teachers College Press.

Barnett, R. (1994), *The Limits to Competence: Knowledge, Higher Education and Society*, Buckingham: Open University Press.

Berrill, M. (1994), 'A view from the crossroads', in *Cambridge Journal of Education*, Vol. 24 (1), pp.113–16.

Bottery, M. (1996), 'The challenge to professionals from the New Public Management: implications for the teaching profession', in *Oxford Review of Education*, Vol. 22 (2), pp.179–97.

Dale, R. (1989), *The State and Education Policy*, Buckingham: Open University Press.

Davies, C. (1996), 'The sociology of professions and the profession of gender', in *Sociology*, Vol. 30 (4), pp.661–78.

DfEE (1998), *Teachers: Meeting the challenge of change*, London: HMSO.

Eraut, M. (1994), *Developing Professional Knowledge and Competence*, London: Falmer Press.

Etzioni, A. (ed.), (1969), *The Semi-Professions and their Organization*, New York: Free Press.

Freidson, E. (1983), 'The theory of professions: state of the art', in R. Dingwall and P. Lewis (eds), *The Sociology of the Professions*, London: Macmillan.

Furlong, J., Barton, L., Miles, S., Whiting, C. and Whitty, G. (2000), *Teacher Education in Transition: re-forming professionalism?*, Buckingham: Open University Press.

Gewirtz, S., Ball, S. and Bowe, R. (1995), *Markets, Choice and Equity in Education*, Buckingham: Open University Press.

Giddens, A. (1998), *The Third Way: The Renewal of Social Democracy*, Cambridge: Polity Press.

Ginsburg, M. B. (1997), 'Professionalism or politics as a model for educators' engagement with/in communities', in *Journal of Education Policy*, Vol. 12 (1/2), pp.5–12.

Hanlon, G. (1998), 'Professionalism as enterprise: service class politics and the redefinition of professionalism', in *Sociology*, Vol. 32 (1), pp.43–63.

Hargreaves, A. (1994), *Changing Teachers, Changing Times: Teachers' Work and Culture in the Postmodern Age*, London: Cassell.

Hargreaves, D. (1994), 'Another radical approach to the reform of initial teacher training', in *Westminster Studies in Education*, Vol. 13, pp.5–11.

Hickox, M. (1995), 'Situating Vocationalism', in *British Journal of Sociology of Education*, Vol. 16 (2), pp.153–63.

Hoyle, E. (1974), 'Professionality, professionalism and control in teaching', in *London Education Review*, Vol. 3 (2), pp.13–19.

Jones, L. and Moore, R. (1993), 'Education, competence and the control of expertise', in *British Journal of Sociology of Education*, Vol. 14, pp.385–97.

Knight, J., Bartlett, L. and McWilliam, E. (eds), (1993), *Unfinished Business: Reshaping the Teacher Education Industry for the 1990s*, Rockhampton: University of Central Queensland.

Kritzman, L. D. (ed.), (1988), *Foucault: Politics/Philosophy/Culture*, New York: Routledge.

Landman, M. and Ozga, J. (1995), 'Teacher education policy in England', in M. Ginsburg and B. Lindsay (eds), *The Political Dimension in Teacher Education: Comparative Perspectives on Policy Formation, Socialization and Society*, London: Falmer Press.

Lawlor, S. (1990), *Teachers Mistaught: Training in theories or education in subjects?*, London: Centre for Policy Studies.

Le Grand, J. (1997), 'Knights, knaves or pawns: Human behaviour and social policy', in *Journal of Social Policy*, Vol. 26, pp.149–64.

Maclure, S. (1993), 'Fight this tooth and nail', in *Times Educational Supplement*, 18 June 1993.

Mahony, P. and Hextall, I. (1996), 'Trailing the TTA'. Paper delivered at the British Educational Research Association Annual Meeting, University of Lancaster, 12–15 September 1996.

Millerson, G. (1964), *The Qualifying Association*, London: Routledge and Kegan Paul.

Neave, G. (1988), 'On the cultivation of quality, efficiency and enterprise: an overview of recent trends in higher education in Western Europe, 1968–1988', in *European Journal of Education*, Vol. 23 (1/2), pp.7–23.

Rose, N. and Miller P. (1992), 'Political power beyond the State: problematics of government', in *British Journal of Sociology*, Vol. 43 (2), pp.173–205.

Whitty, G. and Power, S. (1999), 'Making sense of education reform: global and national influences', in *International Journal of Contemporary Sociology*, Vol. 36 (2), pp.144–62.

Whitty, G., Power, S. and Halpin, D. (1998), *Devolution and Choice in Education: The School, the State and the Market*, Buckingham: Open University Press.

Zeichner, K. and Liston, D. (1987), 'Teaching student teachers to reflect', in *Harvard Educational Review*, Vol. 57 (1), pp.23–48.

11 Performing and conforming

Pat Mahony and Ian Hextall

The performance management model as envisaged in the Green Paper (DfEE, 1998) is firmly embedded within the managerialist ideology which has come to predominate in education and in other sectors of public provision. In this chapter we shall attempt to clarify the value assumptions which underpin performance management and raise an agenda of emerging concerns including some potential implications for patterns of social justice and differentiation. As has been discovered in other countries which have endeavored to introduce such policies there has been a storm of controversy and opposition. We shall illustrate the contours of this in relation to the reactions of unions, governing bodies and local education authorities.

The Green Paper (DfEE, 1998) establishes a quite explicit marker as to the direction in which the government is travelling in its project to modernise the teaching profession. It looks both backwards to a whole swathe of initiatives begun under previous Conservative administrations, and forwards with the particular orientations of Tony Blair's new Labour government. While some of the parts may be familiar, the overall assemblage constitutes something new for teachers in England though perhaps not for some international colleagues. This raises the question as to whether the movements currently taking place in England are symptomatic of wider, global trends. It is an ongoing question of where, if at all, there may be points of international convergence and the extent to which apparent differences are merely illusory.

The roots of performance management

Whilst this is not the context in which to go into detail over the history of performance management it is important to emphasise that its roots lie deep in the private sector and that it was moved into the public sector as a key element in the movement towards new public management or managerialism of the public services during the 1980s and 1990s. This transformation has by now been extensively covered in the literature (Clarke and Newman, 1997; and Blackmore, 1999). In England we now find that there are performance management systems at work in almost all areas of the public service, for example, health, housing, tax collection, employment services, local authority provision, etc.

Performance management constitutes a key element of a managerially-driven version of human resource management (HRM). One of its strongest legitimating devices lies in the presumption that you can move systems of personnel management across from context to context, and that the basic principles and working assumptions remain the same. It is depicted in a technicist form as a free-floating technology capable of being applied in diverse contexts and where the nature of context-specificity is deemed of less relevance than 'techno-universality'. In this sense it works within a universalistic paradigm which accords well with certain deterministic versions of globalisation. A corollary of this universalistic presupposition is the presumption that problems encountered within performance management are issues of presentation, logistics and technique. We can see this in the response which the Labour government made to the consultation resistance it encountered, when it defined most of the problems as issues to be resolved through further adaptation and negotiation. Managerialist ideologies are fundamentally grounded in the notion that there exist sets of principles and procedures, which can be applied to bring about 'effective, efficient and economic' modes of operation. In devising effective operational procedures, specific contextual circumstances have to be taken into account, but the working presumption is that the general principles are pre-eminent and circumstances subsidiary. This is a highly contentious and value-laden point since to most people on the ground it is precisely *context* which gives meaning and flavour to their actions and lives. We find this referred to again and again in the public policy literature; for example, Rogers (1999), writing as a 'critical friend' of the performance management movement, says:

> While performance management aims to increase the capacity of councillors and managers to determine and manage the performance of their own affairs, it is being applied in an environment where both the definition of performance and the operational processes for achieving that performance are being increasingly determined not just by central government but by wholly or partly autonomous audit and inspection agencies. Rather than encouraging an approach

of self-reliance, responsibility and creativity they are likely to produce a culture of compliance and conformity – with worrying consequences. Performing becomes mere conforming.

(Rogers, 1999 p.24)

As an extension of this within performance management, little recognition is accorded to issues of structure, power and conflict which are ever-present in social contexts such as schools but are rendered invisible in managerialist accounts (Angus, 1994; Hextall and Mahony, 1998).

As a discourse, performance management also has deeply 'totalising' characteristics. For example, workers (teachers in our case) are presented as units of labour to be distributed and managed. The characteristics of these labour units are deemed largely irrelevant providing that they comply with certain specifications and meet particular working criteria. This renders the structural characteristics of groups of teachers (or other workers), such as ethnicity, gender, sexuality, and class, marginal. Thus, for example, the Green Paper makes no mention of gender or ethnicity in its proposals. Rather it speaks the language of 'all' teachers, which, given the maldistribution of equal opportunities available to teachers, renders this apparent language of inclusivity potentially socially excluding.

It is also totalising in its reliance on fundamentally individualistic notions of motivation, achievement, performance and progression.[1] Once again its basic operating unit is that of the individual, ambitious for their future, jealous of their achievements and personally motivated in their orientation to teaching. There have, of course, always been teachers like this. But the performance management model elevates this account of being a teacher above a version which emphasises teamwork, collaborative practice and a communitarian, non-competitive orientation. In doing this it takes it as axiomatic that the individualistic model will prove to be more efficient, effective and economical in relation to its outcomes. As Marsden and French put it:

> None of the critical management changes introduced in the last decade and a half can really be expected to work unless there are corresponding changes in the way public servants approach their work, and think about the use of the resources at their disposal.
>
> (Marsden and French, 1998 p.1)

One of the major teaching unions in its response to the Green Paper was quite clear about the hierarchical and divisive presumptions it sees underpinning the government's proposals:

[Performance management] attracts the Government because the premise of payment and reward for excellence and improvement is predicated on it being discriminatory. By definition, not all will fulfil the predetermined criteria. There will be gateways, hurdles and thresholds. A minority will be paid more – perhaps a great deal more – others, a majority, will not.

(NUT, 1999 para. 59)

Parenthetically, the individualising orientation also drives directly to the heart of collective models of organising and protecting teachers, their rights, conditions of service and rewards. Insofar as unions are left with a role within such a model it is to patrol the boundaries of the system to ensure that the practices are conducted in accordance with the established procedures. They are by default themselves painted into an individualistic rather than collectivist purpose *vis-à-vis* their members.

What is performance management and how is it defined?

Getting a clear definition of performance management can prove elusive. What many people provide is a description of the various elements which go to make up an overall account of the technology involved in operating a performance management model or regime. As Ironside and Seifert say:

> . . . unitarist management . . . treats neither the subject nor the process [of performance management] as problematic. All that is left, perhaps, therefore is to describe the functions and activities and skills and then provide some anecdotal examples.
>
> (Ironside and Seifert, 1995 pp.137–8)

Helen Murlis reveals some of the major elements which ground performance management clearly within its human resource management home:

> One of the major lessons emerging . . . is the need for effective performance management to underpin the pay system. A good working definition of performance management is that it is 'the process which links people and jobs to the strategy and objectives of the organisation'. Good performance management is about operating a process that increases the likelihood of achieving performance improvements. Current thinking in this area indicates that management needs to be practised by the integrated operation of four processes . . . planning

for performance, managing performance, appraising performance and rewarding performance.

(Murlis, 1992 p.65)

Armstrong and Baron cite the Institute of Personnel Management (IPM) as having produced the following definition of performance management as a result of a major research project in 1992:

A strategy, which relates to every activity of the organisation, set in the context of its human resources policies, culture, and style and communications systems. The nature of the strategy depends on the organisational context and can vary from organisation to organisation.

(Armstrong and Baron, 1998 p.44)

They go on to say:

It was suggested that what was described as a 'performance management system' complied with the textbook definition when the following characteristics were met by the organisation:
- it communicates a vision of its objectives to all its employees
- it sets departmental and individual performance targets that are related to wider objectives
- it conducts a formal review of progress towards these targets
- it uses the review process to identify training, development and reward outcomes
- it evaluates the whole process in order to improve effectiveness.

In addition, 'performance management organisations';
- express performance targets in terms of measurable outputs, accountabilities and training/learning targets
- use formal appraisal procedures as ways of communicating performance requirements that are set on a regular basis
- link performance requirements to pay, especially for senior managers.

(Armstrong and Baron, 1998 pp.44–5)

Addressing the same issue of definition, Ironside and Seifert once again bring a markedly more critical orientation to their interpretation of the management of human resources. As they say:

One general view of the emergence of HRM as an important part of the management of British enterprises in the 1990s suggests that it, in all its forms, simply represents a modern version of managing resources in a recession. . . . The dominant slogan for managers in the private sector is 'more for less', that is productivity and/or efficiency gains at all costs. If this is the case, in crude terms, then an important issue for the management of recession in public services becomes the implementation of the necessary changes with the minimum of opposition. The main features of the changes based on this model include work intensification, deskilling and lower unit labour costs through reductions in staffing levels and/or lower relative rates of total remuneration. One possible way to minimise opposition to these changes is to try to convince staff of the benefit and/or inevitability of the changes, and this is achieved through isolating staff as individuals and seeking to convince them of the correctness of this new model management.

(Ironside and Seifert, 1995 p.136)

What becomes apparent from such a reading of the theory and practice of performance management is that it has implications at a number of different levels: the personal; the institutional; the systemic; and the societal. However the boundaries and interconnections between these are all too often smudged and presumptions are smuggled in that there is no tension or dissension in moving across such analytical boundaries. Also, any thoroughgoing analysis of performance management would need to take account of a variety of different lenses which, in relation to education, would include: learning, teaching and pedagogy; equity/ social justice and social/political perspectives; a variety of different professional/union perspectives; managerial/economistic; and technical/ logistical standpoints. The official discourse of performance management, as exemplified for instance in the Green Paper, slides across these perspectives without any break of stride even though differentiating between them may serve an important analytical function by revealing ways in which only certain kinds of perspectives are pulled into play in official discourse whilst others are sidelined or completely ignored and by providing a basis for distinguishing between, and/or pulling together critical features derived from different orientations.

We would argue that for our purposes the following elements are of importance in grasping the significance of performance management:

- that it is presented as a way of delivering the purposes and outcomes of the organisation in a way which is transparent and explicitly communicated;
- that from the viewpoint of the management as stakeholders it enables them to identify and differentiate between participants in

terms of the contribution they make to the achievement of these purposes and outcomes. In doing this it enables a more effective distribution of the reward, training and progression resources of the organisation to enhance its capacity to meet established objectives and respond to the demands of change. Profitability, productivity, efficiency, value-addedness, and value-for-money are clearly key concepts in this respect;

- for the employee, performance management is claimed to provide a clear specification as to what is expected, what targets/standards/criteria are to be met and the rewards and other benefits which will result from meeting those criteria. It should also enable an employee to see where their contribution fits within the overall vision or scheme of the organisation. Further to this an effective performance management system should articulate with training provision, professional development, etc. and this in turn should mesh with the organisational models of progression and promotion (see also Lawn, 1995). Taken together, all of these are founded on an organisational map which locates people in various positions within the structure, clarifies the expectations attached to these positions, charts the dynamics of the relationships between the positions and specifies the potential lines of progression which exist between them;

- in relation to the public sector the situation is patently different from that within the private sector. We shall return to some of the detail later, however for the government in its role as 'super-purchaser' of public services, the great promise offered by performance management lies in reductions in public sector expenditure, and hence taxation levels, and the greater visibility of precisely how public resources are being distributed and to what effect. In short, it provides a proxy bottom-line accountability comparable to that operating in the private sector, and also conveys the image of the government operating as a responsible and rational 'consumer' on *our* behalf. All of this is actually centrally driven whilst presented within a culture of decentralisation, delegation and disaggregation of institutional decision-making autonomy to smaller units of delivery.

But as Paul Hoggett has said:

> . . . the British experience indicates that steering by use of incentives and sanctions and the setting of meta-level rules (what DiMaggio

and Powell (1983) call 'the power to set premises') can be an extremely effective form of 'hands-off' control, indeed probably much more powerful than 'hands-on' regulation and direction.

(Hoggett, 1996 pp.25–6)

Major controversies surrounding performance management as an ideology and as a set of working practices

There is a variety of different sources to which one could turn for analysis of performance management. For example, we could delve into the world of management and personnel theory; we could explore the economics of labour and profitability; we could consider some of the historical and contemporary analyses which have been provided within the social policy literature; and, of course, we could look at the educational management literature. We have also found that much of the comment and analysis which is being presented in the academic literature is being echoed in the responses currently being generated from professional associations and unions to the specific proposals currently being made.

While we cannot rehearse all the detailed questions about procedures, logistics, resourcing, timing, duties, responsibilities, training procedures, appraisal mechanisms, etc. around which so many practitioners, unions and professional associations have expressed deep concern,[2] a flavour of the initial response can be indicated by the Professional Association of Teachers' (PAT) concluding comment in its response to the Green Paper:

> The overly complicated and bureaucratic procedures proposed would make the Headteachers' and senior managers' lives a nightmare. The proposals are, quite simply, unworkable!
>
> (PAT, 1999 para. 59)

Marsden and French introduce a rather sanguine view of the relationship between pay and performance which sits uneasily with the speed and lack of forward planning with which the government has proceeded:

> . . . although at first sight tying pay to performance may appear a simple and logical process, in practice there is a large number of problems that management has to overcome . . . The complexity of the linkages between pay and performance are such that only well thought out schemes have any chance of success.
>
> (Marsden and French, 1998 p. 4)

The National Association of Headteachers makes a comparable point when it says:

> The Government is proposing to introduce the world's biggest performance management system without a proper structure to support it. The Green Paper gives the clear impression that it has not grasped the enormity of the exercise or the preconditions, including full costs, which must be met for its success.
>
> (NAHT, 1999 p.21)

In the light of such comments we are lead to question whether performance management is anything but a sophisticated device for restructuring the pay element within the education budget. By claiming to operate a rational and transparent system of pay for performance which is founded on the notion of 'something for something' does it in effect achieve the purpose of getting 'more for less'? The Secondary Heads Association makes it quite clear how it interprets these questions:

> SHA questions whether a system of performance related pay, such as that proposed for teachers, exists in any other profession. Such schemes have been seen to demotivate employees in other fields, especially where the scheme rests upon an inadequate general salary level or is cash-limited, and many schemes in the private sector have been abandoned.
>
> (SHA, 1999 para. 5)

There are also criticisms directed at assumptions being made about what motivates teachers and enables them to improve. There are fears that the demotivating effect for the majority of teachers will far outweigh the rewards for the few unless significantly more money is made available on a long-term basis to enable the majority to access the higher levels of the new pay spine. Related to this are concerns that what motivates teachers is not simply money (though no-one has yet claimed that teachers could do with less of it). Even if self interest were the overriding motivator (rather than a professional commitment to doing the best job possible) it has been pointed out that the proposals may turn out to be self-defeating. Put bluntly, why would I share my good ideas with you when you might use them to achieve progression through the system over me. In reporting its members' responses SHA underlines the general point being made, namely that:

. . . there has been a clear and widespread view that the Government's proposals for performance related pay will not achieve the stated objectives. It is widely believed that the proposals will create divisiveness and jealousies amongst colleagues, threatening the collegiality which has been built up in schools over many years.

(SHA, 1999 para. 10)

The concern is that good educational practice or innovative teaching, far from becoming shared amongst a school staff, will be seen as a personal commodity to be sold in the internal market of the school. The potential implications of this for relations between staff within schools and between schools and their constituent communities are well summarised by these comments from the National Union of Teachers (NUT):

The Government's proposals . . . would profoundly damage the professional culture of co-operation and teamwork that is at the heart of successfully managed schools. The pressures caused by the performance management structure and the tensions between assessors and assessed would generate distrust and counter-productive competition between colleagues. In particular, serious divisions would develop between teachers separated by their success or failure in 'passing' the threshold.

These differences would be exacerbated by their inevitable visibility to pupils – and to parents. Parental pressure would build for pupils to be taught by teachers who had passed. Anxiety and objections would build where pupils were taught by teachers who had not reached, had decided not to apply or, worse, had been failed in their applications.

(NUT, 1999 paras 14/15)

Given limited space we cannot hope to engage with the full range of these issues. However, we have tried to indicate below some of the major general controversies, which are being highlighted.

Defining values, principles and criteria: issues of quality and quantity

This is a key issue because it is on the basis of these that all of the other issues hang. If performance management is to have a significance beyond the narrow question of performance-related pay then the overall value system within which the whole framework is to be located needs to be spelt out. This also has to be something to which employees feel that they can express a commitment otherwise it will not succeed in motivating and encouraging their commitment. Within the private sector this value framework can (arguably) be limited to material factors, eg. profitability, turnover, productivity, design specifications, etc. and the criteria used within the performance management framework can reflect this value structure. This is clearly not the case in the public sector generally, where, as Marsden and French say:

> Determining the relevant dimensions of performance has been a major area of controversy across the public services as staff and their representatives have often argued that quantity is being stressed at the expense of quality . . . deciding on valid criteria for performance measurement management is . . . much more than a simple technical issue, but one which relates to people's beliefs about the goals of the service they work for . . . a great many staff are strongly committed to a certain idea of public service, and there is much disagreement about the suitability of the targets chosen by management.
>
> (Marsden and French, 1998 pp.5–6)

There are echoes here of Australian experience where Smyth and Shacklock (1998) describe how the professional discourses of teachers were often felt to clash with the managerially oriented way in which the standards for ASTs (Advanced Skills Teachers) were couched. As we have indicated in our recent book (Mahony and Hextall, 2000a), the generation, form and content of the national professional standards have been, and continue to be, the subject of intense debate. Defining what is to count as an appropriate outcome in education is difficult enough, finding indices which adequately capture these outcomes is yet more difficult, and developing devices with which to appraise achievement of these outcomes is of yet another order. Certainly this cannot be adequately accomplished by imposing a preordained template and then claiming to have resolved the problem. As we shall see later there is a genuine problem involved in attempting to identify the particular contribution, say to a pupil's performance, which is contributed by any given teacher rather than by a whole history of teachers. There are also real issues about the significance of external factors which are quite literally beyond the control of any school or teacher. Further than this there are legitimate questions to resolve about the extent to which certain key educational values are amenable in principle to conventional appraisal procedures and necessitate quite differently formulated procedures, e.g. collective appraisal, peer appraisal and community involvement (Ladson-Billings, 2000).

Standards and working the system

The performance management model envisaged in the Green Paper will be delivered via an appraisal system within which explicitly articulated sets of national standards will play a central part. It will be against these standards that the individual teacher's performance will be appraised and they will provide the foundation criteria for the evaluation of the various forms of evidence which the teacher is meant to present. There are various ways in which they can be analysed in order to get a grip on the work they are intended to do in the delivery and legitimation of policy (not only in the field of education but more widely in the domain of public policy).

At the level of detail, professional standards can be analysed in terms of their clarity, consistency, coherence, and in terms of the values, principles and assumptions which characterise them as conceptual systems. In relation to their stated purposes, they can be considered in terms of their 'fitness for purpose' – are they capable of doing the work they are intended to do and, if they are, is what they accomplish consistent with the wider purposes of the organisation within which they are located? Procedurally standards can be interrogated at different levels, both in terms of their mode of establishment and formation, with all the questions of accountability and transparency which this entails. Also, they can be questioned in terms of the manner in which they are translated into practice and the consequences, both manifest and latent, which follow from these procedures. Culturally and socially there is a whole set of issues to address in relation to the ideology of standards as an ubiquitous form. These include consideration of their underlying values and principles which operate both at the personal level of those deemed successful in meeting the standards and at the level of delivery in terms of the values communicated or instilled in those who are being taught. In both cases the standards construct a world within which people are meant to act and they define ways of acting within that world. The struggles which take place over standards are then conflicts over definitions of the nature of the world and society and what is important within them. The denial of a space within which disagreement is allowed about the 'facts' of effective teaching becomes an exercise in domination and exclusion; and the placing of firm boundaries around the scope for debate or disagreement becomes an exercise in limitation or consensus management (Hextall and Mahony, 2000).

A part of the reason why standards can undertake this cultural work so unproblematically is because they are so overlaid with a cloak of technicism. They do not appear to be a part of the exercise of constructing cultural or educational achievements but only of measuring or assessing them. But in order to meet the standards you have to be the kind of person that the standards have in mind, capable of accomplishing the activities that the standards entail, of performing within the relationships presumed at different levels, and of conforming to the principles which form the boundaries. The procedures and practices (e.g. appraisal) which provide the dynamics of standards become the processes through which the positions designated within the performance management structure get populated. In doing this they accomplish both a *distributional* and *relational* function at one and the same time (Gewirtz, 1998).

Equity issues

The last point leads us into issues of equity and social justice. Quite apart from the criticisms that have been made about the content of the standards (Ainsworth and Johnson, 2000; Mahony, 1999), a range of concerns have been expressed that the implementation of the system will be inconsistent and unfair. Though at a common sense level it seems legitimate that people who work harder should receive greater rewards, in practice there is a host of problems associated with this assumption. For example despite the apparent transparency of appraising staff against national standards, in practice interpretation of the standards means that judgement is a subjective process, grounded partly in the needs of the school as well as on the perceived talents of the individual teacher concerned. That at least has been our finding from a recent project on the impact of the national standards (Mahony and Hextall, 2000b). In addition, Australian evidence (Down *et al.*, 1997; Smyth and Shacklock, 1998) has indicated that those who 'succeed' are likely to be those in possession of 'valuable' (policy-enhanced) skills, e.g. ICT capability. Leaving aside questions of favouritism or the tendency of managers to over-rate their own staff in an effort to retain them, those who have experienced the enhanced pay element of performance management seem less than sanguine about its supposed transparency. A recent letter to the *Times Educational Supplement* reads:

> As someone who has worked under a performance pay system for the whole of the 1990s, I would reassure teachers that performance-related pay will be nothing as simple as a crude relationship between results and payments. Payments there will be, for some, but such is the complexity of PRP, no-one will know why they did or did not get the money.
>
> (TES, 23 July 1999)

Related to this is the concern that those groups who have traditionally suffered discrimination within the labour market will experience even greater difficulty in negotiating the hoops and hurdles integral to the system being introduced. The National Association of Schoolmasters and Union of Women Teachers (NASUWT) devoted a whole section of its consultation response to an analysis of the discriminatory potential of the new system:

> It is highly regrettable that equality issues are not addressed, particularly when within the teaching profession there are recognised, significant imbalances in gender, race and disability. Consequently, as this factor is not acknowledged within the proposals, no system is set out to ensure discrimination does not occur in their application or to prevent the current imbalances being perpetuated or aggravated.
>
> (NASUWT, 1999 para. 6.2 p.24)

As we have indicated there is no explicit reference to a recognition of the salient structural categories as significant in patterns of progression and promotion. Nor, in the accompanying Technical Documents (DfEE, 1999a–d) is there any reference to the skills required to monitor or deliver an equal opportunities element within the performance management model. This is despite the fact that, as the NUT argues, evidence in other occupational areas:

> . . . suggests that those points in the PRP system where management bias and subjectivity can enter – the appraisal, and the subsequent translation of the performance rating into a pay award – are the areas where discrimination can and will occur.
>
> (NUT, 1999 para. 157)

Conclusion

As we have pointed out earlier in this chapter, public sector employees are increasingly working within regimes of performance management. This raises significant contemporary questions about the forms of regulation and control which are embedded within such transformations of occupational relations and their broader consequences for social relations in general. Brian Hoggett expresses some of the dilemmas:

> The paradox of Britain in the 1990s therefore is the co-existence of an unregulated economy with an excessively regulated public sphere. . . .

unlike the Utopia of high trust, high skill, participatory firm commitment to quality drawn by some variants of the flexible-specialization thesis, what we seem to be heading towards in both the private and public sectors in the UK is the development of a high output, low commitment work culture in which trust has become a value of the past and where quality counts far less than quantity . . .

(Hoggett, 1996 p.28)

Addressing the kinds of content, structure, positioning and social relationships raised in our argument cannot be approached without reflecting on questions of control and governance. Such reflections would have to take account of the ways in which our societies are increasingly diversified. Within most official documentation, it would be very surprising not to find lip-service being paid to the interests of parents, students, employers and the much vaunted 'community interests'. However, the significance of this, when fleshed out, often appears somewhat tokenistic. Clearly this is no easy issue even though, for some politicians, policy-makers, administrators, and educationists, the resolution to the dilemmas seems straightforward. You form a defined policy (perhaps after officially sponsored exploration of alternatives and consultation) and then implement it with clarity and determination. Policies on standards, quality and effectiveness would be good contemporary exemplars of such an approach. All too often, however, such policies are insufficiently grounded in the nature of the educational experiences which most people encounter, have consulted on too narrow a base, have failed to access or hear the voices of those who are most marginalised; fail to reflect upon or leave adequate space for the detailed specificities of circumstances; privilege certain interests over others, and operate with totalising orientations which fail to take account of structural, sectional and regional differentiations. We have got to this point, because the values, purposes, content and distribution of education have been rendered beyond debate, and stifled by a world view in which:

. . . 'performance' appears to have achieved an almost magical significance, and has led to the creation not just of Performance Management but also performance reviews, performance audits, performance plans and performance appraisals.

(Rogers, 1999 p.1)

Questions of the most enormous democratic significance are being raised by the increasingly porous nature of the relationships between what we used to call the public and private sectors. The boundary lines between these, which have never been watertight, are becoming increasingly blurred under the impact of privatisation, market relations, deregulation, various forms of devolution and delegation of powers and responsibilities, and the emergence of what is sometimes described as the contract state. Into this catalogue we would now add the performance management system as yet another example of these transformations in which an elusive and ambivalent discourse of 'professionalism' is being used to accomplish the task of redefining both the activity of teaching and the structural relationships between teachers. Whilst such debates will take us well beyond the confines of education policy, let alone the even more specific terrain of teacher education and professional development, addressing such issues is vital if there is to be a sustainable public debate about 'effective' schooling and its potential contribution to social formations characterised by equity and social justice.

Notes

1 The interaction between the 'self' and transformations in contemporary forms of work and occupational relationships are intriguingly explored in Clarke and Newman (1997), Casey (1995) and Gee, *et al.* (1996).
2 For full details of initial responses from unions and professional associations see Chapter 3 Mahony and Hextall (2000a). Also see the recent analysis of responses to the Green Paper in Storey (2000).

References

Ainsworth, S. and Johnson, A. (2000), 'The TTA Consultation Documents on ITT: What no Values?', in D. Lawton, J. Cairn and R. Gardener (eds) *Education for Values: Morals, Ethics and Citizenship in Contemporary Teaching*, London: Kogan Page.

Angus, L. (1994), 'Sociological Analysis and Education Management: the social context of the self-managing school', in *British Journal of Sociology of Education*, Vol. 15, No. 1, pp.79–91.

Armstrong, M. and Baron, A. (1998), *Performance Management: The new realities*, London: Institute of Personnel and Development.

Blackmore, J. (1999), *Troubling Women: Feminism, Leadership and Educational Change*, Buckingham: Open University Press.

Casey, C. (1995), *Work, Self and Society after Industrialism*, London: Routledge.

Clarke, J. and Newman, J. (1997), *The Managerial State*, London: Sage.

DfEE (1998), Green Paper, *Teachers: Meeting the challenge of change*, London: TSO.

DfEE (1999a), *Teachers meeting the challenge of change: technical consultation document on pay and performance management*, London: DfEE.

DfEE (1999b), *Teachers: Taking forward the challenge of change – detailed summary of responses to the Green Paper consultation exercise*, London: DfEE.

DfEE (1999c), *Performance Management Framework for Teachers: Consultation Document*, London: DfEE.

DfEE (1999d), *Explanatory note on how we expect the performance threshold to operate in 2000–2001* (submission to the STRB), London: DfEE.

Down, B., Hogan, C. and Chadbourne, R. (1997), 'Making Sense of Performance Management in Schools: Official Rhetoric and Teachers' Reality'. Paper presented at the Australian Association for Research in Education Conference, Brisbane, December 1997.

Gee, J. P., Hull, G. and Lankshear, C. (1996), *The New Work Order: behind the language of the new capitalism*, Sydney: Allen & Unwin.

Gewirtz, S. (1998), 'Conceptualizing social justice in education: mapping the territory', in *Journal of Education Policy*, Vol. 13, No. 4, pp.469–84.

Hextall, I. and Mahony, P. (1998), 'Effective Teachers for Effective Schools', in G. Weiner, R. Slee and S. Tomlinson (eds), *School Effectiveness for Whom?*, pp.128–43, London: Falmer Press.

Hextall, I. and Mahony, P. (2000), 'Consultation and the management of consent: standards for Qualified Teacher Status', in *British Education Research Journal*, Vol. 26 (3), pp.323–42.

Hoggett, P. (1996), 'New Modes of Control in the Public Service', in *Public Administration*, Vol. 74, Spring, pp.9–32.

Ironside, M. and Seifert, R. (1995), *Industrial Relations in Schools*, London: Routledge.

Ladson-Billings, G. (2000), *The Validity of National Board for Professional Teaching Standards (NBPTS) Assessment for Effective Urban Teachers (Final Report)*, University of Madison: Wisconsin-Madison.

Lawn, M. (1995), 'Restructuring teaching in the USA and England: moving towards the differentiated, flexible teacher', in *Journal of Education Policy*, Vol. 10, No. 4, pp.347–60.

Mahony, P. (1999), 'Teacher Education Policy and Gender', in J. Salisbury and S. Riddell (eds), *Gender Policy and Educational Change*, pp.229–41, London: Routledge.

Mahony, P. and Hextall, I. (2000a), *Reconstructing Teaching: standards, performance and accountability*, London: RoutledgeFalmer.

Mahony, P. and Hextall, I. (2000b), *The Impact on Teaching of the National Professional Qualifications and Standards: Summary of Findings*, London: University of Surrey Roehampton.

Marsden D. and French S. (1998), *What a Performance: Performance related pay in the Public Services*, London: Centre for Economic Performance, LSE.

Murlis, H. (1992), 'PRP in the context of Performance Management', in H. Tomlinson (ed.), *Performance Related Pay in Education*, London: Routledge.

NAHT (1999), *Response to the Green Paper 'Teachers: Meeting the Challenge of Change' and Technical Consultation Paper on Pay and Performance Management*, Haywards Heath: NAHT.

NASUWT (1999), *Response to the Green Paper . . . working hard to make it work*, Birmingham: NASUWT.

NUT (1999), *Teaching at the Threshold*, London: NUT.

PAT (1999), *Teachers: Meeting the Challenge of Change*, Derby: PAT.

SHA (1999), *Response to the Government's Green Paper 'Teachers: Meeting the Challenge of Change'*, Leicester: SHA.

Smyth, J. and Shacklock, G. (1998), *Re-Making Teaching: Ideology, Policy and Practice*, London: Routledge.

Storey, A. (2000), 'A Leap of Faith? Performance Pay for Teachers?', in *Journal of Education Policy*, Vol. 15, pp.509–23.

12 Characteristics of performative cultures

Their central paradoxes and limitations as resources for educational reform

John Elliott

Introduction

Under New Labour the previous government's project of replacing 'inefficient' bureaucratic systems of governance within the public sector with the new public management, based on ideas derived from the private sector, has proceeded with a much firmer and more confident resolve. Although decentralisation and organisational autonomy are key ideas for the new performance management, it facilitates a new form of indirect regulatory control which paradoxically concentrates governance at the centre. It achieves this by divorcing power from responsibility and reinterpreting accountability as a mechanism for securing regulatory compliance from public service professionals.

In the field of education, the solution to the problem of sustaining the welfare state has not been a New Right shift towards the privatisation of schooling but the emergence of the evaluative state. Such a state indirectly regulates the performance of schools and teachers through a technology of audit. The establishment of a so-called independent watchdog in the form of OfSTED, and the introduction of quasi-market mechanisms, are simply devices to strengthen this indirect regulation of performance by central government. The impact of a progressive tightening of accountability through such devices has been profound. Primary schools, for the first time, and also secondary schools, are keenly aware of the impact of the publication of league tables, and their position in them, on their recruitment of pupils and increasingly of staff. With respect to the latter, recently-publicised problems of teacher recruitment in some schools may be viewed as at least a partial consequence of rendering the performance of schools increasingly transparent through the publication of OfSTED inspection reports, and the deployment of quasi-market mechanisms like league tables.

The emergence of the evaluative state, and a technology for auditing the performance of educational institutions in a form which renders them transparent to the public gaze, is transforming the organisational cultures which shape the professional practices of teachers. The new organisational cultures may be described as performative cultures inasmuch as they are all underpinned by the principle of performativity.

The principle of performativity

Within performative organisational cultures, *quality* is defined as the best equation achievable between inputs and outputs (Lyotard, 1979). The organisation's overriding goal is to optimise performance by maximising outputs (benefits) and minimising inputs (costs) and thereby provide 'value-for-money'. Lyotard calls this the 'principle of performativity'. It is well captured in Michael Barber's account of the UK government's 'important strategy innovations' in the educational field:

> Each year the professional development programme will be based on an analysis of what pupils and teachers have (and have not) been able to do well the previous year. Precision-targeting of professional development across a system is, I believe, one of our most important strategy innovations, ensuring both quality and cost-effectiveness.
>
> (Barber, 2000)

In terms of the principle of performativity, quality and cost-effectiveness are not separate goals but one and the same. Barber's account is somewhat ambiguous in this respect.

This ambiguity reflects a certain instability in the operational definition of quality within performative cultures. Power (1997 pp.49–50) argues that when quality is defined as 'value-for-money' it incorporates three operational characteristics for quality audit; namely, economy, efficiency and effectiveness. Economy refers to the acquisition of resources on the best possible terms. Efficiency refers to the utilisation of these resources to achieve a given level of output. Effectiveness refers to the match between outcomes and intentions. Power argues that 'a fundamental tension exists between the effectiveness and the economy/efficiency components' of the 'value-for-money' concept (Power, 1997 p.50), inasmuch as they depend on different evaluative logics. One originates from a tradition of socio-scientific inquiry which engages with the complexities of 'connecting service activities to outcomes', both intended and unintended. The other stems from accountancy and the business disciplines. Here, outcomes are simply equated with outputs or 'measures of the measurable' features of activities – such as examination results and truancy rates – in relation to the activities of schooling. Outputs are identified independently of any understanding of the contextual complexities which shape such activities. In this respect they lack empirical verification as indicators of effectiveness (Power, 1997 pp.114–15). Quality audits tend to gravitate, Power argues, towards evaluation designs that emphasise economy/efficiency while claiming to be concerned with effectiveness. This is because they are shaped 'to suit a particular skills base' (Power, 1997 p.51) which is inadequate for the task of verifying the empirical connection between outcomes and outputs.

Transparency through performance indicators

Performative cultures presume that the performance of core activities within organisations can be made transparent to the public's gaze on a continuous and sustainable basis through technologies of audit. Such technologies aspire to provide perfect information about the workings of the organisation through highly selective objectifications of performance known as performance indicators (PIs). PIs presume propositions about the relationship between cause and effect as if it can be captured in a timeless form, in the here-and-now. Information about performance is supposedly perfect when it is shaped by timeless propositions about the relationship between inputs and outputs. PIs therefore leave little room for a view of causality as a time-dependent phenomenon, the understanding of which changes over time and is never perfect (Strathern, 2000).

Technologies of audit rest upon the assumption of fixed and immutable standards against which to judge performance. In this context the quality of an organisation's core activities can only be described in the audit language of indicators. If quality cannot be measured against timeless, fixed and immutable standards or targets, it does not exist. Outcomes which escape the gaze of the technologies of audit are not the bearers of real quality.

Descriptions of social organisations in the language of indicators are endemic to performative cultures and reflect a fundamental interest in making such organisations objects of social engineering. Barber makes this interest very explicit in relation to the UK government's Excellence in Cities educational programme. He writes:

> Ultimately the programme should result in a complete re-engineering of secondary education. Instead of fitting students into the system as

we did in the 20th century, we would build the system around the needs and aspirations of students.

(Barber, 2000)

The social engineering of performance to meet human needs, as Strathern points out, involves a paradox. The more activities are shaped by 'the timeless logic of a standardised indicator' the less they meet the real needs they are intended to serve. People's needs change over time and circumstance, and Strathern's example of services to the elderly is a good illustration of this. The more the elderly ask their local authority to respond to their need for meals, the more the authority responds by attempting to match its performance to the standardised indicator of 'home helps per thousand of population'. The problem is that the elderly want microwaves and freezers rather than home helps at this particular point in time. Similarly, one could argue that meeting school attendance requirements and attaining good GCSE grades is not well matched to the learning needs of adolescents at a time when they are preoccupied with 'emotional work'.

The more totalising the engineering of the educational system around standardised performance indicators becomes, the more difficult it is for schools and teachers to provide flexible responses to their students' learning needs. For example, teachers have tended to allow their students a measure of space and time for 'informal learning', through freedom of association within the organisational boundaries of the school and classroom. In exchange many students were prepared to play the formal learning game. This trade-off was evidenced in an interview transcript I recently read. A student was explaining why she liked her Maths lessons. She was able to perform the problem-solving tasks her teacher set to the required level of attainment in 20 minutes, leaving her 15 minutes to talk with her friends before the end of the lesson. The more pervasive the gaze of performance audit on the activities of teachers, the less it becomes possible for them to balance formal learning requirements against the need of their students for non-formal space and time in which to pursue their own 'learning agendas'.

The unintended consequences that might reasonably be predicted from the intensification of the social engineering that Barber so applauds, are yet further increases in the levels of disaffection from formal learning manifested by students in schools. Rather than enhancing levels of achievement in schools, there is a point at which the intensification of performance auditing and management becomes counter-productive. In practice, the UK New Labour government has become aware of this (Elliott, 2000). In its proposals to revise the national curriculum for the new century, it linked the disaffection of a significant minority of students to an over-prescriptive national curriculum that gave teachers few opportunities to make flexible responses to the learning needs of students (DfEE, 1999). The revisions involve reductions in the level of prescriptive detail for most subjects and the introduction of more curricular flexibility. They also provide new opportunities at key stages 3 and 4 for school initiatives in the areas of Personal, Social and Health Education (PSHE), and Citizenship Education. There is the clear intention to give teachers more space to explore ways of preventing and overcoming disaffection, and in doing so to construct bridges between formal and non-formal learning.

The revisions are perhaps a good example of the kind of 'oscillatory management' (Strathern, 2000) which accompanies attempts to render systems totally transparent to the gaze of audit. Paradoxically, from time to time, the demands for accountability and quality assurance have to be uncoupled to a degree from making provision for the real needs of those whom the system is designed to serve. Moreover, the oscillation should itself not become too transparent to the public gaze. Hence, we find the national curriculum proposals for PSHE and Citizenship Education being fitted into outcomes-based frameworks, along similar lines to other national curriculum subjects. The message conveyed is that teaching and learning will be made fit for audit. What this message conceals is that worthwhile learning outcomes in these areas cannot be pre-standardised and reduced to a limited set of measurable outputs.

The lists of actual outcomes specified in the proposed frameworks refer not so much to measurable outputs of teaching and learning as to the procedural values and principles which ought to infuse these processes. For example, 'learning to discuss and debate topical issues and events' could have been formulated as the principle that 'students ought to learn through discussion and debate'; which says and implies a great deal about how students ought to learn, and indeed how teachers ought to teach. The transformation of this principle into a learning outcome adds little to its meaning but obscures a great deal. Of course, 'learning through discussion' implies learning how to discuss in the process. It is rather confusing to call the latter an 'outcome' of the process since it is an intrinsic aspect of it. However, in doing so what is concealed is the nature of discussion as an open-ended and unpredictable learning process.

The concealment of paradox is a characteristic of the management of the oscillations which accompany attempts to render performance in educational systems totally transparent to the gaze of audit. It does however provide teachers who are able to decode the messages with opportunities to forge new directions for education in their organisations.

The promise of predictability and control

The conceptual conflation of outputs, as measured by performance indicators, and outcomes is part of the control ideology which underpins the culture of performativity. What is going on is the concealment of one kind of reality about human activities in order to construct another kind of reality about them, one which renders them amenable to social and economic control in the name of 'quality assurance'. Paradoxically, making performance visible by measuring it against indicators depends on making evidence about its real impact invisible, since such evidence would reveal the dependence of outcomes on time and context, and limits on their predictability.

Strathern (2000) cites the case of audits of research and teaching performativity in higher education institutions within the UK. Research productivity is measured against such outputs as the quality of selected publications, holding on to research-active staff, success in obtaining funds for projects, attracting high quality young researchers. What this kind of visibility conceals, Strathern argues, 'are the "real" facts about how the organisation operates'. This includes the department's investment of time and energy in supporting the research of its members, and the social skills involved in growing influence networks and transmitting, over the generations, the tacit knowledge which constitutes the basis of a dynamic and creative research culture or tradition. For Strathern it is these 'invisible-to-audit' processes that are critical for the production of research quality, and that are essentially marked by relationships of trust within the organisation.

With respect to teaching quality assessments, Strathern also shows how a focus on 'clarity in communicating information to students', as an audited goal of teaching, presumes that if something is clearly stated then it is understandable and reproducible by students. Teaching is audited as if 'immediate assimilability' is its goal. Yet, she argues, we know that learning takes place over time and 'may manifest itself weeks, years, generations, after teaching, and may manifest itself in forms that do not look like the original at all', for 'the student's experiences will introduce his or her own "indirection"'. For Strathern it is far from clear that understanding, the process that transforms information into knowledge, 'is a simple consequence of clarity itself'. Quality assessments that focus on the latter conceal the complexities of the teaching–learning process and in doing so fail to yield evidence about the real impact of teaching over time. At any point in time evidence of impact will inevitably be partial and provisional.

Evidence about the impact of human activities yields provisional and tentative insights rather than conclusive and certain knowledge, and its usefulness consists in its capacity to inform rather than displace the judgements of practitioners. Such evidence is antithetical to the construction of knowledge in the interests of economic or social control. Instead it supports self-generative reflective action precisely because it implies that the workings of an organisation can never be grasped in their entirety (Strathern, 2000). This also implies accountability on the part of the practitioners concerned, but not in the sense of compliance to regulatory norms established by performance indicators. Practitioners exercise accountability for the impact of their activities at particular times, by demonstrating their ability to make 'transient use' (Strathern, 2000) of the available evidence to improve their practical judgements.

The use of indicators as a basis for audit promises control by concealing rather than reducing risk, and in doing so functions to comfort the fainthearted. It is a kind of panic reaction which stems from a sense of crisis.

The intolerance of time and the construction of the 'ever active performer'

Performative cultures place organisations in a continuous state of fending off an impending crisis.

> The sense of urgency comes, not just from the belief that every passing day when a child's education is less than optimal is another day lost, but also from the belief that time is running out for public education to prove its worth.
>
> (Barber, 2000)

Performative cultures are intolerant of time because disaster is always imminent and things have to be done now to ward it off. People within the organisation therefore have to be kept in a continuous state of activation. This implies changes to the way in which the teacher's 'professional self' is conceptualised, to 'promote the auditable, competitive and ever active performer' in the place of the 'inspiring teacher' (Strathern, 2000).

In the case of schools, the continuous state of activation based on an intolerance of time becomes most evident in those identified by OfSTED as failing schools. They go into special measures which, as a recently-interviewed teacher in such a school points out, leaves little time and space for teachers to reflectively develop their practice.

In the emergency atmosphere generated by Special Measures colleagues want strong leadership and to be told what to do. . . . As a school we seem always to have been in a hurry, without the time to gather research data on what might be effective practice, because of a need to be seen to be acting. The research process seems too slow when our masters are insisting that failing schools have to be turned round within two years.

(Teacher interviewee, 1999)

The constant state of activation engendered by the gaze of OfSTED has now been further reinforced by the new performance management in schools, which stems from linking teachers' pay to their performance.

The central challenge for us, as for many other educational systems, is to recruit good people into teaching, enable those who are demonstrably successful to rise rapidly and improve the status of teachers in their own eyes and those of the public. Linking teachers' pay to their performance is the key to achieving these objectives. The flashpoint has been the Government's insistence that pupil outcomes must be taken into account in assessing a teacher's performance. We have done so partly because, to anyone outside the teaching profession, it is simply not credible to leave the central purpose of an activity out of the assessment of it, and partly because the wider objective is to create a culture in the education service in which everyone, whatever their role, takes responsibility for pupil performance.

(Barber, 2000)

The architecture of this new professional self for teachers has been constructed on the basis of research carried out in a mere ten months for the UK government by Hay McBer (2000) at a price of £4 million. In itself it is a good illustration of the principle of performativity in action, and the 'intolerance of time' which characterises performative cultures. The Hay McBer research represents the construction of yet more layers of indicators to supplement national curriculum targets and attainment levels.

The methodology of the research, on which the architecture of a new professional self for teachers has been designed, is shaped by a policy context which demands a technology for auditing teaching as a basis for implementing its performance-related pay proposals. From the outset, the researchers presumed that the outcomes of effective teaching could be measured against pre-standardised outputs in the form of exam/test results and classroom climate variables, such as clarity, order, safe learning environment, etc. They had 'value-added' data on each teacher in their representative sample in the form of start-of year and end-of year test/ exam results. On this basis they identified 'effective teachers' within their sample and then, through classroom observation and behavioural event interviewing, set out to describe the specific skills and professional characteristics which made them effective and differentiated them from the less effective.

The researchers then proceeded to validate their findings against academic achievement data, gathered independently, on the pupils of the teachers in their sample. The analysis focused on the extent to which teachers whose pupils displayed high gain scores exhibited the skills and characteristics of effective teachers that had been identified. It led to the conclusion that 'pupil progress is most significantly influenced' by a teacher who exhibits the skills and characteristics identified by the research. Moreover, the research also concluded that the creation of a good classroom climate is also significantly influenced by the teacher who possesses these skills and characteristics.

The researchers and policy-makers do not question the ambiguous idea of quality and the conceptual conflation of outputs with outcomes, the confusion of logics embedded in the research design. They are therefore not asking what this architecture of multilayered indicators of effective teaching conceals, and whether the professional self it constructs will have dysfunctional consequences for education in schools. Such questions would render teaching effectiveness a complex and time-dependent phenomenon and, given the crisis and urgency that Barber expresses, there is apparently no time anyway to consider them. Only performativity, the continuous state of activation to match the indicators, can bring comfort in crisis. The construction of auditable professional identities must be insulated from independent inquiry. As Power argues, the 'mood which has led to the reshaping of the public sector in recent years could not be described as very sensitive to empirical inquiry'. Power also believes that the insulation of audit from independent inquiry can be explained by its genesis 'in a broader politics of fear and anxiety'.

I shall argue later that this broader politics is about sustaining economic growth in the face of international competition. In English-speaking countries, like the UK, governments tend to deal with their anxieties about globalisation by continuously reaffirming the belief that sustainability depends on their capacity to re-engineer and re-regulate every sphere of society, including the public services, by introducing market mechanisms. Such reaffirmations of belief to ward off anxiety about the consequences of globalisation involve the 'continual reintensification of available instruments of regulatory control' (Power, 1997).

Audit and the draining of trust

Performative cultures within public service organisations imply a low level of trust in the professionalism of their employees: the more pervasive the gaze of audit the less the trust invested in the moral competence of its members to respond to the needs of the people they serve.

The internalisation of audit functions as an intrinsic part of the system is often rationalised as a process of self-evaluation which restores the trust displaced by external audit. Hence, in welcoming the Hay McBer descriptions of effective teachers as a basis for instituting performance-related pay in the UK, Estelle Morris, Minister for Education and Employment, asserts their value as a tool for 'self-evaluation' (see http://www.dfee.gov.uk/news/2000/268.htm, June 2000). Yet at the same time she asserts that they demonstrate 'what the government has always maintained, that there are measurable factors that have a significant impact on teacher performance'. It would be better to regard the development of forms of self-evaluation regulated by indicator systems as yet another stage in the leaking away of trust in professional organisations.

An increasing capacity for managerially orchestrated self-inspection is indicative of an organisation which has moved into a state of continuous doubt about the trustworthiness of those engaged in its core activities: such is the extent to which it has assimilated the performative culture. This enhances the conditions for perfecting the visibility of those activities, since managers inside the organisation will have greater access to them than outsiders. The latter are only necessary when the managers act in the belief that their people should be trusted, and that their activities should be protected from the unremitting and timeless gaze of audit. Once these beliefs have been sufficiently eroded, then the transparency of the organisation is enhanced by handing audit functions over to its managers. We are now witnessing such a transition in our schools, with the new 'performance management systems' being instituted around performance-related pay, and the replacement of external inspections by so-called 'light-touch' self-inspections. The latter will be structured by OfSTED's revised framework of indicators (in the light of the Hay McBer 'research').

Efforts to render performance totally visible through the language of indicators, in draining away 'trust' within the organisation, transforms it in counter-productive ways. Power (1997, p.95) uses the term colonisation to depict the possibility of any audit process disseminating and implanting 'the values which underly and support its information demands'. For Power it represents one type of audit failure, inasmuch as an audit process which 'disseminates and implants the values which underly and support its information demands' creates side-effects that 'may undermine performance'. Colonisation through audit fosters 'pathologies of creative compliance' in the form of gamesmanship around an indicator culture.

With respect to academic audit in HEIs (higher education institutions), for example, Power argues that 'orientations towards teaching and research have been affected and colonized by a hard managerialism' (Power, 1997 p.103). However, he contends, 'academics in their new role as auditees are hardly "totalized" and "docile" subjects' (Power, 1997 p.103). Strathern makes a similar point when she asserts that everyone knows that performance indicators are 'a highly constructed and artificial means of measuring real output'. Yet they still accede to the prevailing practices of audit, quality assurance and accountability. This state of affairs depicts a kind of passive resistance to colonisation as a totalising process that expresses itself as 'creative compliance'. The creative aspect resides in the ability to play games with indicators. The well-documented evidence of the games people play around an indicator culture testifies to the extent to which performance auditing provides a fatal remedy (Power, 1997 p.119) to the problem of rendering the core activities of professional organisations visible and accountable. Such games involve the cynical production of auditable performances, such as when teachers 'teach to tests' in the full knowledge that the outcomes of good teaching are rarely made visible by test results.

Another type of audit failure, identified by Power, is when organisations strategically attempt to prevent this from happening by decoupling the audit process from the 'core organizational activities' which give it point.

> Through the creation of compartmentalized organizational units for dealing with external assessment, audit and evaluation can be rendered ceremonial in such a way as to deflect a rational questioning of organizational conduct.
>
> (Power, 1997 p.96)

From this point of view audits are 'rationalized rituals of inspection' that produce comfort and organisational legitimacy (Power, 1997 p.96). According to Power neither decoupling nor colonisation is a pure possibility; both tend to be unstable processes. In the case of decoupling, the audit process rarely remains permanently buffered from core organisational activities. For example, internal managers of audit may change sides and 'use their new-found power to advance internal changes' (Power, 1997 p.97). However, in time the side-effects of this type of colonisation are likely to produce an oscillation back towards decoupling. Power's thesis, about the tendency for the decoupling process to be inherently unstable, need not imply that grassroots initiatives cannot be sustained over time. They can provide a source of powerful resistance to managerially orchestrated colonising tendencies. Such resistance requires an eternally vigilant and self-reflexive stance on the part of communities of practitioners.

The global significance of performativity

Performative cultures tend to represent the performance of an organisation or system in terms of its global significance. The term 'world-class' recurs with almost monotonous frequency as part of its rhetoric: 'Our vision is a world class education service; one which matches the best anywhere on the planet' (Barber, 2000).

The development of a performative culture within the public services is an integral part of the neo-liberal project of re-engineering society as a free market for goods and services. John Gray (1999) has pointed out that constructing a free market demands that all intermediary institutions, such as trades unions and professional associations, be weakened. They are weakened in ways which prevent them from standing between individuals and market forces. Gray argues that 'only a strong centralised state can wage war on such powerful intermediary institutions' (Gray, 1999 p.26). This power is exercised by injecting market mechanisms such as 'competitive tendering, performance-related and profit-related pay' into all the public services. The role of the state is ' to supply a framework of rules and regulations within which the free-market, including crucially the labour market, would be self-regulating' (Gray, 1999 pp.26–7). The model that shaped this re-engineering of the public services in the UK, Gray argues, was the US labour market 'with its high levels of mobility, downward flexibility of wages and low costs for employers' (Gray, 1999 p.27).

The re-engineering of public services on a free-market model is assumed to be a condition of competitiveness in an increasingly globalised economy. Moreover, it is further assumed that that this global economy will be increasingly shaped by the same free-market mechanisms, as nation-states generally begin to realise that the growth of their economies depends on a universal consumer of its goods and services. The performance of educational systems, for example, must therefore be shaped in a form that permits international comparisons. This implies universal standards in the form of indicators, against which to compare the performance of different systems, and an increasing convergence of educational practices.

> In this decade we will see educational reform globalizing. We will see the globalization of large elements of the curriculum. Media and communications organizations will prepare and market internationally excellent interactive materials which will influence curriculum, standards, pedagogy and assessment across international boundaries.
> (Barber, 2000)

Within the above scenario there is decreasing room for diverse conceptions of education that are embedded in different societal cultures. According to Barber, the international comparisons of the 1990s (e.g. TIMSS) had a profound impact, inasmuch as they extended the horizons of policy-makers and researchers 'beyond national boundaries in the search for solutions'. However, it can be argued that this search ignored the way culture shapes the relationship between pedagogy and learning outcomes. The cultural embeddedness of the performance of far eastern educational systems moulded in the Confucian work ethic was uncritically neglected when the UK benchmarked the 'tiger economies'. It was assumed that unfavourable comparisons could simply be explained in terms of teaching methods e.g. whole-class teaching. This assumption neglected the cultural significance of the class for socialising students into a work ethic that requires the individual to identify with a group as a source of worth and self-esteem. Educational attainment in this context is a means of securing acceptance as a member of a group. It is Confucian culture that supplies the motivation to achieve, and shapes teaching methods and conceptions of standards.

Barber's vision of a global educational market presumes that the American model of a free society will become the basis for a new universal civilisation, which will supersede the plurality of cultures. But according to Gray the vision of the global free market is a utopia that can never be realised. It is based on the illusion that economic modernisation, 'the spread of industrial production into interconnected market economies throughout the world', implies the 'inexorable advance of a singular type of western capitalism: the American free market' (Gray, 1999 p.3). Gray argues that the opposite is the case. Economic modernisation on a global scale works against the Anglo-American project of creating a global free market. It does so by spawning a variety of capitalisms that are culturally indigenous (Gray, 1999 p.4). For Gray, the growth of a world economy does not result in a universal civilisation modeled on western ideas of individualism and rationality. Rather it produces 'regimes that achieve modernity by renewing their cultural traditions' (Gray, 1999 p.193).

If Gray's thesis is correct then there are no universal standards against which to judge the performance of educational systems. The principle of performativity currently shaping the UK education service is simply an Anglo-American project with little prospect of global transferability. In this light Barber's assumption, that an educational system re-engineered according to the performativity principle will match any other system on the planet, is questionable.

Beyond centralised engineering and performative cultures in education

The principle of performativity stems from a societal context in which the economic functions of social systems, like education, are separated from their personal and social functions and rendered superordinate to them. This abstraction of economy from society is largely an Anglo-American phenomenon operating in the USA, the UK, Australia and New Zealand (Gray, 1999). It stems from a desire to emancipate markets, including labour markets, from state and other forms of societal control. This desire rests on the belief that free markets are a necessary condition of sustainable growth in a global economy. In English-speaking countries educational knowledge, both 'knowing that' and 'knowing how', has become valued primarily for its utility in the smooth functioning of a free labour market. The value of knowledge resides in its commodity value for such a market. Audit processes in education, both external and internal, function as guarantors of the cost-effective production of commodity value.

However if, as Gray argues, the costs of free markets to families, communities and jobs renders them inherently unstable, then the belief that they are a necessary condition of sustainable economic growth collapses. In which case, the logic of defining educational processes in terms of indicators of the cost-effective production of commodity value also collapses. The attempt of governments to sustain economic growth by re-engineering the educational system in a form that renders its production of commodity value for the free market predictable is based on an illusion. The economic value of educational outcomes cannot be separated from the broader personal and social needs they serve. The view that they can stems from what Gray (1999 p.192) calls a theological perspective on market institutions in which they are treated as ends in themselves. He contrasts this doctrinal perspective in English-speaking countries (itself embedded in a culture of possessive individualism) with the instrumental or pragmatic view of markets in Asian countries. The latter is a view of markets as a means of serving the values and stability of society.

Gray argues that it is a mistake to view the Asian economic crisis in terms of the failure of Asian economies to embrace the free-market ideal (Gray, 1999 pp.218–21). The Asian crisis 'is the first historical demonstration that unrestricted global mobility of capital can have disastrous consequences for economic stability' in all societies, including those that embrace free-market doctrines. It indicates the emergence of an international market that tends to a state of anarchy and disorder, its behaviour impacting on particular sovereign states across the globe in different, unpredictable, and uncontrollable ways (Gray, 1999 pp.70–71). Gray predicts that all economies will now be mutating continuously 'with unpredictable consequences for social cohesion and political stability'. The Asian crisis is simply a 'prelude to a time of major dislocation for global capitalism' (Gray, 1999 p.220).

Gray contends that western ideas of free markets will play little part (1999 p.220) in the way Asian societies respond to the economic fluctuations caused by anarchic global markets. This implies that, given their pragmatic outlook on market institutions, they will give priority to monitoring the impact of these fluctuations on 'the values and stability of society' (Gray, 1999 p.192). In this context the educational reform proposals in post-colonial and post-crisis Hong Kong are interesting (Elliott and Morris, 2000). They constitute a response to globalisation in two respects. First, with respect to the spread of new technologies of production and communication across national frontiers. The proposals aim to wean teachers and students off textbooks as a sole source of knowledge, and to make use of new technologies in accessing multi-medial learning resources. Second, with respect to the fact that the society's economy is networked with other economies across the world and can no longer exist in isolation. This implies that its future citizens must learn to live in a dynamic and constantly changing economic environment, which will impact on their lives in largely unpredictable ways. The reform proposals emphasise the importance of life-long and life-wide learning as aims of education for the twenty-first century, in a world which is undergoing fundamental economic, technological, social and cultural change.

With respect to life-long learning, the development of generic transferable skills is stressed above the acquisition of specific subject-based knowledge. This involves a shift from passive learning processes to active ones, in which students are given opportunities to organise and manage their own learning. In line with this shift of emphasis are proposals to reduce the amount of high-stakes testing of learning output, and to introduce more school-based curriculum development and formative assessment (assessment for temporary use). With respect to life-wide learning the development of multiple abilities through activities that cannot be confined to formal classrooms is stressed. This involves transcending 'the constraints of academic subjects and examinations' by avoiding the compartmentalisation of learning outcomes in terms of subjects. Instead, it is proposed that subjects be integrated into eight key learning areas for whole-person development.

The Hong Kong curriculum reforms constitute a response to globalisation which is rather different from the western response in its emphases. Indeed they can be read as seeking to reduce the western influence on the educational system through less high-stakes testing, downgrading the subject-based academic curriculum, and trusting teachers with the tasks of curriculum development and assessments of student progress. As a response to globalisation the reforms imply limits on the extent to which the government can predict and control the commodity value of learning outcomes. They also imply that the development of the society's economic resources in response to the phenomenon of globalisation may well reside in the development of its social and cultural capital. An educational system that is open to the life-long development of multiple abilities, which are valued within the society and culture, may in the end prove to be more economically functional than one which reifies specific economic goals. Hong Kong could be said to be adopting a Darwinian model of the relation between education and the economy. This can be contrasted with the engineering model that drives educational reform through technologies of audit within the UK. Commodity value is naturally selected from the cultural capital a society accumulates through its educational system, rather than being centrally engineered.

If the educational reforms in Hong Kong and other societies in the Asia–Pacific region are indicative of the changes one might expect in the wake of a major dislocation in global capitalism, then the educational system within the UK would do well to prepare itself. Spaces beyond the reach of technologies of audit, however inherently unstable and without guarantee of permanence they may be, need to be created for activating an alternative vision of educational development.

Conclusion: from the evaluatory state towards the self-evaluating community of educational practitioners

Educational organisations, like schools and higher education institutions, need to create spaces for their professionals to develop a form of performance evaluation that is more sensitive 'to the complexities of connecting . . . processes causally to outcomes' (Power, 1997). These would include elements of self, peer and student/parent evaluation, in addition to evaluation support from external agencies. Within this form of collaborative evaluation research, indicators of effectiveness become 'things' to be empirically verified, refined and discovered in particular contexts of practice. They will also include qualitative as well as quantitative indicators. Considerations of cost-effectiveness would not be ruled out, but instead of simply measuring the costs of achieving a given level of output they would involve a more sophisticated weighing up of costs against evidence of impact.

Although yielding only imperfect information at any point in time, evaluations of an educational institution's or practitioner's effectiveness nevertheless have an important formative function; namely, as feedback which can be used by practitioners to further develop their practice. Accountability for the effectiveness of teaching involves a willingness on the part of teachers to publicly demonstrate, when called upon to do so, how evidence about the impact of their teaching on learners has been used to further develop practice. This type of accountability presupposes a growth of evidence-based practice, where teachers engage both with and in research into the quality of their teaching. It lies at the heart of quality development in classrooms and schools, and should not be confused with audit-based accountability. The idea of evidence-based teaching as a process of rectifying deficiencies, identified by measuring performance against a normative template of fixed indicators, rests on a distorted conception of what constitutes relevant evidence about the relationship between teaching and its outcomes. Evidence of measurable improvement, defined as bringing performance up to a fixed standard, is not the same as evidence of development, defined as an open-ended and ongoing process over time.

Accountability for the development of true quality in teaching is conditional upon teachers being trusted to engage in the process free from the unremitting gaze of audit. This is because it is a process which is essentially invisible to audit. The more the technology of audit – the creation of information systems and audit trails for the purposes of inspection – encroach on and shape teaching and learning the less space teachers have for quality development and for becoming effective teachers.

It is precisely because quality development in teaching requires an investment of trust in teachers, that society – in the form of its representational bodies – has the right, at particular points in time, to call them to account for their practice in terms of its outcomes for students and others. This kind of accountability implies trust but not unconditional trust.

There comes a point at which the strengthening of performance audit at the level of classrooms becomes counter-productive. At this point it disrupts rather than enhances the development of teaching quality, drains away the necessary amount of trust on which such development depends, and renders teachers largely unaccountable for the outcomes – as opposed to the outputs – of their teaching. The constant intensification of accountability through audit may bring more comfort to policy-makers, and perhaps parents, as a guarantor of minimal standards, but it is likely to depress the quality of educational development for the new millennium. It is not that accountability within the educational system is not in need of further strengthening. However, this strengthening should be based on a different logic of evaluation from the one that shapes performance auditing. In asserting this, one does not have to deny the importance of a certain level of performance audit as a guarantor of minimal standards. A better balance between evaluation as performance audit and evaluation for quality development needs to be achieved when global forces are making it increasingly difficult for governments to steer the relationship between educational outcomes and the economy. In such a situation, excellence in education requires a government to acknowledge its limitations by investing more trust in the teaching profession.

References

Barber, M. (2000), 'High expectations and standards for all – no matter what', edited version of a speech delivered to The Smith Richardson Foundation in Washington. www.tes.co.uk.

DfEE (1999), *Achieving Excellence through the National Curriculum*, London: DfEE.

Elliott, J. (2000), 'Revising the national curriculum: a comment on the Secretary of State's proposals', in *Journal of Education Policy*, Vol. 15, No. 2, pp.247–55.

Elliott, J. and Morris, P. (2000), *Educational Reform, Schooling, and Teacher Education in Hong Kong*, Hong Kong: Hong Kong Institute for Education.

Gray, J. (1998), *False Dawn: the delusions of global capitalism*, London: Granta Books.

Hay McBer Report and DfEE (2000), *A Model of Teacher Effectiveness*, Department for Education and Employment, The Teaching Reforms Site, http://www.dfee.gov.uk/teachingreforms/mcber/intro.htm.

Lyotard, J-F. (1979), *The Post-Modern Condition: A Report on Knowledge*, UK edn: Manchester University Press.

Power, M. (1997), *The Audit Society*, Oxford: University Press.

Strathern, M. (2000), 'The Tyranny of Transparency', in *British Educational Research Journal*, Vol. 26, No. 3, June, pp.309–21.

13 Performativities and fabrications in the education economy

Towards the performative society

Stephen Ball

> Each time I have attempted to do theoretical work it has been on the basis of elements from my experience – always in relation to processes that I saw taking place around me. It is in fact because I thought I recognised something cracked, dully jarring or disfunctioning in things I saw in the institutions in which I dealt with my relations with others, that I undertook a particular piece of work, several fragments of autobiography.
>
> (Foucault, cited in Rajchman, 1985 p.36)

This chapter joins in a burgeoning conversation concerned with performativity in education and social policy. It looks at both the capillary detail and the bigger picture of performativity in the public sector. Ideally it should be read in relation to the multitude of performative texts and 'texts of performativity' with which we are continually confronted and which increasingly inform and deform our practice. The chapter is intended to be both very theoretical and very practical, very abstract and very immediate.

Performativity is a technology, a culture and a mode of regulation, or even a system of 'terror' in Lyotard's words, that employs judgements, comparisons and displays as means of control, attrition and change. The performances – of individual subjects or organisations – serve as measures of productivity or output, or displays of 'quality', or 'moments' of promotion or inspection. They stand for, encapsulate or represent the worth, quality or value of an individual or organisation within a field of judgement. 'An equation between wealth, efficiency, and truth is thus established' (Lyotard, 1984 p.46). The issue of who controls the field of judgement is crucial. 'Accountability' and 'competition' are the lingua franca of this new 'discourse of power' as Lyotard describes it. A discourse which is the emerging form of legitimation in post-industrial societies for both the production of knowledge and its transmission through education.

My aim is to begin work on and towards an analytics of this discourse of power, and the resistances and accommodations to it. This is both an exercise in critical ontology and the analysis of new regulative forms.

In referring to various texts or data, I am not attempting in any simple sense to mobilise proof of my arguments. I am trying to establish the existence of an attitude and an ethical framework within which teachers and researchers in schools, colleges and universities are having to work and think about what they do and who they are. I am interested in the way in which these texts play their part in 'making us up' (Hacking, 1986 p.231) by providing 'new modes of description' and 'new possibilities for action'. Thus are new social identities created – what it means to be educated; what is means to be a teacher or a researcher. This remaking can be enhancing and empowering for some but this has to be set over and against the various inauthenticities discussed below.[1] It is productive as well as destructive. There are 'winners' and 'losers' in the 'struggle for the soul of professionalism' (Hanlon, 1998), which is embedded in this remaking. We make ourselves up within the information we provide and construct about ourselves. We articulate ourselves within the representational games of competition, intensification and quality.

The argument focuses upon a struggle over visibility. I shall explore a paradox, arguing that tactics of transparency produce a resistance of opacity, of elusivity; but that this resistance is also paradoxical and disciplinary. In general terms I want to outline a new mode of social (and moral) regulation that bites deeply and immediately into the practice of state professionals – reforming and 're-forming' meaning and identity, producing or making up new professional subjectivities. This new mode involves, as Deleuze (1992) puts it, a shift from 'societies of discipline' to 'societies of control': 'controls are a modulation, like a self-deforming cast that will continuously change from one moment to the other, or like a sieve whose mesh will transmute from point to point' (Deleuze, 1992).

Within this new mode of regulation, the organisation of power within definite forms of time-space (e.g. factory or office production systems) is now less important. It is the database, the appraisal meeting, the annual review, report writing and promotion applications, inspections, peer reviews that are to the fore. There is not so much, or not only, a *structure* of surveillance, as a *flow* of performativities both continuous and eventful – that is *spectacular*. It is not the possible certainty of always being seen that is the issue, as in the panopticon. Instead it is the uncertainty and instability of being judged in different ways, by different means, through different agents; the 'bringing-off' of performances – the flow of changing demands, expectations and indicators that make us continually accountable and constantly recorded – 'giving the position of any element within an open environment at any given instant' (Deleuze, 1992 p.7). This is the basis for the principle of uncertainty and inevitability; it is a recipe for ontological insecurity, posing questions such as – are we doing enough? are we doing the right thing? how will we measure up?

Nonetheless, clearly, controls overlay rather than displace disciplines in most educational organisations even if the emphasis is shifting. There is at work here a combination of two things: first, of *rituals* (grandiloquent pronouncements and spectacular events) which serve to naturalise the discourses of control (such as inspections, audits, promotion applications, job interviews); second, of *routines* (record-keeping, committee and taskforce meetings, interactions) which address forms of identity by treating people in terms of the identities of the discourses of performativity (Corrigan and Sayer, 1985).

Different identities and performances are more or less possible, more or less available, in different locations (Blackmore and Sachs, 1999). However, whatever our location, we now operate within a baffling array of figures, performance indicators, comparisons and competitions – in such a way that the contentments of stability are increasingly elusive, purposes are contradictory, motivations blurred and self worth slippery. Constant doubts about which judgements may be in play at any point mean that any and all comparisons have to be attended to. What is produced is a state of conscious and permanent visibility (or visibilities) at the intersection of government, organisation and self-formation. And one key aspect of the steering effects of judgement and comparison is a gearing of academic production to the requirements of national economic competition, which are in turn supported by: 'Policies which pursue the general goal of reorganizing, maintaining and generalising market exchange relationships' (Offe, 1984 p.125).

Performativity works from the outside in and from the inside out. As regards the latter, performances are, on the one hand, aimed at culture-building, the instilling of pride, identification with and 'a love of product or a belief in the quality of the services' provided (Willmott, 1992 p.63). On the other hand, ratings and rankings, set within competition between groups *within* institutions, can engender individual feelings of pride, guilt, shame and envy – they have an emotional (status) dimension, as well as (the appearance of) rationality and objectivity. As regards the former, we can consider a teacher who appears in Jeffrey and Woods' powerful, moving and indeed terrifying book *Testing Teachers* which deals with the UK regime of school inspections and examines teachers' experience of these inspections as a conflict of values, a colonisation of their lives, and deprofessionalisation of their role:

I don't have the job satisfaction now I once had working with young kids because I feel every time I do something intuitive I just feel guilty about it. 'Is this right; am I doing this the right way; does this cover what I am supposed to be covering; should I be doing something else; should I be more structured; should I have this in place; should I have done this?' You start to query everything you are doing – there's a kind of guilt in teaching at the moment. I don't know if that's particularly related to Ofsted but of course it's multiplied by the fact that Ofsted is coming in because you get in a panic that you won't be able to justify yourself when they finally arrive.

(Jeffrey and Woods, 1998 p.118)

Here then is guilt, uncertainty, instability and the emergence of a new sub-jectivity[2] – a new kind of teacher. What we see here is a particular set of 'practices through which we act upon ourselves and one another in order to make us particular kinds of being' (Rose, 1992 p.161). Crucially, and this is central to my argument, together, these forms of regulation, or governmentality,[3] have a social and interpersonal dimension. They are folded into complex institutional, team, group and communal relations – the academic community, the school, the subject department, the univer-sity, for example). *We* sit on peer reviews, *we* write the accountability reports, *we* assign grades to other departments, *we* berate our colleagues for their 'poor' productivity, *we* devise, run and feed departmental and institutional procedures for monitoring and improving 'output'.

Within this economy of education, material and personal interests are intertwined in the competition for resources, security and esteem and the intensification of public professional labour – the changing conditions of and meanings for work.[4] The focus here is primarily on performance itself as a system of measures and indicators (signs) and sets of relation-ships, rather than on its functions for the social system and the economy. The starting point is Lyotard's concept but my use of the concept of performativity moves beyond his presentation of the principle of perform-ativity 'as the optimising of performance by maximising outputs (benefits) and minimising inputs (costs)'. For I also want to differentiate between perform*ativity* in Lyotard's sense, to 'be operational (that is, commensur-able) or disappear' (Lyotard, 1984 p.xxiv); and in Butler's (1990) sense, as enactment or perform*ance*. That perverse form of response/resistance to and accommodation of performativity that I call *fabrication* is also a major concern.

While at times I will talk about schools and school teachers in this chapter, and refer to other public sector organisations, I can claim no luxury or objectivity of distance in all this. My daily practice within a university is the most immediate reality for what I am attempting to analyse. Thus, some of my illustrations are taken from documents, events and observations within my own institution. Some of the oppressions I describe are perpetrated by me. I am agent and subject within the regime of performativity in the academy. As signalled by the opening quotation, this is in part an exercise in autobiography.

Social relations of practice

As represented by Lingard and Blackmore (1997 p.13) the policy duality of accountability and enterprise in higher education produces tensions which 'are played out in the everyday/everynight lives of individual academics, in the form of demands made upon their time to provide feedback and accountability upwards to their institutions, through performance management, quality assurance and research quantums and productivity agreements under enterprise bargaining'. Two points follow from this. First, there is the contradiction – what Lyotard calls the law of contradiction. This arises between intensification, as an increase in the volume of first-order activities, and the 'costs' of second-order activities themselves, like performance monitoring and management. Thus, as a number of commentators have pointed out, acquiring the performative information necessary for perfect control, 'consumes so much energy that it drastically reduces the energy available for making improvement inputs' (Elliott, 1996 p.15; also Blackmore and Sachs, 1997). Survival and competitive advantage in the economy of education rests equally upon the energy of first-order activities and the energy of second-order activities – producing what Blackmore and Sachs (1997) call 'institutional schizophrenia'. However, there is no simple 'realist' relationship between the former and the latter and they are mediated by the effort devoted to the production of personal and institutional 'fabrications'. Furthermore, as noted already, it is important to recognise the extent to which these activities enter into our everyday relations. These are most apparent in the pressures on individuals, formalised by appraisals, annual reviews and data bases, to make their contribution to the performativity of the unit. Again in this there is a real possibility that authentic social relations are replaced by judgemental relations wherein persons are valued for their productivity alone. In Deleuze's terms, 'individuals have become "dividuals" and masses, samples, data, markets or "banks"' (Deleuze, 1992 p.5). This is part of what Lash and Urry (1994 p.15) call the 'emptying out' of relationships, which are left flat and 'deficient in affect'.

In relation to individual practice we can also identify the development and ravages of another kind of 'schizophrenia'. There is the possibility that commitment, judgement and authenticity within practice are sacri-ficed for impression and performance. There is a potential *splitting* between the teacher's own judgements about 'good practice' and students' 'needs' on the one hand and the rigours of performance on the other. Again this can be illustrated by quoting teachers from Jeffrey and Woods' study of UK school inspections. One teacher, Veronica, talked about resenting 'what I've done. I've never compromised before and I feel ashamed. It's like licking their boots'; and another, Diane, talked about a loss of respect for herself:

> My first reaction was 'I'm not going to play the game', but I am and they know I am. I don't respect myself for it; my own self respect goes down. Why aren't I making a stand? Why aren't I saying, 'I know I can teach; say what you want to say', and so I lose my own self-respect. I know who I am; know why I teach, and I don't like it: I don't like them doing this, and that's sad, isn't it?
>
> (Jeffrey and Woods, 1998 p.160)

There is a lot here. There is an indication of the particular performativity – the management of performance – which is called up by the inspection process. What is produced is a spectacle, or what we might see as an 'enacted fantasy' (Butler, 1990), which is there simply to be seen and judged. And as the teacher also hints the heavy sense of inauthenticity in all this may well be appreciated as much by the inspectors as the inspected; Diane is 'playing the game' and 'they know I am'. Nonetheless, the effects here in terms of discipline and control are powerful indeed; as are the costs to the self. Jeffrey and Woods note the 'most dramatic' example of Chloe:

> She was the only year 6 teacher at Trafflon and after criticism of their SATs results she resolved to go down the path of 'improvement of results'. She changed her curriculum, and achieved her aim by getting the second best results the following year in her LEA. She justified this by saying that she was 'now just doing a job'; and had withdrawn her total involvement to preserve her 'sanity'. 'The results were better because I acted like a function machine'.
>
> (Jeffrey and Woods, 1998 p.163)

Again the alienation of self is linked to the incipient 'madness' of the requirements of performativity: the result, inauthentic practice and relationships. We also see here the emergence of 'new forms of social relations' – social structures are replaced by 'information structures' (Lash and Urry, 1994 p.111).

We might find a similar splitting and personal and social inauthenticity as teachers and researchers in higher education when we apply for grants in which we have no academic interest but will look good on departmental returns or earn income; or give conference papers or submit journal articles which are unready or unoriginal in order to chalk up another count in the annual output review. This may exemplify a situation that Giddens sees as endemic in late modernity. Where there is an institutionalised 'existential separation' from 'the moral resources necessary to live a full and satisfying existence' (Giddens, 1991 p.91). He suggests as a result the individual may experience personal meaninglessness. However, there are mixed motives at work here – we tell ourselves 'necessary fictions' which rationalise our own intensification or legitimate our involvements in the rituals of performance.

Nonetheless, this tension, this structural and individual 'schizophrenia', and the potential for inauthenticity and meaninglessness is increasingly an everyday experience for us all. The activities of the technical intelligensia drive performativity into the day to day practices of teachers and into the social relations between teachers. They make management ubiquitous, invisible, inescapable – part of, embedded in, everything we do. We choose and judge our actions and they are judged by others on the basis of their contribution to organisational performance. And in all this the demands of performativity dramatically close down the possibilities for 'metaphysical discourses', for relating practice to philosophical principles like social justice and equity. And 'fables' of promise and opportunity such as those which attend democratic education are also marginalised. Even so, we are all expected to make our contribution to the construction of convincing institutional performances. Which brings us to the issue of fabrication.

Fabrications

The fabrications that organisations (and individuals) produce are selections among various possible representations – or versions – of the organisation or person. Complex organisations like schools and universities are multi-faceted and diverse, indeed they are sometimes contested and often contradictory. Clearly, particular groups or individuals will be able to privilege particular representations. However, these selections and choices are not made in a political vacuum. They are informed by the priorities, constraints and climate set by the policy environment. To paraphrase Foucault, fabrications are versions of an organisation (or person) which does not exist – they are not 'outside the truth' but neither do they render simply true or direct accounts – they are produced purposely 'to be accountable'.

Truthfulness is not the point – the point is their effectiveness, in the market or for the inspection, as well as the work they do 'on' and 'in' the organisation – their transformational impact. As Butler (1990 p.136) puts it, in a rather different context: 'Such acts, gestures, enactments, generally construed, are *performative* in the sense that the essence or identity that they otherwise purport to express are *fabrications* manufactured and sustained through corporeal signs and other discursive means'. However, as Butler is swift to point out, such fabrications are paradoxical, and deeply so. In one sense organisational fabrications are an escape from the gaze, a strategy of impression management that in effect erects a facade of calculation. But in another sense the work of fabricating the organisation requires submission to the rigours of performativity and the disciplines of competition – resistance *and* capitulation. It is, as we have seen, a betrayal even, a giving up of claims to authenticity and commitment, it is an investment in plasticity. Crucially and invariably acts of fabrication and the fabrications themselves act and reflect back upon the practices they stand for. The fabrication becomes something to be sustained, lived up to. Something to measure individual practices against. The discipline of the market is transformed into the discipline of the image, the sign.

All of this keeps the gaze in place – the 'professional' teacher and lecturer are here defined by their grasp of and careful use of systems and procedures, and by the particular rewards and new identities that this delivers through a regressive, self-regulation. It is in these ways that we become more capable, more efficient, more productive, more relevant; we become user-friendly; we become part of the 'knowledge economy'. We learn that we can become more than we were. There is something very seductive about being 'properly passionate' about excellence, about achieving 'peak performance'.[5]

Apart from their official functions, as responses to accountability, both main aspects of educational performativity – comparison and commodification – are linked to the provision of information for consumers within the education market forum. And they are thus also different ways of making schools and universities more responsive or appear to be more responsive to their consumers.

However, the work of fabrication points to a second paradox. Technologies and calculations which appear to make public sector organisations more transparent may actually result in making them more opaque, as representational artefacts are increasingly constructed with great deliberation and sophistication.

Within all this (some) educational institutions will become whatever, seems necessary to become in order to flourish in the market. The heart of the educational project is gouged out and left empty. Authenticity is

replaced by plasticity. Within the education market institutional promotion
and representation take on the qualities of postmodern depthlessness – yet
more floating signifiers in the plethora of semiotic images, spectacles and
fragments that increasingly dominate consumer society. Indeed, the
particular disciplines of competition encourage schools and universities
to fabricate themselves – to manage and manipulate their performances
in particular ways. Increasingly educational institutions are taking the
position that part of what they offer to choosers/consumers is a physical
and semiotic context which is no longer 'left to chance, but has to be
heavily designed' (Lash and Urry, 1994 p.204). Certainly, schools have
become much more aware of and attentive to the need to carefully organise
the ways in which they present themselves to their current and potential
parents through promotional publications, school events, school productions, open evenings, websites (Abbott, 1999)[6] and local press coverage.
Furthermore, there is a general tension or confusion in the education
market between information-giving and impression management and promotion. This blizzard of hype and (pseudo) information also contributes
to opacity rather than transparency.

Again, individually, we also fabricate ourselves. We produce versions of
ourselves for and at job interviews – and increasingly may have to 'perform'
a presentation for our potential colleagues – for promotion and for grant-
getting.

Let me try to be even more specific with some more examples, and in
doing so begin to develop an analysis of the 'poetics of fabrication'. This
might allow us to think about how plausibility and believability are
achieved, or brought off, both tactically and creatively. It might be
useful to distinguish between trivial or *representational* fabrications
(which is not meant to underplay their effects) and those which are
constitutive and arise from *organising* principles.

The routine selection (or manipulation) of statistics and indicators

Systems of calculability almost always leave latitude for representational
variation (Ball 1997):

> I'm rushing around like a loony today trying to put together this exam
> results display she [the headteacher] wants . . . I didn't have any data
> to do it with and I've had to collect that and then I've had to find a
> way of presenting the results in a way that looks good . . . GCSEs
> and A level results against the national average . . . that's presented
> us with some problems, because obviously with four subjects the

results are uneven . . . I've found a way of doing the A-level that looks alright, I'm struggling a bit with the GCSE.

(Secondary School Head of Faculty)

In higher education the dual-authoring of papers with less productive colleagues is another fairly innocuous method of massaging publications returns. Leo Walford, Journals Editor at Sage Publications, has recently talked about the research assessment exercise (RAE) in the UK leading to what he calls the 'salami-slicing of strong research papers in several thinner articles' (Headline 'RAE can "corrupt" research', *THES*, 26 March 1999). In addition the republication of just slightly different versions of essentially the same paper seems to be becoming more common. Publishers are harassed to organise their production schedules to ensure publication before the RAE cut-off date. The choice of indicators, where more than one is available, is another routine act of fabrication And in the UK the run-up to each RAE is now marked by a flurry of transfers of star performers to institutions wanting to boost their chances of a better grade – another form of instant fabrication.

In the school sector we can point to the introduction of baseline testing in UK schools as another point of struggle over and manipulation of indicators. Primary schools are eager to test early – despite advice to 'let the children settle down' – to produce maximum 'under-performance', against which 'value-added' gains can be made, and attributed to the schools. Some parents on the other hand are preparing their children for the tests to ensure a good showing, or are shocked by the poor performance of their 'unprepared' children. The interests of good schooling and good parenting are made antithetical by the demands of performativity. And the way in which performativity can easily become totally divorced from service is dramatically demonstrated by a UK private rail company which on several occasions has reportedly run trains without stopping at scheduled stations to ensure that they meet their punctuality targets. Or we might note the impact of the publication of the morbidity rates of individual surgeons in the USA which has led to many doctors refusing to operate on difficult or high-risk cases. The same may happen in the UK – 'Surgeons may refuse high-risk cases' was a headline in *The Independent* newspaper (*The Independent*, 7 October 1999).

The stage management of events

A colleague in London described to me a situation where two schools rented extra computers for their open evening, the idea being to give parents the impression of a hi-tech learning environment. Another colleague at the Chinese University of Hong Kong described a practice in mainland China in which schools about to be inspected rented plants and bushes from local nurseries, in order to meet the requirement that they should provide a pleasant and conducive learning environment for students. In both cases, the rented items were returned once the event was finished. Jeffrey and Woods (1998) again, describe a school preparing for inspection by rehearsing the inspectors' questions: 'We practised ensuring that we presented a consensus for any interviews we had. It was very helpful. I want them to say that the Senior Management Team has a shared clear view' (Grace, quoted p.155). School open evenings are now typically carefully choreographed events, sometimes with professional support.

Constructing accounts of the institution

Increasingly, public sector institutions are required to construct a variety of textual accounts of ourselves in the form of development plans, strategic documents, sets of objectives etc. (as are individuals). Symbolism is as important as substance here, in at least two senses. First, such texts symbolise and stand for the corporate consensus of the institution, and indeed these exercises in institutional extrapolation can also work as a means of manufacturing consensus (Ball, 1997), the focusing of activities around an agreed set of priorities. Second, they provide a touchstone of shared endeavour which displaces or subsumes differences, disagreements and value divergences. Of course they are also a version of the institution constructed for external audiences. They may deploy discursive tactics to convey order and coherence, consensus and dynamism, responsiveness and careful self-evaluation or, to other audiences, a synthetic personalism, 'a caring institution'. By such means the organisation is written into being.

Performance as performativity

All of these examples of what I have called *representational* fabrications do in different ways have *organising* effects. As I argued more generally earlier fabrications act back on their producers. And indeed as technologies of accountability some of the requirements referred to here are intended to work as much as formative interventions as they are as summative indicators. The other sense of fabricating an institution as *constitutive* – in relation to certain organising principles – is the way in which performativities are achieved by the adoption of particular policies and practices. One way in which we can see this, which also points up the relationship between market incentives, market values and market information, is in the generation of GCSE examination results and league table positions in certain UK schools. The logic of market incentives would suggest that any school or university which can select its clients will do so – either formally or informally. Those schools which do select their students, either formally or informally, are more able to control their league table position and their reputation generally. Furthermore, those students who offer the best chance of GCSE success tend to be the cheapest to teach, and easiest to manage. Students who threaten the reputation or performance of the school will be deselected (excluded) and indeed we have seen a massive growth in the number of students excluded from school in the UK since 1991. Generally, as explained by headteachers in our research on many occasions, the most effective long-term strategy for improving GCSE performance is to change the student intake. Thus, GCSE attainment percentages and local league table positions do not in any simple sense represent the outcomes of 'good' teaching and 'effective' learning; they are instead artefacts produced out of a complex set of policy strategies and practical tactics which underpin the fabrication of performance.

Individual fabrications

In addition to these organisational fabrications, as noted earlier, we are increasingly required to fabricate ourselves. While there have always been performance and 'impression-management' aspects of rituals like inter-views and lectures, they are increasingly a part of organisational routines, in annual appraisal interviews, in students' assessments of their tutors, and in promotion and job applications. The point is to make yourself different and, in the case of representational texts, to express yourself in relation to the performativity of the organisation. This is an aspect of what Blackmore and Sachs call self-management – 'the issue was as much what was seen to be done, rather than substantively what was done' (Blackmore and Sachs, 1999 p.10).

The application or promotion text is increasingly an artifice of high order. A career is reconstructed within these texts as a seamless, develop-mental progression to the present, with lines of further development, a potential value-added, streaming off into the future. We rehearse our national and international reputation, quote from reviews of our books, highlight the excellence of our teaching and our contributions to adminis-tration and the institutional and academic communities. We become rounded paragons with multiple strengths and infinite possibilities for further work, adept in the studied art of convincing exaggeration. We make fantasies of ourselves,[7] aestheticise ourselves. Appraisal documents can be equally fantastical in setting and reporting on personal targets.

But again we are increasingly caught up in the logic of our own representations. We are engaged in an indexing, a tabularising, of the self. Increasingly we represent and enact our academic selves in terms of productivities and tables of performance. We work on ourselves and each other, through the micro practices of representation/fabrication, judgement and comparison. A new kind of practical ethics is articulated and realised. In all this, what we are seeing, I want to argue, is 'a general change in categories of self-understanding and techniques of self-improvement' (Rose, 1992 p.161).

The performative society

> . . . the generalisation of an enterprise form to all forms of conduct may of itself serve to incapacitate an organisation's ability to pursue its preferred projects by redefining its identity and hence what the nature of its project actually is.
>
> (Du Gay, 1996 p.190)

This is also Lyotard's point. It is not that performativity gets in the way of real academic work, it is a vehicle for changing what academic work is! At the heart of Lyotard's thesis is his argument that the commodification of knowledge is a key characteristic of what he calls 'the postmodern condition'. This involves not simply a different evaluation of knowledge but fundamental changes in the relationships between the learner, learning and knowledge, 'a thorough exteriorization of knowledge' (Lyotard, 1984 p.4). Knowledge and knowledge relations, including the relationships between learners, are desocialised.

Underlying this is the dissemination of the market or enterprise form as the master narrative defining and constraining the whole variety of relationships within and between the state, civil society and the economy. As far as public sector activities are concerned: '. . . the emphasis shifts from the state as provider to the state as regulator, establishing the conditions under which various internal markets are allowed to operate, and the state as auditor, assessing their outcomes' (Scott, 1995 p.80). As Bernstein (1996 p.169) puts it 'contract replaces covenant'. Within the public sector this process of exteriorisation also involves a profound shift in the nature of the relationship between workers and their work. Service commitments no longer have value or meaning and professional judgement is subordinated to the requirements of performativity and marketing; though obviously there is an important element of cynical compliance at work in the processes of individual and institutional fabrication. This is part of a larger process of ethical retooling in the public sector which is replacing concern for client need and professional judgement with commercial decision-making. The space for the operation of autonomous ethical codes based on a shared moral language is colonised or closed down. Embedded here is what Hanlon calls 'a struggle for the soul of professionalism' (Hanlon, 1998 p.50) – a contest over the meaning of professionalism which has at its centre the issue of trust – 'who is trusted, and why they are trusted is up for grabs' (Hanlon, 1998 p.59). The ethos of traditional professionalism is no longer trusted 'to deliver what is required, increasing profitability and international competitiveness' (Hanlon, 1998 p.52) and is being replaced by a 'new commercialised professionalism' (Hanlon, 1998 p.54).

The new structures and roles for organisational management with a central core for policy, audit and regulation and separate 'service delivery units' – the rim and the hub – increasingly mirror the steering-at-a-distance role of the 'small state' or what Neave (1988) calls 'the new evaluative state'. In this way, the state also provides a new ethical framework and general mode of regulation, a much more hands-off, self-regulating regulation, which nonetheless enables and legitimates the dissemination of the commodity form as we are required to commodify ourselves and our academic productions. This is, in Aglietta's (1979 p.101) terms, a new 'regulative ensemble' or a 'particular mode of social coherence', a historically distinct form of labour organisation. This ensemble of performative technologies is an improvised and polyvalent mix of physical, textual and moral elements which 'make it possible to govern in an "advanced liberal" way' (Rose, 1996 p.58).

Within the framework of performativity, academics and teachers are represented and encouraged to think about themselves as individuals who calculate about themselves, 'add value' to themselves, improve their productivity, live an existence of calculation. They are to become 'enterprising subjects', who live their lives as 'an enterprise of the self' (Rose, 1989). This is not simply a set of changes in the nature of public sector professionalism and social relations. Rather these changes encapsulate a more general and profound shift in the way we are coming 'to recognise ourselves and act upon ourselves as certain kinds of subject' (Rose, 1992 p.161) and 'the nature of the present in which we are' (Rose, 1992 p.161); and thus a certain form of life in which 'one could recognise oneself' (Foucault, 1988 p.49) is threatened or lost. Instead we are presented with other ways of saying who we are and representing ourselves. We have an opportunity to be enthused. We also have everyday opportunities to refuse these ways of accounting for ourselves, not as apathy, rather as 'a hyper- and pessimistic activism'. As Foucault puts it: 'I think

224   *Ball*

that the ethico-political choice we have to make every day is to determine which is the main danger' (Foucault, 1983, p.232).[8]

Notes

1 The idea of authenticity, as a discursive practice in its own right, needs to be worked upon. It is deployed here in a neutral sense or at least as a 'nonpositive affirmation . . . an affirmation that affirms nothing' (Foucault, 1997 p.197) – an act of exiting. However, I might go as far as saying that while 'authenticity' is certainly not intended as a normative condition it is intended to indicate a stance towards, an anticipation of the effects of, the discourses we employ – 'a refusal to be mindlessly complicitous' (Pignatelli, 1993 p.430), the generation of 'inventive responses' and an honouring of 'disqualified knowledges' (Foucault, 1980; see also Ball, 1999).
2 Subjectivity is: 'patterns by which experiential and emotional contexts, feelings, images and memories are organised to form one's self-image, one's sense of self and others, and our possibilities of existence' (De Lauretis, 1986 p.5).
3 As Mitchell Dean explains: 'The notion of governmentality implies, then, first a project for the analysis of the state which would no longer rely on the juxtaposition of micro and macrolevels of power, and the conceptual autonomy of an analytics of micropower and the theory of sovereignty' (Dean, 1994 p.160).
4 The pressures of performativity and performance act, in particular and heightened forms, on those academic workers who are without tenure or on fixed-term contracts.
5 Erica McWilliam pointed out to me the importance of trying to capture a sense of the seductive possibilities of performativity. See McWilliam, Hatcher *et al.* (1999) on the role of awards in higher education.
6 Abbott distinguishes between those sites which are promotional and those which are educative.
7 A colleague in another university recently described her application for promotion to me 'as a form of prostitution'.
8 An extended version of this paper was given as the Frank Tate Memorial Lecture at the Australian Association for Research in Education conference in Melbourne, 1999. It was later published in the *Australian Educational Researcher* 27(2), 1–24.

References

Aglietta, M. (1979), *A Theory of Capitalist Regulation: The US Experience*, London: New Left Books.
Ball, S. J. (1997), 'Good School/Bad School', in *British Journal of Sociology of Education*, Vol. 18 (3), pp.317–36.
Ball, S. J. (1998), 'Performativity and Fragmentation in "Postmodern Schooling"', in J. Carter (ed.), *Postmodernity and the Fragmentation of Welfare*, London: Routledge.

Ball, S. J. (1999), 'Global trends in educational reform and the struggle for the soul of the teacher!', Education Policy series: Occasional Paper. Hong Kong: Chinese University of Hong Kong.

Baudrillard, J. (1998), *The Consumer Society*, London: Sage.

Bernstein, B. (1996), *Pedagogy, Symbolic Control and Identity*, London: Taylor & Francis.

Blackmore, J. and Sachs, J. (1997), 'Worried, Weary and Just Plain Worn Out: Gender, restructuring and the psychic economy of higher education', Brisbane: AARE Annual Conference.

Blackmore, J. and Sachs, J. (1999), 'Performativity, passion and the making of the academic self: women leaders in the restructured and internationalised university', in A. McKinnon and A. Grant (eds), *Academic Women*.

Butler, J. (1990), *Gender Trouble*, London: Routledge.

Corrigan, P. and Sayer, D. (1985), *The Great Arch: English State Formation as Cultural Revolution*, Oxford: Basil Blackwell.

Dean, M. (1994), '"A social structure of many souls": Moral regulation, government, and self formation', in *Canadian Journal of Sociology*, Vol. 19 (2), pp.145–68.

De Lauretis, T. (1986), 'Feminist Studies/Critical Studies: Issues, Terms and Contexts', in T. De Lauretis (ed.), *Feminist Studies/Critical Studies*, Bloomington: University of Indiana Press.

Deleuze, G. (1992), 'Postscript on the Societies of Control', October, Vol. 59, pp.3–7.

Du Gay, P. (1996), *Consumption and Identity at Work*, London: Sage.

Elliott, J. (1996), 'Quality Assurance, the Educational Standards Debate, and the Commodification of Educational Research', BERA Annual Conference: University of Lancaster.

Foucault, M. (1977), *Language, Counter-Memory, Practice: Selected Essays and Interviews*, Ithaca, NY: Cornell University Press.

Foucault, M. (1979), *Discipline and Punish*, Harmondsworth: Peregrine.

Foucault, M. (1980), Two Lectures. *Power/Knowledge*, New York: Pantheon Books.

Foucault, M. (1981), *The History of Sexuality: An Introduction*, Harmondsworth: Penguin.

Foucault, M. (1983), 'On the Genealogy of Ethics: An Overview of Work in Progress', in H. Dreyfus and P. Rabinow (eds), *Michel Foucault: Beyond Structuralism and Hermeneutics*, Chicago: University of Chicago Press.

Gewirtz, S. and Ball, S. J. (1999), 'Schools. Cultures and Values: the Impact of the Conservative Education Reforms in the 1980s and 1990s in England', ESRC Values and Cultures project paper, King's College London.

Gewirtz, S., Ball, S. J. *et al.* (1995), *Markets, Choice and Equity in Education*, Buckingham: Open University Press.

Hacking, I. (1986), 'Making People up', in T. Heller, M. Sosna and D. Wellbery (eds), *Autonomy, Individuality and the Self in Western Thought*, Stanford CA: Stanford University Press.

Hanlon, G. (1998), 'Professionalism as Enterprise', in *Sociology*, Vol. 32 (1), pp.43–63.

Jeffrey, B. and Woods, P. (1998), *Testing Teachers: The Effect of School Inspections on Primary Teachers*, London: Falmer Press.

Lash, S. and Urry J. (1994), *Economies of Signs and Space*, London: Sage.

Lingard, B. and Blackmore, J. (1997), 'The "Performative" State and the State of Educational Research' (Editorial), in *The Australian Educational Researcher*, Vol. 24 (3), pp.1–20.

Lipietz, A. (1985), *The Enchanted World, Credit and World Crises*, London: Verso.

McCollow, C. and Lingard, B. (1996), 'Changing discourses and practices of academic work', in *Australian Universities' Review*, Vol. 39 (2), pp.11–19.

McWilliam, E., Hatcher, C. *et al.* (1999), 'Developing Professional Identities: Re-making the academic for corporate time', Queensland: Queensland University of Technology.

Neave, G. (1988), 'On the cultivation of quality, efficiency and enterprise, an overview of recent trends in Higher Education in Western Europe 1986–88', in *European Journal of Education*, Vol. 23 (1), pp.7–23.

Offe, C. (1984), *Contradictions of the Welfare State*, London: Hutchinson.

Pignatelli, F. (1993), 'What Can I do? Foucault on Freedom and the Question of Teacher Agency', in *Educational Theory*, Vol. 43 (4), pp.411–32.

Rajchman, J. (1985), *Michel Foucault: The Freedom of Philosophy*, New York: Columbia University Press.

Rose, N. (1989), *Governing the Soul: the shaping of the private self*, London: Routledge.

Rose, N. (1992), 'Governing the enterprising self', in P. Heelas and P. Morris (eds), *The values of the Enterprise Culture*, London: Routledge.

Rose, N. (1996), 'Governing "advanced" liberal democracies', in A. Barry, T. Osborne and N. Rose (eds), *Foucault and Political Reason: Liberalism, neo-liberalism and rationalities of government*, London: UCL Press.

Scott, P. (1995), *The Meanings of Mass Higher Education*, Buckingham: Open University Press.

Slater, D. (1997), *Consumer Culture and Modernity*, Cambridge: Polity Press.

Willmott, H. (1992), 'Postmodernism and Excellence: The De-differentiation of Economy and Culture', in *Journal of Organisational Change and Management*, Vol. 5 (1), pp.58–68.

Conclusion

An agenda for action and evidence-related policy

Denis Gleeson and Chris Husbands

We end our exploration of the performing school. Our survey has raised wide-ranging questions about educational processes, educational change and the relationship between the education system and society. Perhaps predictably, we have, as yet, few clear answers. We are left instead – as after all truly effective performances – with a whirl of images, a combination of pitfalls and potentials, possibilities and constraints. At one end of our continuum of possibilities lies the managed school, ever more closely mandated and directed by an assertive government, seeking from its headteacher, teachers and pupils, predefined outcomes and efficiency in attaining those outcomes. At the other end of our continuum lies the renewed school, in which open, collaborative and self-critical professional cultures produce a renewed focus on teaching and learning and on affirming professional development. Between these extremes lie endless compromises and balances. Beyond them too lie other issues: the extent to which governments are prepared to cede their own direct control over the micro-level of educational change, the extent to which they are prepared to accept the implicit trade-offs between competing educational purposes and the extent to which they are prepared to negotiate a new settlement for schooling with teachers, parents and learners. All of these are unclear. What is clear is that the purposes, structure and internal dynamics of education and schools are being systematically redefined.

There are a number of features which emerge and which connect with wider educational and public policy processes. There is much current emphasis in government and policy research circles on the need for policy to be 'evidence-based' or 'evidence-informed'. However, as the contributors to this book point out, the relationship between policy and educational practice is complex, involving disputes about the nature of schooling and teacher professionality as well as the agenda of inspection, standards and management. The result may well be curious paradoxes –

one of a government paying teachers more but losing teacher commitment; or one of a government placing educational change at the centre of its social inclusion strategies but demoralising educational leaders and managers. At one level, we are faced with a government impatient to raise standards of pupil achievement as part of its drive for modernisation in a globally competitive economy. Here, the twin pressures of political economy and policy underpin the managerialist drives linking performance management with predefined expectations for teachers and learners. At another level, schools struggle to respond to the changing conditions of learning influenced by cultural shifts in family, community and the workplace. The agendas do not appear to mesh: it is as if we have two education systems: one defined by prescribed tests, targets and standards from the top; and the other drawing on experience, practice and the challenges of day-to-day educational change. Whilst those endowed with cultural capital are predisposed to connect the two systems to their advantage, the terms on which the connections are made are contested. The challenge of raising educational standards for all without resolving the disparities between these two systems is enormous.

The challenge requires a balance of consultation and consensus among government, professionals and the communities they serve about the ways in which the conditions for an educated community can be established. At the moment, a low-trust view of teaching and learning still prevails, despite the shifts in policy rhetoric. One reason for this is that experience and practice are, still, considered pollutants to the grand narrative, in terms either of the inimical influences of professional cultures or the past failures of educational reform efforts. But the failure to recognise the connections between professional and policy agendas – the failure to recognise *simultaneously* the connections between situational or contextual learning (Lave and Wenger, 1991) and the wider aspirations for a high achieving education system – may prove fatal. The danger is that schools and teachers work in an increasingly test- and outcome-driven society where targets and credentialism thrive often at the expense of genuinely useful and usable learning. Performance management could, then, be the most recent example of this construction of a 'fabricated' society. At the same time, a commitment to professional renewal, long-term professional development, and an open dialogue involving all sectors of the educational community, holds the promise of genuine educational improvement. To secure control of performance management, to secure control of the opportunities provided by a government committed to education, requires policy–practice initiatives that ensure that learning and human agency drives policy, and that research, policy and professional agendas can be productively engaged. This will involve giving greater democratic voice to professionals and community, in anticipation that both government and professionals are up to the challenge.

Reference

Lave, J. and Wenger, E. (1991), *Situated Learning*, Cambridge: Cambridge University Press.

Index